"Internet Plus" Pathways to the Transformation of China's Property Sector

Shusong Ba · Xianling Yang

"Internet Plus" Pathways to the Transformation of China's Property Sector

Springer

Shusong Ba
HKEx Central
Hong Kong

Xianling Yang
Lianjia Real Estate Research Institute
Beijing
China

Translated by Feng Yue, Junying Yu and Hanxiong Zhu

ISBN 978-981-10-1698-1 ISBN 978-981-10-1699-8 (eBook)
DOI 10.1007/978-981-10-1699-8

The print edition is not for sale in China Mainland. Customers from China Mainland please order the print book from: Xiamen University Press

Library of Congress Control Number: 2016944376

Printed on acid-free paper

This Springer imprint is published by Springer Nature
The registered company is Springer Science+Business Media Singapore Pte Ltd.

Preface

The Forthcoming "Golden Age"
Of the Internet and the Existing Home Market

Here I am now in Hong Kong, looking out of my window at a forest of high-rises.

While looking at this city with a mature real estate market and contemplating the development of China's property sector, I wonder what changes are burgeoning as various sectors of the Chinese economy are using "Internet plus" strategy to explore new frontiers.

China's property market is undergoing a dramatic shake-up. A fundamental change is that a market dominated by new homes is giving way to a market of existing homes. In this age of mobile Internet, China's industrial transformation, which used to feature standardized products, is now characterized by nonstandardized services. Mobile Internet is germinating changes in the property sector, although a drastic transformation has not yet started.

Under these circumstances, a shake-up in the property market is duly expected, with the old order receding and the new order being established. This book is my effort to visualize the future in China's property market. The views expressed in it are my own and do not represent those of any organization.

I. Crossover Fusion of the Internet and Property Sector

The advent of this new age is marked by these three events:

First, a market dominated by new homes is giving way to a market of existing homes, which is the fundamental change.

Second, China's mobile Internet users have outnumbered PC users. This means the Internet's influence over the traditional industries is no longer about standardized products, but nonstandardized service. The Internet, now providing all sorts of services in real-life situations, is no longer simply a virtual world, but part of the real world. Mobile Internet is germinating changes in the real estate brokerage industry, although a drastic transformation is yet to be expected.

Third, the new rules of the real estate brokerage industry are established. The boundaries between different business models are blurring. Real estate developers and traditional brokerages are becoming more and more Internet-based, Internet companies are engaging in brokerage, and media companies are transforming into e-commerce businesses. The formerly different businesses that used to operate within their own territories are now competing severely on the same battlefield.

II. What Does a Booming Market of Existing Homes Mean to Us?

Existing homes are already a dominant presence in the markets of the USA, the UK, France, and Australia, where the numbers of existing home sales are, respectively, 9 times, 8.1 times, 1.9 times, and 3.5 times those of new home sales. While this ratio is only 0.6 in Japan at large, existing home sales are much more active in Japan's capital region and Kinki region than the rest of the country, the numbers of which are 3 times and 1.9 times those of new home sales, respectively.

In 2013, although the ratio of existing home and new home sales is only 35 % in China at large, the former already surpassed the latter in all first-tier cities and a few second-tier cities. According to the statistics of Centaline Home, first-tier cities account for 16 % of the total transacted area of existing homes and 39 % of the transaction volume.

Although existing homes have not yet dominated the housing market in most Chinese cities, due to a large enough existing housing stock, relatively high homeownership rate and the increasing population mobility, the boom of the existing home market is but inevitable.

What, then, does a booming market of existing homes mean to us?

1. Balance Between Supply and Demand

As real estate development process consists of many complicated steps like land acquisition, design and construction, the cycle of development can be as long as three years or longer. As a result, in a new home market, the supply of homes does not synchronize with demand. When demand elasticity is much greater than supply elasticity, developers at the supply end of the industrial chain has the final say in the market, with consumers and real estate agents at the disadvantaged end. The result is elevated home prices and reduced commissions.

However, in a market dominated by existing homes, supply and demand are both decentralized, with no individual or organization monopolizing the supply. Supply elasticity and demand elasticity are more balanced and synchronized. If not impacted by a macroeconomic cycle or financial business cycle, home prices will not experience any momentous rise or fall. The fluctuation in home prices will be smaller and more constant. Therefore, consumers need to be constantly attentive to the ever changing market. In the existing home market, home buyers are mostly owner-occupiers rather than investors, and naturally they will be more concerned about the location, transportation, and neighborhood of the property. Houses to them are not just concrete structures—they are homes to live in. That explains the highly complicated and intensive information cluster each housing transaction is. Furthermore, people may opt to rent a home as an alternative to buying one. The demand for information will be even greater given the shorter cycle of house rental and higher frequency of information exchange.

2. The Emergence of Large Matchmaking Platforms

The prerequisite for a trading platform is balanced and decentralized buyers and sellers. As real estate sector is becoming a buying market, developers' clout is on the decrease as consumer power rises. This will pave the way for trading platforms and e-commerce businesses in the new home market. What's more, in the existing home market where buyers and sellers are more decentralized than in the new home market, even larger trading platforms will emerge.

There was no trading platform in its true sense in China's new home market before 2014. The prevalent business model then was media e-commerce businesses, which were in essence with media companies offering advertising services. Internet companies were merely developers' platforms for advertisement.

However, in 2014, with the hesitant housing market, the long-drawn sales cycle and home-buying process and the limited effect of advertisement in traditional media, traditional brokerages found it difficult to expand its customer base. Trading platforms for both new homes and existing homes then heaved into sight. Furthermore, the group-buy deposits these platforms charge guarantee immediate commission payment, which used to be a headache for traditional brokerages, and these platforms thus thrived.

However, no real trading platform is in sight in the existing home market. Media companies offer advertising channels or platforms for real estate agents or brokerages to disseminate their information, but they are not involved in or have much control over transactions. On the other hand, although traditional brokerages participate in transactions, they have not evolved from brokerages to platforms. Given the complexity of the existing home market and the indispensability of agents, trading platforms are bound to switch from solely matchmaking platforms to platforms with their own brokerage operations and then the other way round. In the next two or three years, there will emerge one or several huge regional trading platforms for existing homes, which provide information, match buyers and sellers and provide extended services centering around transactions.

Finally, there will be competition between trading platforms for new homes and those for existing homes, because from a consumer's point of view, new homes and existing homes are not much different, but it remains to be seen which will get the upper hand.

Hong Kong
June 2015

Shusong Ba

Contents

Chapter 1
Existing Homes to Take Over China's Housing Market

Readers Guide

- The next 10 years will witness a transition in China's housing market from new homes to existing homes. The robust rise of the existing home market is also an inevitable trend in the international context.
- Although existing homes are not yet a dominant presence in the housing market of most cities, due to a large enough existing housing stock, relatively high homeownership rate and the increasing population mobility, the boom of the existing home market is but inevitable.
- The enormity of US existing home market, with its 5 million transactions each year, owes much to the fact that most homes in the US are single family homes, which, in most cases, meet people's demands for better housing conditions than what they already have. Comparatively speaking, the slow growth of Japan's existing home market is partly due to the low quality and small floor space of its existing homes.

The next 10 years will witness a transition in China's housing market from new homes to existing homes. A robust rise of the existing home market is also an inevitable trend in the international context. Existing homes already dominate the markets of the US, the UK, France and Australia, where the numbers of existing home sales are respectively 9 times, 8.1 times, 1.9 times and 3.5 times those of new home sales. While this ratio is only 0.6 in Japan at large, existing home sales are much more active in Japan's Capital Region and Kinki Region than the rest of the country, the numbers of which are 3 times and 1.9 times those of new home sales respectively (see Fig. 1.1).

S. Ba and X. Yang, *"Internet Plus" Pathways to the Transformation of China's Property Sector*, DOI 10.1007/978-981-10-1699-8_1

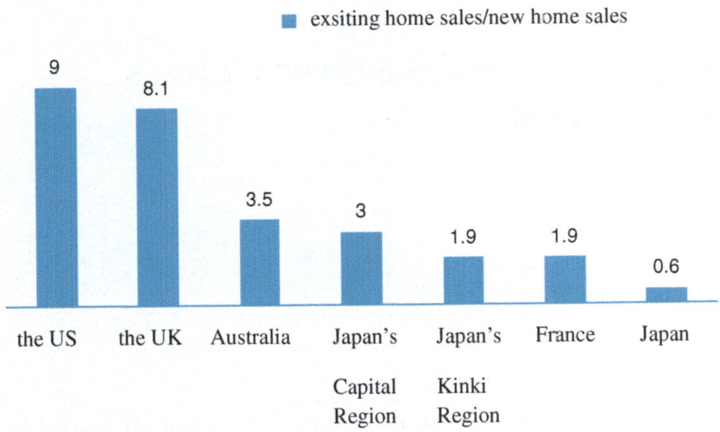

Fig. 1.1 The Ratio of existing home transaction over new home transaction. *Source* The Authors

1.1 The Conditions for a Booming Market of Existing Homes

Now these questions present themselves: On what conditions and at what point in time will existing homes dominate the housing market? What are the causes of such marked differences in the development of the existing home market in different countries? The answer lies in the following three areas.

First, the number of self-owned homes determines the number of homes to be circulated in the market. This is the precondition. Only a fairly high homeownership rate and a considerable number of self-owned homes can stoke a market for existing home sales and rentals. The sharp contrast between the existing home markets in the US and the UK sheds some light on the matter in hand.

In the US, although the real estate brokerage industry appeared in as early as 1880, it did not flourish until 1950 and mature until 1980. The number of housing starts and existing homes stabilized after the boom of the new home market in the 1940s, with homeownership rate stabilizing at above 60 % in long periods (see Fig. 1.2). These facts, together with the large-scale sub-urbanization and human migration since the 1950s, dramatically raised the circulation rate of existing homes, which gradually took the shares from new homes and became a dominant presence, maintaining an 80 % market share over a long period of time, hence boosting the growth of thereal estate brokerage industry.

By contrast, the UK's existing home market did not emerge until the 1980s. This comparatively retarded growth is attributed to the UK's low homeownership rate, which did not rise above 60 % until the 1980s (see Fig. 1.3). The UK government used to exercise intensive intervention in the housing market. With more than 50 % of the homes provided by the government, the UK's homeownership rate grew exceedingly slowly, allowing little room for existing home circulation.

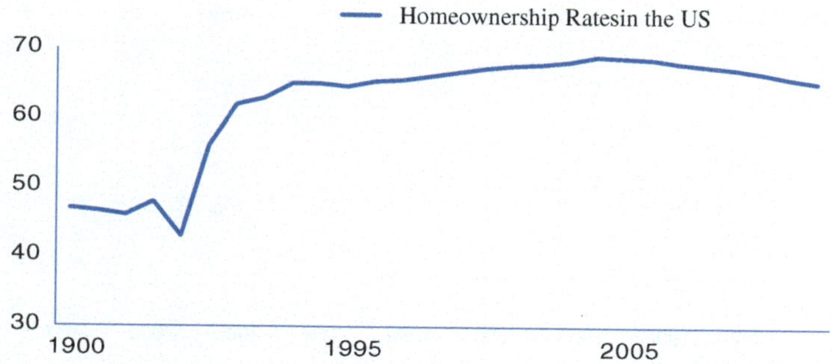

Fig. 1.2 Homeownership rates in the US. *Source* Ferguson (2012). The ascent of money (C. Gao, Trans.). Beijing Citic Press; the Authors

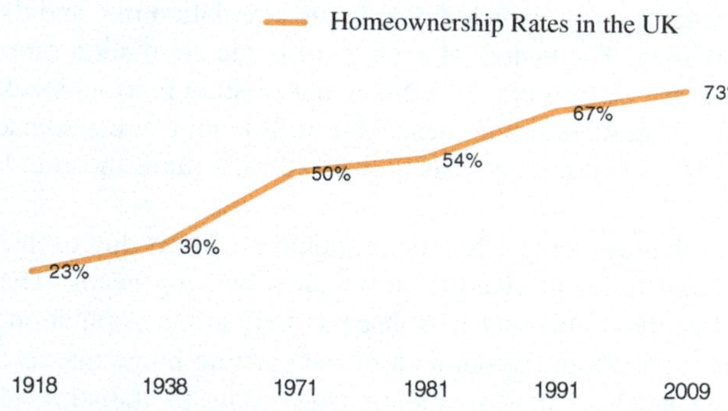

Fig. 1.3 Homeownership rates in the UK. *Source* Office for National Statistics, the Authors

According to statistics, 1/3 of the UK's houses were built by city councils from 1959 to 1964 and the homeownership was still less than 50 % in 1971. In 1983, the more radical Conservative Party under Margaret Thatcher initiated a housing reform. Council houses were sold to 1.5 million working class families at a low price so that more people can possess homes of their own. Consequently the UK's homeownership rate rose to 54 % in 1981 and 67 % 10 years later. The number of self-owned homes is now 18 million, up from 11 million in 1980, providing rich soil for the UK's existing home market to thrive.

The second cause of such a difference lies in the quality of existing homes. Houses of poor quality cannot enter the market,where new homes can better meet people's demands. The enormity of US existing home market, with its 5 million sales each year, owes much to the fact that most US homes are single family homes, which, in most cases, meet people's demands for better housing conditions than what they already have. Comparatively speaking, the slow growth of Japan's existing home market is partly due to the low quality and small floor space of its existing homes.

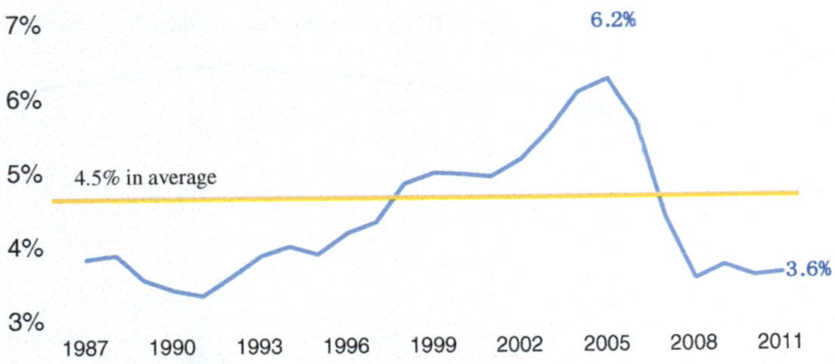

Fig. 1.4 Home circulation rates in the US. *Source* Realogy yearly reports, the Authors

The third reason lies in the different population mobility and different frequency of residence change, which define home circulation rate and the size of the existing home market. The historical average of home circulation rate in the US is 4.5 %, peaking at 6.2 % (see Fig. 1.4). Since the existing housing stock is 120 million units, a 4.5 % circulation rate means 5.4 million units are sold each year. The turnover rate in US rental market is as high as 30 %, 6 times the circulation rate in the sales market.

The high circulation rate in US existing home market is due to the great population mobility and frequent changes in people's housing needs. The sub-urbanization trend after the 1940s and its subsequent suburban population growth rate of over 50 % brought about the outburst of the existing home market. In addition, people's housing needs change frequently. According to statistics, from 2001 to 2011, only 16 % of the US families remained tenants; 13 % of them, who had been tenants, became home owners; 7 % of them, who had been home owners, became tenants; and 9 % of them frequently shift between being tenants and home owners. The frequency is even higher for age groups under 30 (see Fig. 1.5).

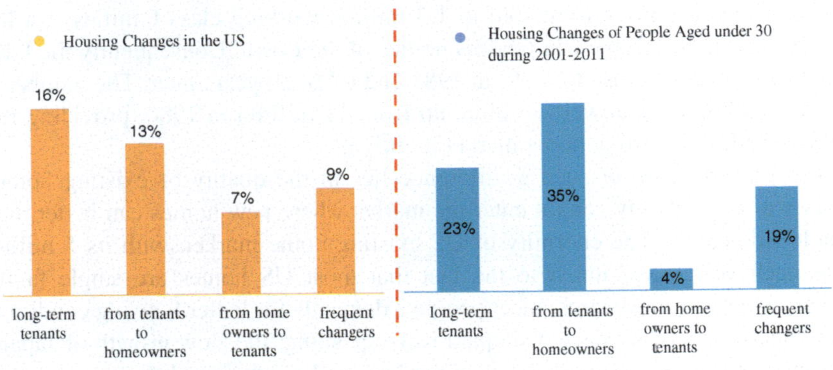

Fig. 1.5 Housing changes in the US. *Source* United States Census Bureau; the Authors

1.2 Why Will China's Existing Homes Take Over the Market?

In 2013, although the ratio of existing home and new home sales is only 35 % in China at large, the former already surpassed the latter in all first-tier cities and a few second-tier cities. According to the statistics of Centaline Home, first tier cities account for 16 % of the total transacted area of existing homes, and 39 % of the transaction volume.

Although existing homes are not yet a dominant presence in most cities' housing market, due to a large enough existing housing stock, relatively high homeownership rate and the increasing population mobility, the rise of the existing home market is but inevitable.

First, China has a large enough existing housing stock. The development of private-ownership housing started in the 1980s and thrived after 1998. Existing housing stock is now over 100 million units. This number will rise to 125 million in 2015 if the scale of current construction is taken into consideration. Supposing new homes are developed at 50 % of the current rate after 2015, the number of existing homes will still reach an astronomical 160 million in 2020 (see Fig. 1.6), ranking first in the world.

Second, homeownership rate is already high in China's cities. Two hundred and fifty millions of China's urban dwells are migrants from rural areas who are not registered as permanent residents and have not entered the real estate market. If migrant population is not taken into account, the homeownership rate of China's registered permanent residents in cities will exceed 70 % in 2015, which will translate into the boom of the existing home market.

Third, China is undergoing a tidal wave of population movement and changes in housing needs. To begin with, although China has had mass population movement throughout history, migrants from rural areas have not entered the home market. However, this is bound to change. As a result of industrial restructuring, migrant population will move from manufacturing industry to service industry,

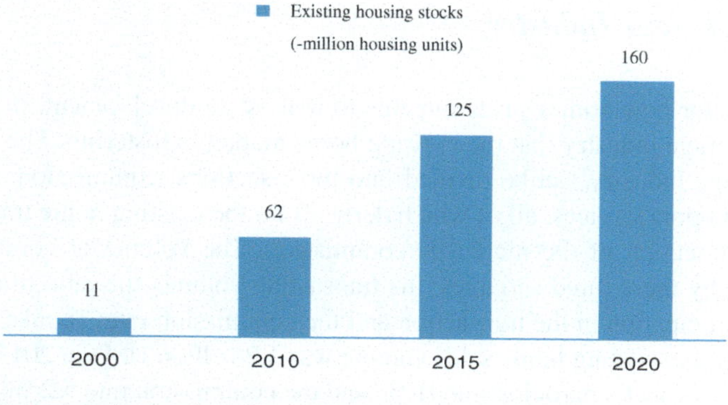

Fig. 1.6 Existing housing stocks in China. *Source* Wind; the Authors

which is concentrated in densely populated areas of cities. These people will need places to live and will either buy or rent homes, as opposed to living in dormitories in factories when they work in the manufacturing sector. Furthermore, while a pure urbanization process used to be the case China, she is now also undergoing a sub-urbanization process and a rapid development of metropolitan regions, resulting in the redistribution of population between a central city and its satellite cities and between a city's center and its outskirts. Finally, China's current reform of household registration system will accelerate the above mentioned processes.

1.3 What Is the Potential for the Existing Home Market?

People's demand for the real estate brokerage industry stems from their demand for houses. Therefore, the real estate brokerage industry should be examined in the big picture of housing market in order to determine the room for its development. The boom of the existing home market is the driving force for the development of the real estate brokerage industry, as is evidenced by the cases in the US, Japan, the UK and Australia. Due to the difficulties in the correlation and dissemination of information as well as the expertise needed all through the process of buying and selling homes, a real estate broker's assistance is much needed to the two parties of a transaction. By contrast, land developers' advertisement, marketing and promotion are effective and accessible to buyers without the assistance of real estate agents, whose service is therefore not as much needed.

The profit of the real estate brokerage industry comes from three areas: commission, advertisement, and support services, which are respectively occupied by traditional real estate brokerages, Internet companies and title insurance companies and financial services companies.

1.3.1 The Three Sections in the Market of the Real Estate Brokerage Industry

As demand for new homes gives impetus to real estate development, it is the real estate brokerage industry that the existing home market is fostering. The market of the brokerage industry can be divided into three sections: commission, advertisement and support services, all of which derive from the existing home transactions.

The first section of the market is commission. The volume of commission is determined by these three variables: the transaction volume, the ratio of real estate broker's participation in the transaction and the commission rate. To take the US as an example, the existing home sales volume was 1.2 trillion USD in 2013, the ratio of real estate broker's participation 91 %, and the commission rate 5.2 %; hence the total volume of commission was the product of the three figures: 56.8 billion USD (see Fig. 1.7).

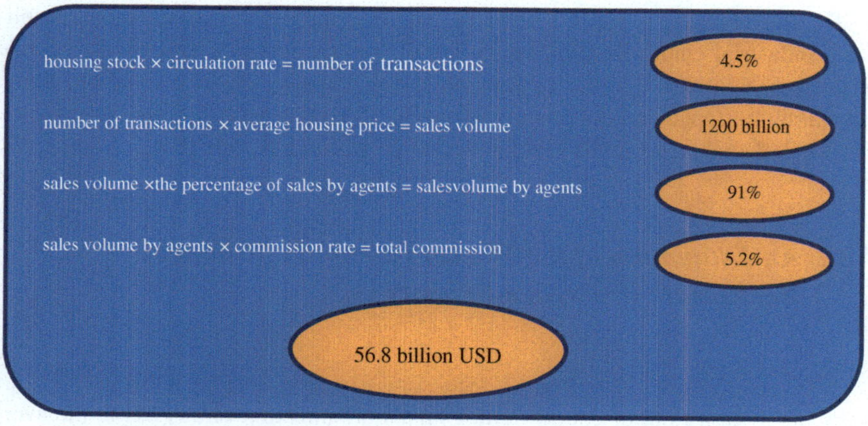

Fig. 1.7 The total commission in the US in 2013: 56.8 billion USD. *Source* The Authors

The second section of the market is advertisement. It includes real estate brokers' ad spending, which usually accounts for 10–20 % of the commission, mortgage brokers' ad spending and the ad spending of rental agents and home decoration businesses. In 2013, American real estate agents spent 11.1 billion USD on advertisement, which was 15.8 % of the total commission, 56.8 billion USD, while rental agents and home decoration businesses spent 11.1 billion USD. The total volume of US advertisement section in 2013 was 38 billion USD, over 50 % of which came from online advertisement (Fig. 1.8).

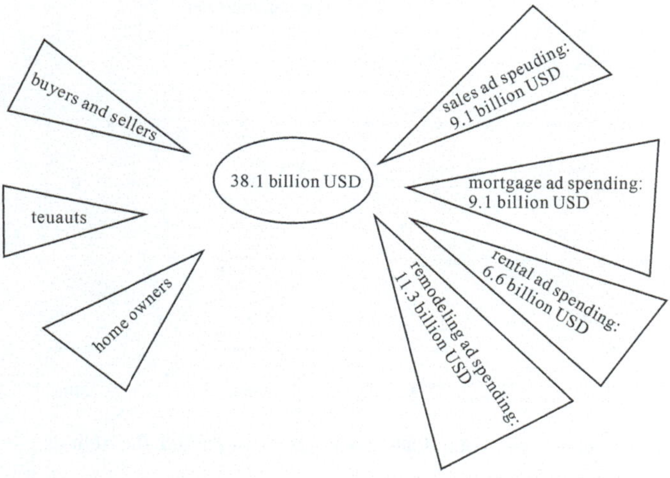

Fig. 1.8 Ad spending in the real estate brokerage industry in the US in 2013: 38 billion USD. *Source* The Authors

The third section is support services. The existing home market has a complicated industrial chain, involving a variety of support services: title service, home inspection, contract signing, settlement, utility payoffs, credit evaluation, home valuation, mortgage and duty memo service etc., each generates a transaction cost. The total of such costs in the USmounted to 20 billion USD in 2013.

1.3.2 An Estimation of the Market Potential of China's Real Estate Brokerage Industry

Basic postulates

Postulate 1: In a state of equilibrium, China's urbanization rate is 65 %, the average number of persons per household is 2.5, and therefore the total number of urban households is 360 million.

Postulate 2: In a state of equilibrium, 60 % of the households own the houses they are living in, 20 % of them rent houses, and the rest 20 % low-income households live in public housing.

Postulate 3: The circulation rate of the existing home market is 3–5 %, and the turnover rate of rental market is 30 %. (Author's note: 3 % is almost the lowest in the world, roughly equaling Japan's circulation rate (see Fig. 1.9). In fact, China's current turnover rate is probably much higher than 30 %, as average lease is rarely longer than 3 years.)

Postulate 4: The commission charged on an existing home transaction is 2 % (see Fig. 1.10), and the commission on a rental is half a month's rent.

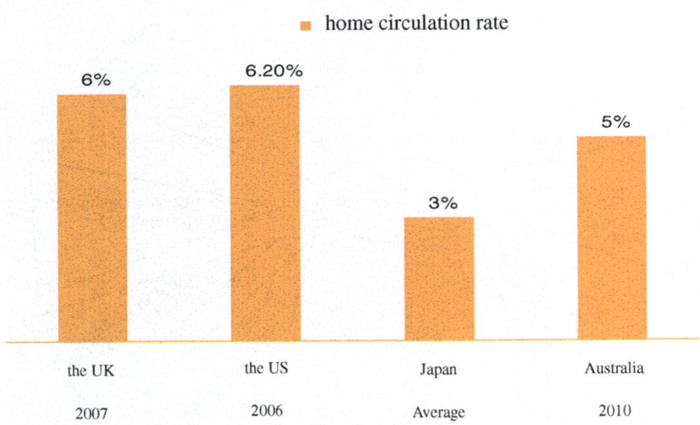

Fig. 1.9 Home circulation rates in different countries. *Source* Wind; the Authors

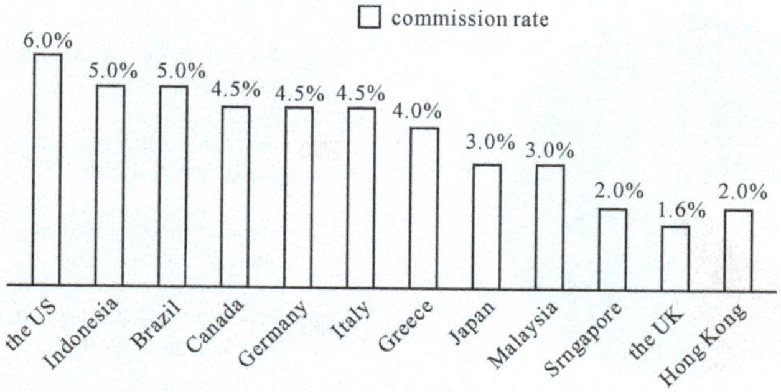

Fig. 1.10 Commission rates in different countries. *Source* Wind; the Authors

The results of the calculation

1. The total commission charged on existing home transactions will range between 83 and 140 billion RMB

According to the above postulates, in a state of equilibrium, the number of existing self-owned houses will be 218 million units. If the circulation rate is 3 %, the average price is 800 thousand per unit in a state of equilibrium, 80 % of the transactions are handled through real estate agents, and the commission rate is 2 %, then the lower limit of the potential commission volume is 83 billion RMB (see Fig. 1.11).

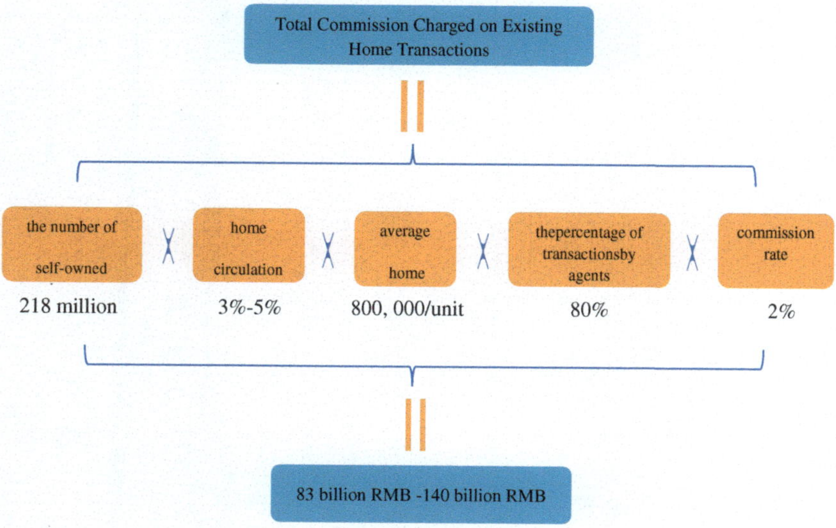

Fig. 1.11 The estimated total commission charged on existing home transactions. *Source* Wind; the Authors

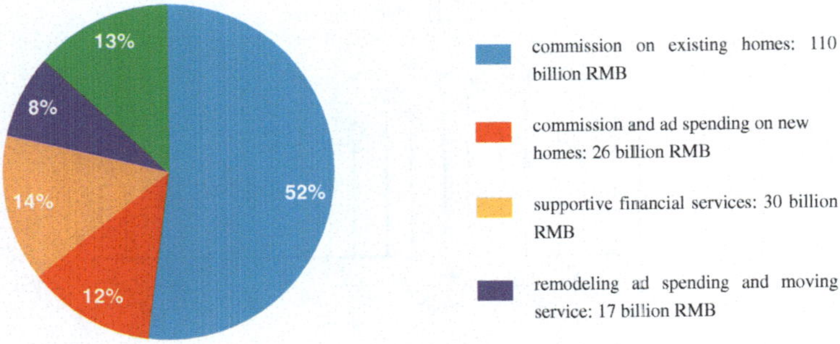

Fig. 1.12 The shares occupied by the participators in industrial chain. *Source* The Authors

2. The total commission charged on rentals will range between 29 and 50 billion RMB

According to the above postulates, the number of existing homes for rent is 73 million units in a state of equilibrium. If the turnover rate is 30 %, the return on rental homes is 4 %, and the commission charged on rentals is half a month's rent, then the lower limit of the total rental commission is 29 billion RMB.

3. If support services like financial service, title insurance, home inspection, settlement and moving service are taken into account, the market of the whole industrial chain will exceed 200 billion RMB (see Fig. 1.12).

Chapter 2
Changes in Pre-internet Real Estate Brokerage Industry in the US Over the Century

Readers Guide

- The nature of real estate brokerage business is correlating buyer and seller information. Given the highly decentralized, locally specific and non-standardized housing supply and highly differential and individualized market demand, the nature of the real estate brokerage industry and the primal issue it is confronted with is the correlation of information.
- Even in today's America, where the internet is a pervasive presence, nearly 90 % of the real estate transactions are closed with the assistance of real estate agents, with only 9 % done by the sellers themselves, and the ratio is still on the decrease (down from 18 % in 1997 and 9 % in 2013). In the UK, Australia and China, the ratio of broker-assisted transactions is over 80 %.
- Information products cost a lot to produce but little to duplicate and disseminate. That is why the real estate brokerage industry has always been confronted with information paradox.

The nature of real estate brokerage business is correlating buyer and seller information. Given the highly decentralized, locally specific and non-standardized housing supply and highly differential and individualized market demand, the nature of the real estate brokerage industry and the primal issue it is confronted with is the correlation of information.

2.1 The Characteristics of Real Estate Transactions

The characteristics of real estate transactions render real estate service a highly information-intensive business.

First, buying or selling a home is usually the biggest and most important assets deployment in a family life cycle. Such decisions are few and far between and have to be made with great discretion, hence the demand for adequate, up-to-date and accurate information.

S. Ba and X. Yang, *"Internet Plus" Pathways to the Transformation of China's Property Sector*, DOI 10.1007/978-981-10-1699-8_2

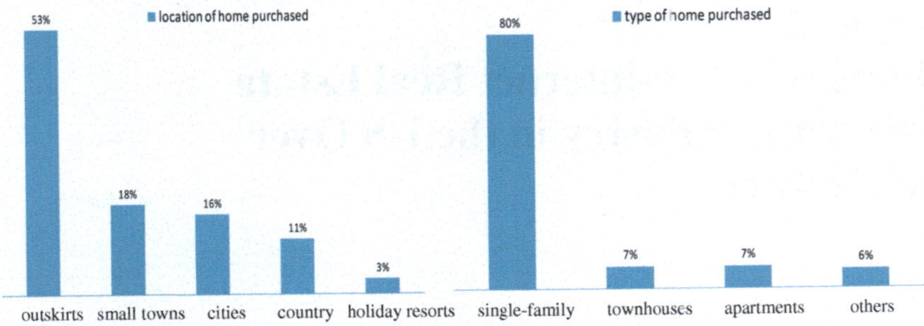

Fig. 2.1 The locations and types of homes purchased in the US. *Source* NAR (2014)

Second, homes are highly non-standardized and localized properties. Every home is different due to its different location, neighborhood, supporting facilities and transportation. In addition, buyer resources are diversified. It is extremely difficult to match the right seller with the right buyer. In America, 71 % of the transacted homes are in the outskirts and small towns, and 87 % of them are single family homes (see Fig. 2.1). Selling or buying homes is mostly about processing a store of highly locally specific and non-standardized information.

Third, real estate transactions involve a series of important steps, including consulting, home search, home viewing, contract signing, financing, settlement, moving and insurance, all of which can be excruciating for buyers with no expertise in these areas. Real estate broker's professional service is much needed.

2.2 The Roles of Real Estate Brokers

Even in today's America, where the internet is a pervasive presence, nearly 90 % of the real estate transactions are closed with the assistance of real estate agents, with only 9 % by the sellers themselves, down from 18 % in 1997 and 9 % in 2013 (see Fig. 2.2), and the ratio is still decreasing. In the UK, Australia and China, the ratio of broker-assisted transactions is over 80 %.

Why then, do buyers and sellers hire real estate brokers? What essential parts do they play?

2.2.1 Why Do People Hire Real Estate Brokers?

Whether a home seller will hire a real estate agent or not depends on the cost of the transaction. In other words, as selling a home is time consuming, he has to

Fig. 2.2 The decrease of sales by owners in the US. *Source* The Authors

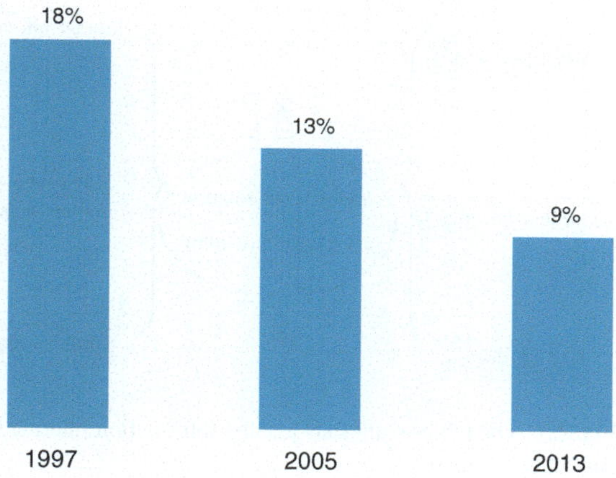

weigh the cost of time against the commission he has to pay if he chooses to hire a agent. High-income home sellers and those moving out of the area are more ready to hire real estate agents. For home buyers, on the other hand, their access to local market information and the cost of time are the major concerns. High-income home buyers and those moving into the area are more likely to use agents.

Both sellers and buyers decide to use real estate agents because of their lack of information about the local housing market and their concerns over the cost of time.

2.2.2 *What Essential Part Do Real Estate Agents Play?*

Real estate broker's part in a transaction can be divided into two sections.

First, the correlation and dissemination of information. Three kinds of information are disseminated and correlated: information about the property, including the location, floor area, layout and listed price; information about the neighborhood, including locally specific information like the surrounding schools, transportation, public facilities, crime rates and natural disasters; information about the existing home market, including the historical development of the local home prices and the valuation of the property in question.

Second, support services. Support services fall under the following three categories: accompanying buyers on their property viewing tours, negotiating price on behalf of the clients, helping through the procedures after a contract is signed (see Fig. 2.3).

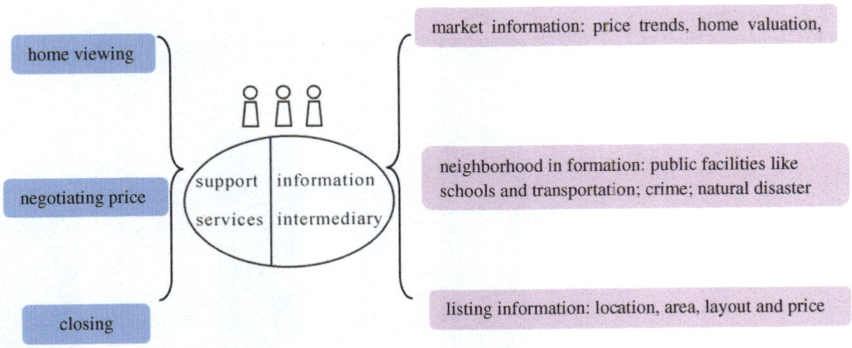

Fig. 2.3 The job of real estate agents: Information Intermediary + Support Services. *Source* The Authors

2.3 The Process of a Real Estate Transaction

Traditionally, a typical real estate transaction conducted with the help of an agent involves three important steps: choosing a real estate agent, signing listing agreement and marketing. A transaction kicks off at the choice of a real estate broker; next, listing information is obtained and commission rate officially stated according to the type of listing agreement; and then the real estate agent helps buyers and sellers find each other through his marketing effort, which is the crucial step in the process of real estate transactions (see Fig. 2.4).

2.3.1 Choosing a Real Estate Broker

The choice of real estate agents is based on a potential client's assessment of the agents, which is made according to two essential criteria. The first is whether they are trustworthy and whether they can act in their client's best interests. The second is whether they are capable enough to effectively market their client's homes and find the highest bids.

However, the assessment is not an easy job, because the performance of real estate agents is difficult to monitor and evaluate. As people do not buy or sell houses frequently, it is difficult for them to assess real estate broker's service and professionalism based on one or two transactions. Clients cannot assess real estate broker's abilities before a transaction, nor can they objectively appraise the transaction price after one, for they are much less informed than real estate agents. This is a typical case of information asymmetry.

Due to the limited information on the client's part, finding trusty agents who can act in their client's best interests is extremely difficult. In the history of US real estate brokerage industry, there were three solutions to this problem: First, a

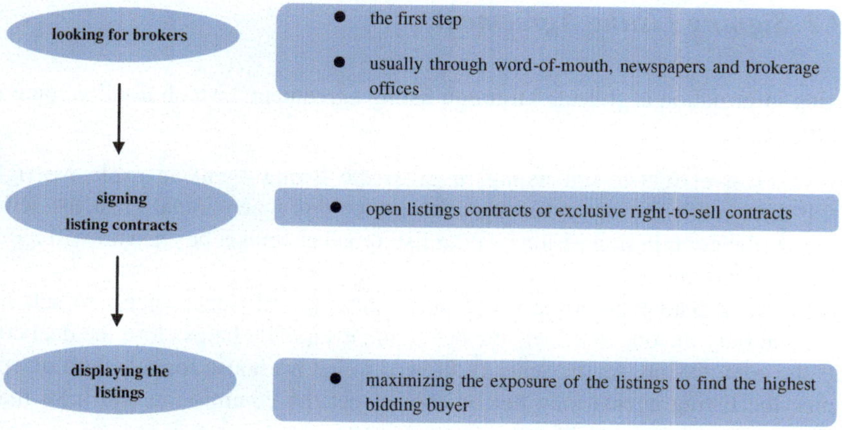

Fig. 2.4 Three important steps in a real estate transaction. *Source* The Authors

licensing system for real estate agents was launched in 1913 to establish qualification threshold and ensure service quality. Second, the practice of open listing is adopted. Home sellers can use more than one real estate agent to help sell their homes, while the sellers themselves can also find buyers on their own, without paying commission to the real estate agents. Third, real estate agents build up their reputation through franchising. There were around 15 thousand real estate franchisees in the US in 1979. Fourth, people mostly rely on s from friends to find good agents. In 1983, 54 % home sellers found their agents through their friend's referrals (see Fig. 2.5). Finally, real estate agents advertise themselves on newspapers, magazines and TV, which boosts the development of classified ads on print media.

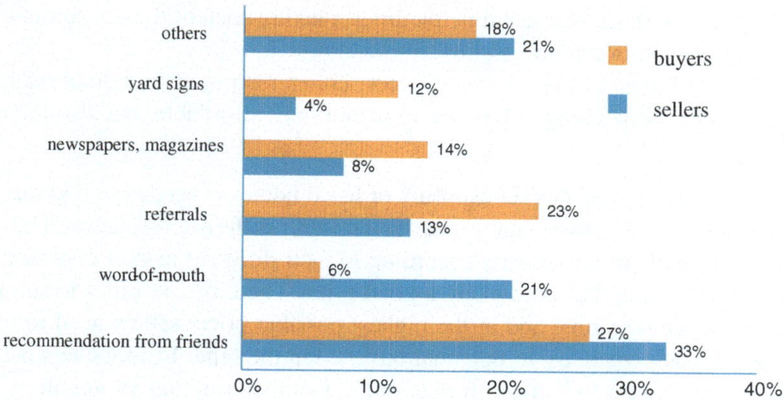

Fig. 2.5 How buyers and sellers look for real estate agents. *Source* FTC (1983)

2.3.2 *Signing Listing Agreement*

Listing information is collected through listing agreements, which usually come in three types.

First, exclusive right-to-sell listing. It gives the listing agent an exclusive right to sell the client's. property. Listing contracts of this type stipulate that the seller must pay the commission as long as the listing agent finds a buyer who will agree to the selling terms.
Second, open listing. A home seller uses multiple real estate agents to sell his home, but only the one that finds the buyer and eventually helps close the deal collects the commission. As the seller is allowed to list his house for sale with several agents, the listing agents may not be able to get the commission and have their marketing expenses covered.
The third, exclusive brokerage listing. It contracts one agent to sell the home. Its difference from exclusive right-to-sell listing is that, as with an open listing, no sales commission is owed if the home seller finds a buyer by himself.

Open listing is the most widely used listing contract in the US in the 1920s and the 1930s, in the UK before the 1980s and in today's China. The major drawback of open listing is that it leads to excessive or even unhealthy competition and a rather chaotic practice. Professionalism is thus improbable among agents who do not have control over their commission.

2.3.3 *Marketing the Homes for Sale*

Real estate transactions are substantially different from transactions of ordinary commodities in the following ways.

First, every home is different. Houses differ from each other in locations, layouts, neighborhoods and accessible public facilities, making each of them a complicated concentration of information.
Second, every buyer has his own resources, either for rational or emotional reasons. The home he is going to buy has to be not only affordable, but also the most satisfactory.

Consequently, a great market exposure of listed homes is needed to find matches between diversified housing units and buyers with different resources. The selling prices of the homes may vary according to their different market exposure; the greater the exposure, the more likely a good price. Therefore, in order to sell their homes in the shortest time and at the highest possible price, sellers need to maximize their home's visibility to potential buyers. On the other hand, buyers need to maximize their access to listing information, so that they can find affordable as well as the most suitable and the most satisfactory homes in the shortest time.

2.3.4 *Information Paradox*

Information products cost a lot to produce but little to duplicate and disseminate. That is why the real estate brokerage industry has always been confronted with information paradox.

On one hand, for the sellers and the real estate brokerage industry at large, widely disseminating the listing information will generate a scale effect and therefore help find potential buyers in the shortest time possible.

On the other hand, the producer of information, for example, a real estate agent or brokerage who has spent time and money accumulating information and advertising the house, may not be able to collect the commission for his previous hard work because once the information is made public, the potential buyer may make a deal with the seller without him, and other real estate agents may take the information for free.

As a result, in order to cover the cost of information, a real estate agent has to limit other broker's access to his listing information. However, this will reduce or even cancel out the chances of finding potential buyers, because one agent or one brokerage has only a limited market share, with access to only part of the market.

2.4 Changes in the Pre-internet Real Estate Brokerage Industry in the US Over the Century

Given the highly decentralized, localized and non-standardized information about housing supply and demand, the evolution of the real estate brokerage industry in the US over the century centers around these essential issues: finding trusty real estate agents, signing listing agreements and while endeavoring to solve the so called "information paradox", maximizing the market exposure of the listed homes in order to find the highest bidding buyers.

2.4.1 *Accidental Matching of Information Before 1880*

There was virtually no real estate brokerage industry in the US before 1880, and the housing market was dominated by rapidly emerging new homes, with negligible number of transactions of existing homes. No real estate agents ever participated in such transactions, and sellers and buyers find each other by chance, which is a typical C2C model (see Fig. 2.6). The correlation of the buyer information and seller information was very inefficient. There were hardly any professional real estate agents, and their work was done by local lawyers or authorities.

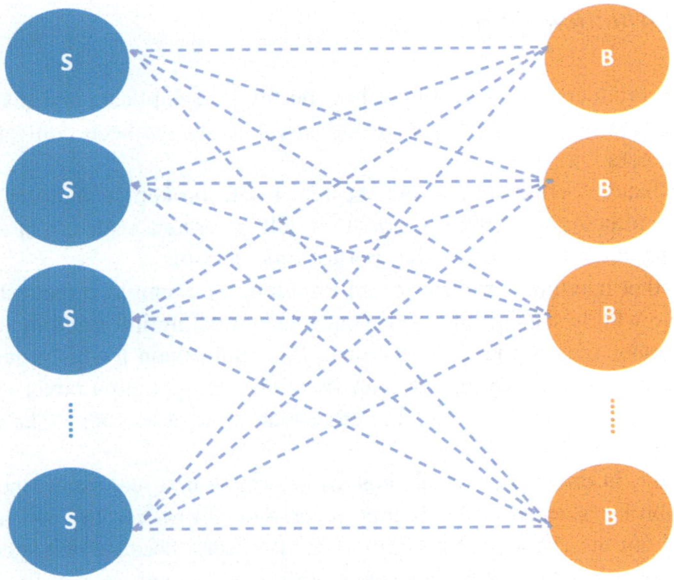

Fig. 2.6 Accidental matching of information before 1880. *Source* The Authors (*S* for sellers; *B* for buyers)

2.4.2 The Appearance of Real Estate Agents and the Dominance of Open Listing Agreement During 1880–1950

The real estate brokerage industry in the US began after 1880, when existing home sales began to grow in some cities. Open listing was the first type of listing agreement to appear, with its heyday in the 1930s. A home seller may use several, even as many as 20 real estate agents to sell his home (see Fig. 2.7), but only the one that finds the buyer and eventually helps close the deal collects the commission.

The background of the dominance of open listing and its features are as follows.

First, with new homes dominating the housing market, the supply of existing homes fell short of the demand; therefore, listing information was the most essential part of the real estate brokerage industry. Second, sellers could only maintain a very limited market exposure. Listing information could only be visible to part of the market and part of the potential buyers even if 20 real estate agents were doing the job at the same time. Third, as real estate agents worked individually and independently from each other, buyers need to contact each of the real estate agents in order to gather adequate information, which was very inefficient. Fourth, an open listing agreement allows a home seller to use multiple real estate agents to sell his home, but only the one that finds the buyer and eventually helps close the deal collects the commission. The other agents who have spent time and money looking

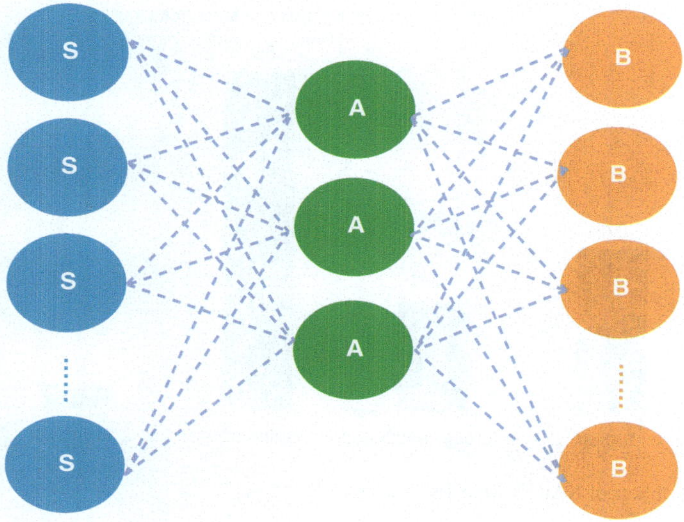

Fig. 2.7 The open listing model. *Source* The Authors (*A* for agents)

for prospective buyers will not be able to get the commission nor have their marketing expenses covered. A market with professional real estate agents is unlikely to take shape under these circumstances.

Although an open listing agreement is extremely inefficient, with its protection over the sellers and the small volume of transactions back then, it sustained over a long period and was not replaced by exclusive right-to-sell agreements until 1950.

2.4.3 The Prevalence of Multiple Listing Services From 1950 to 1995

Multiple listing services have definitely been playing the leading role in the evolution of the real estate brokerage industry in the US. The birth, the growth and finally the boom of Multiple listing services (MLS) overlap the evolution of US real estate brokerage industry. One has to study Multiple listing services first before he can understand the changes of industrial chain in the real estate brokerage industry in the US and the impact of the Internet.

2.4.3.1 What Is an MLS?

An MLS is a suite of services created by local association of real estate agents and are only accessible to its members, who are required to add all their listings to the service database.

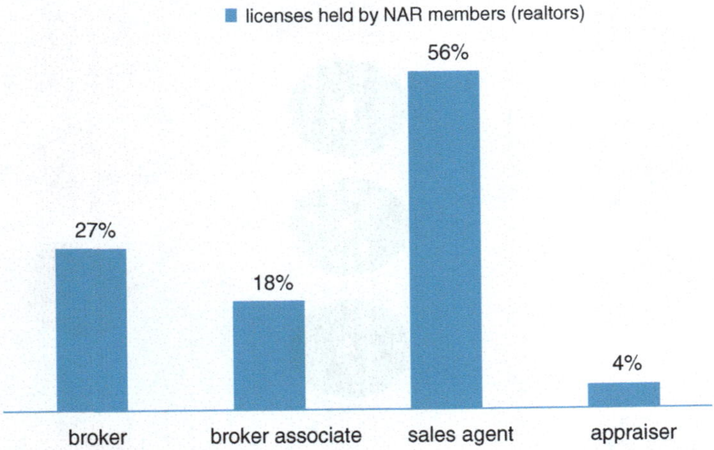

Fig. 2.8 Members of NAR. *Source* The Authors

Multiple listing services restrict membership and access to realtors, who are concurrently members of the local, state and national association of realtors. US National Association of Realtors (NAR) has 1.1 million members holding different licenses (see Fig. 2.8). The realtors have passed real estate license exams and are pledged to a code of ethics. NAR and MLSes, so to speak, are "broker's clubs", where they observe common codes and enjoy common interests.

As a common database, an MLS accepts listing information from exclusive right-to-sell agreements only. It requires that a member release listing information to the service within 72 h after an exclusive right-to-sell agreement is signed. The listing information includes the location and layout of the property, listed price, term of agreement (usually 90 days), commission rate and commission splits (see Fig. 2.9). A selling agent is supposed to up-to-date change the status of a listing from "active" to "sold" or "rented" after a transaction and input the transaction price in the database.

2.4.3.2 How Did Multiple Listing Services Prevail in America?

he first local MLS was created in New York in 1907. However, Multiple listing services had no significant development in the following decades until the outburst of existing home market in the US in 1950, which translated into flourishing Multiple listing services and local associations of realtors. After the 1970s, MLS prevailed in the whole country. Today, there are approximately 900 Multiple listing services created and operated by local associations of realtors in America (Fig. 2.10).

According to statics, although Multiple listing services and local associations of realtors developed rapidly, the growth of MLS membership lagged behind.

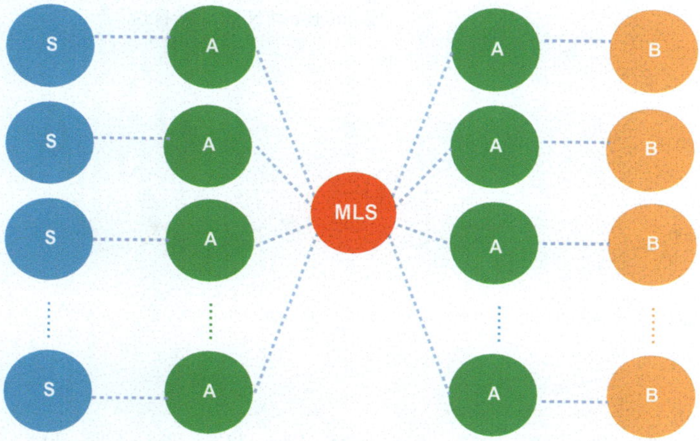

Fig. 2.9 The distribution of information in MLS and exclusive-right-to-sell model. *Source* The Authors

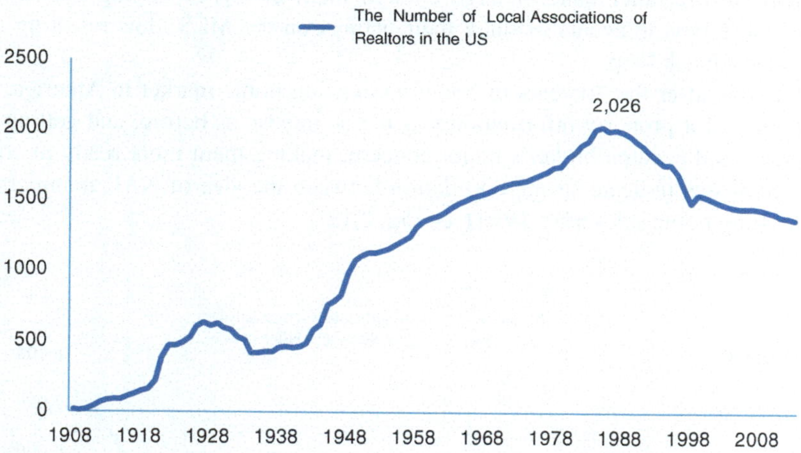

Fig. 2.10 The number of local associations of realtors in the US. *Source* NAR

In fact, the MLS membership roster did not soar to 800 thousand until the early 1970s, up from 130 thousand (see Fig. 2.11). There are two underlying reasons.

Members clubs are typically characterized with network effects. Joining the club does not have much significant value until the membership roster grows to a certain critical number. Therefore MLS membership needs to grow over a long period of time until it can produce "positive feedback" loop. An MLS is a mutually benefiting platform for its members. "Help me sell my inventory and I'll help sell yours." Then the cooperating agents split commission between them. Buying agents will want to join an MLS only when it offers a large enough number of

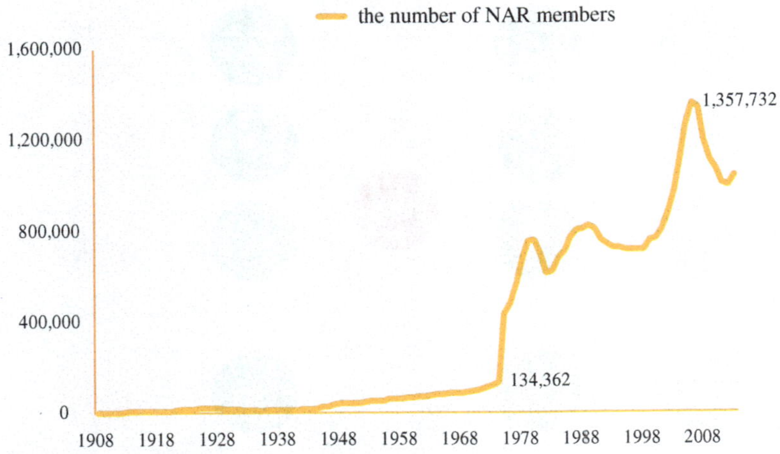

Fig. 2.11 The number of NAR members. *Source* NAR

listings. On the other hand, a large enough membership of buying agents will attract more buying agents to share their listings on the MLS, thus resulting in a positive feedback loop.

In 1970s, after the 10 years of booming existing home market in America, the competition for property information was not as intense as before, and getting the inventory sold became broker's major concern, making them more ready to cooperate. Statistics indicate strong correlation between the size of NAR membership and existing home sales after 1970 (see Fig. 2.12).

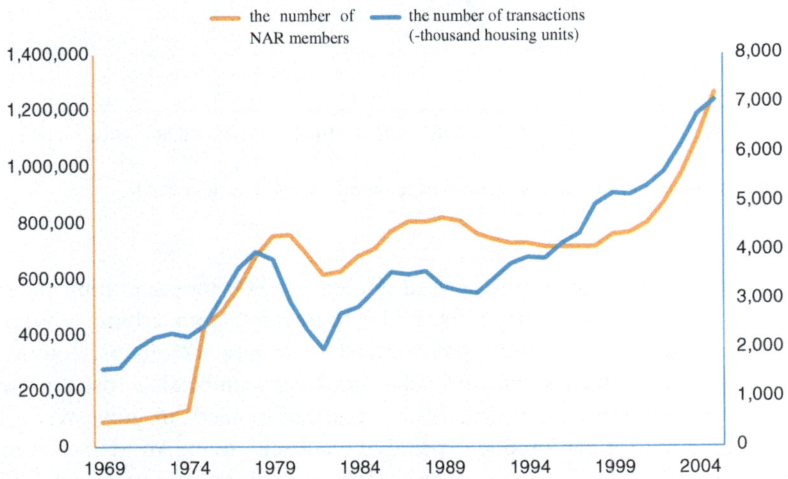

Fig. 2.12 The number of NAR members and the number of existing home transactions. *Source* NAR

2.5 How Does an MLS Connect the Links in the Industrial Chain of the Real Estate Brokerage Industry?

Multiple listing services reorganized the industrial chain of the real estate brokerage industry in late 1970s, when 92 % agents input their listing information into MLS database. Exclusive right-to-sell agreement completely replaced open listing agreement. The new way of operation and new value spread were established according to the new rules.

First, the major changes brought about by Multiple listing services are as follows: exclusive right-to-sell agreements have become the dominant type of listing agreement; listing information is displayed on a common database that ensures maximum market exposure; individual agents are gathered on a common information matching platform. Supposing all selling agents release their listings to Multiple listing services for all buying agents to see, then the job of Multiple listing services is to increase the exposure of listed properties by displaying them to a greater number of buying agents while reducing the cost of home search on the buying broker's part. In theory, buyers only need one single buying agent to access all market information.

In this way, each of the "part of the market" that individual agents have access to are connected to form "the whole market", and a seller or a buyer needs only one agent to disseminate his supply or demand information to the whole market. The faster dissemination and wider exposure of listing information help match buyers and sellers with more precision and efficiency.

Second, Multiple listing services have established the new rules of the trade and become the "market-makers" that dominate the real estate brokerage industry. Instead of competing with each other as they had used to when they worked by open listing agreements, agents began to cooperate. A typical process of real estate transaction in an MLS system is as follows: A seller hires a selling agent, who feeds his property information into the MLS database. Then a buyer goes to a buying agent, who searches for the matching listing information on the MLS. If he finds a suitable home and helps close the deal, the seller will pay the commission to his agent, who will split the commission with the buying agent (commission split is usually 50/50 unless specified otherwise in the listing agreement, see Fig. 2.13).

In the late 1970s, 81 % of the sellers hired selling agents (the ratio approaching 90 % in 2013), 92 % of whom would share the listing information on an MLS. On the other hand, 66 % of the buyers used buying agents, the ratio being 88 % in 2013 (see Fig. 2.14), who would access the MLS database to find suitable homes.

Third, Multiple listing services changed the commission splits in the real estate brokerage industry. In an MLS, the first commission split is between a buying agent and a selling agent at the rate of 50/50, each getting 3 % of the selling price as the regular commission rate in the US is 6 %. The second split is between a brokerage and its franchise company. A agent or a brokerage in the US usually chooses to franchise with a national or regional brand. The franchisor gets 6 % of

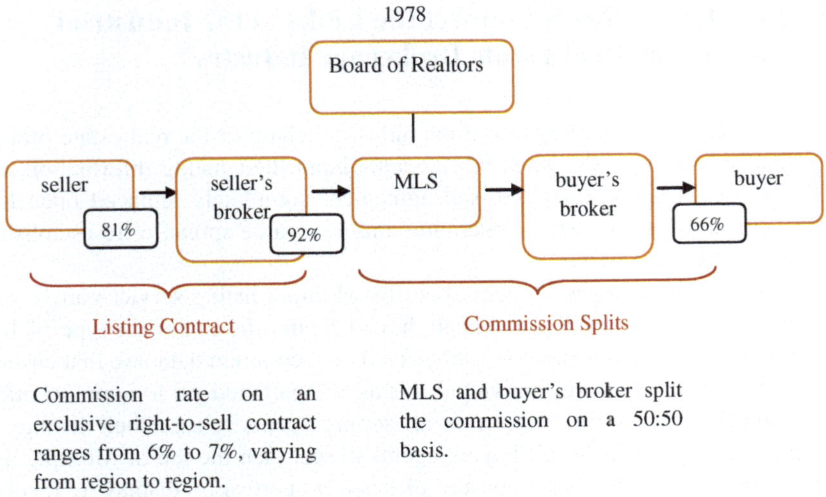

Fig. 2.13 MLS established the rules of the industry. *Sources* Federal Trade Commission (1983); The Authors

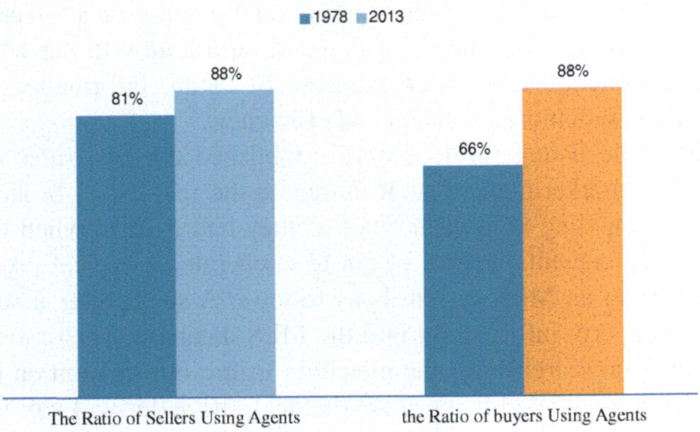

Fig. 2.14 The ratio of buyers using real estate agents versus the ratio of sellers using real estate agents. *Source* NAR (2014)

the 3 % and the brokerage gets the rest 94 %. The third split is between a agent and the brokerage he is working with. Since it is the agent who does most of the work, the brokerage does not get much of the commission, usually 10–30 % (see Fig. 2.15) or even lower. The more able and experienced the agent, the less commission split he offers the brokerage. Only inexperienced entrants will give 50 % or more of his commission to the brokerage. This is a dilemma on the part of the brokerage: brokerages must recruit more new agents in order to get more commission, but more new recruits usually means less satisfactory service.

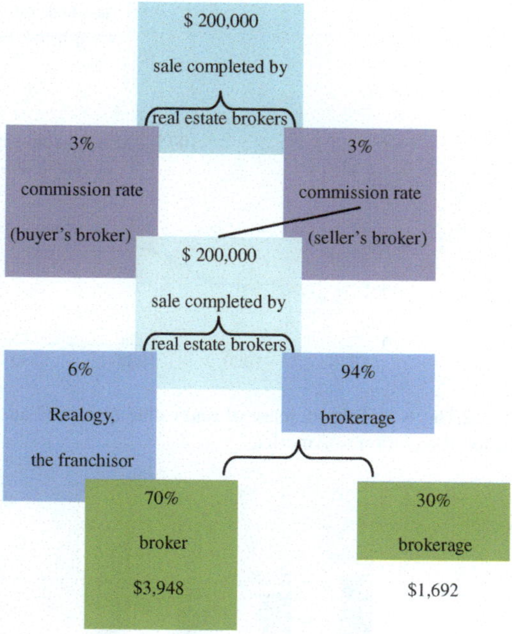

Fig. 2.15 Commission splits in MLS systems. *Source* The Authors

Forth, the thriving Multiple listing services indirectly facilitated the development of franchising companies and increased classified ads on property sales or rentals in print media. As a closed system, an MLS restricts accessibility to its member agents. Buyers or sellers have to contact the agents or read their ads to get listing information and other market information. The purpose of broker's ads, however, is not to disseminate the listing information, but to market himself and attract clients. They pay for the franchising companies for the same reason—to distinguish themselves from other agents by identifying with brand names like "21st Century". This acts as a screening mechanism for the clients, who are the disadvantaged side of information asymmetry. However, it seems that less able agents, rather than experienced ones, need more of such proofs of their professionalism. Although the benefit of franchising with a well-known brand is open to dispute, it remains a popular choice for many agents over long periods. Many companies grew to be business giants through franchising.

Statistics show that in 2005, real estate classified ad spending on newspapers was 6 times the spending in 1975 (see Fig. 2.16), and that a large number of franchising companies emerged (see Fig. 2.17). 21st Century Real Estate in her prime had over 130 thousand franchised agents, making her the largest franchisor in the world.

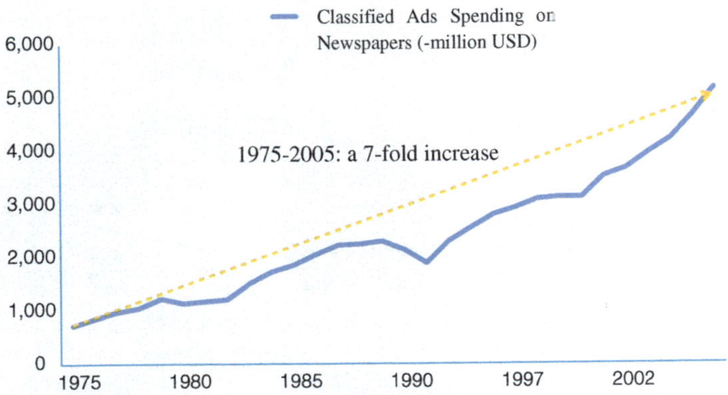

Fig. 2.16 A sixfold increase of real estate classified ads spending on newspapers. *Source* Newspaper association of America

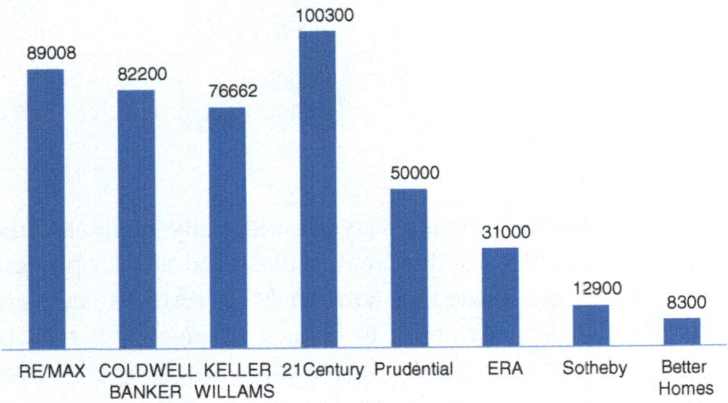

Fig. 2.17 Franchising companies thriving in the MLS model: the number of real estate agents in each Franchising company. *Source* Realogy yearly report (2013)

2.6 Much Discussed Issues in an MLS-Dominant Market

2.6.1 Smaller Brokerages and Increased Concentration Ratio

As Multiple listing services prevail, housing market is gradually dominated by medium-sized or small enterprises for the following reasons:

First, in the real estate brokerage industry, business expansion alone does not result in economies of scale. Agents rely heavily on their independent judgment and expertise. One cannot break down a broker's work and form an automated work flow. Therefore, expansion of a brokerage is nothing more than having more people doing the same job, achieving practically no scale merit.

Second, it is difficult for big brokerages to make quick adjustments to business slowdowns or reduced market demand. On the contrary, small brokerages with small fixed costs can better survive economic cyclical changes.
Third, the real estate brokerage industry has rather low barriers to entry. Only a small amount of capital is needed to open a brokerage. In addition, new brokerages can use the listing information provided by Multiple listing services.

Smaller brokerages are naturally decentralized. A real estate agent usually works within a limited region, because the information about the local market is of the greatest value to him.

The real estate brokerage industry is highly labor-intensive, the fee or commission for the agents being the greatest expense, accounting for 60 % of a brokerage's total income. Brokerages will offer favorable commission splits, 70 % for example, to productive agents. Professional agents are a brokerage's major asset. A brokerage hardly has any assets besides its agents and the brand name. Therefore, in order to study the brokerage industry, one has to examine the motivation of agents and their relationship with Multiple listing services first.

With smaller brokerages comes increased concentration ratio. As the largest franchisor, 21 Century Real Estate expanded rapidly in 1979. Thirty eight percent of the broker-assisted real estate transactions were handled by franchised brokerages, 48 % of which were completed by 21 Century Real Estate. Agents can quickly raise their profiles in the market by franchising with well-known brands, which in return stokes the rapid expansion of franchising companies.

2.6.2 Fixed-Percentage Commission: Reasonable or Unreasonable?

In the circle of economic studies, it is generally believed that fixed-percentage commission that US brokerage industry generally adopts causes much waste and is inefficient. Local MLS members monopolize the market and adopt a commission rate above market equilibrium. In addition, the easy entry to this industry gives rise to non-price competition, which does not raise the productivity of the brokerage industry, hence the lower economic profits.

Another widely held opinion is that since the cost of selling a property is not correlated with its price, a fixed-percentage commission based on the property's selling price suggests a monopolist's price discrimination.

The opposing opinion is that a fixed commission rate does not necessarily lead to monopoly and lack of price competition. For example, in competition with other agents, a agent will promise his client that he will sell the property in a shorter time and at a higher price, which, according to some economists, is part of the selling proceeds. In this case, the "net commission" the seller pays is fixed commission minus this part of the proceeds. The fixed-percentage commission rate is in fact variable.

Some economists prove with convincing statistics that fixed-percentage commission rate is counter-cyclical in a competitive market. It falls when home prices go up. Although big brokerages sell faster than smaller brokerages, they do not charge extra commission.

The cost of a buyer and his broker's home search will affect home prices, commission rates and commission splits. Multiple listing services reduce the cost of a home selling search for agents and home buying search for homes. If this reduction in cost is taken into account, again, the commission rate is in fact variable.

Some hold that agents do not just match buyers and sellers, and that they facilitate the buyer's consumption of houses. The lowered cost of home search will bring more of such searches and thereby increase buyer's chances of finding a suitable home and the seller's chances of getting their homes sold. As advertisements promote consumption, so does brokerage service.

Another researcher studied the different effects of flat-fee, fixed percentage commission rate and split commission. First, sellers may shorten terms of agreement in order to give agents stronger impetus, as agents will not get the commission if they fail to sell the property before the agreement expires. However, sellers need to spend more time to negotiate with agents to get them sign the agreement, as most agents are not willing to accept such harsh terms. Sellers have to strike a balance between the cost of this negotiation and the benefits from the impetus it may give the agents. Second, if the listing agreement specifies that the first agent to find a buyer collects all the commission, then agents will make the greatest "joint effort" to find a buyer. If the listing agreement specifies that the commission is to be split, then the agents get the greatest "joint profit" for their cooperation. Most selling agents would rather take a smaller split instead of a larger split or even full commission that entails fierce competition. If sellers insist on paying full commission only to the agent who brings the buyer, then selling agents may refuse such an agreement, or refuse to share the listing information. Multiple listing services eliminate the excessive competition between agents and increase the chances of sales when they disseminate the listing information to the whole market. The sellers, while enjoying these benefits, must pay full commission.

2.6.3 Traditional Broker's Boycott Against Nontraditional Brokers

In the early 1980s, discount agents were participated in only 2 % of the real estate transactions. However, nontraditional business models like discount brokerage service, internet-based brokerages and flat-fee service probably represent the trend in the future real estate brokerage industry.

Traditional agents boycott nontraditional agents in ways including denying their access to traditional broker's listing information. Traditionally, consumers believe that commission rate is set by law and trade rules and is supposed to be the same in every brokerage.

A survey made in 1983 suggests that 34 % of the nontraditional agents admitted that they were boycotted by traditional media (mostly newspapers), who refused to advertise for them because of the joint threat from traditional agents.

Many traditional agents believe that discount is not a sustainable policy and that the regular commission rate traditional agents adopt is a reasonable level for the sustainable development of the industry. In fact, most nontraditional brokerages are new firms. A survey made in 1983 suggests that only 10 % of the 154 nontraditional samples were set up before 1974.

Some traditional agents point out that the interdependence between brokerages makes price competition a vain effort.

Buying agents are usually compensated with a split of the commission paid by sellers, so if a selling agent discounts his commission, the split that goes to the buying agent will be smaller, and he will be reluctant to show homes with discount commission to potential buyers.

The advantage nontraditional agents enjoy is that they rely on advertisements and discounts instead of referrals to acquire selling information, but selling homes remains a difficult task for them, which, sometimes has to be undertaken by home owners themselves.

According to a survey made in 1979, 68 % of the nontraditional agents did not regularly use Multiple listing services, and 75 % of them adopted a fixed commission rate, about 1.6 % of the selling price. Eighty four percent of the non-traditional agents required home owners to manage marketing and home showing themselves after the agents list their homes on an MLS.

Most of the 32 % of the non-traditional agents who used multiple listing services provided full service, with average commission rate at 4.2 %, but they had to cooperate with other agents in order to keep the business coming in the door.

Chapter 3
What Changes Has the Internet Brought to the Real Estate Brokerage Industry?

Readers Guide

- In a market where buyers and sellers are both highly decentralized, a market maker acts as a neural center, establishing the rules of the trade and integrating the decentralized information channels. For one thing, it can acquire listing information and control the supply; for another, it can attract buyers and control the demand, providing a highly centralized platform for buyers and sellers to find each other.
- Since 1995, the Internet has fundamentally changed people's ways of communicating, acquiring information and buying products or services. Buyers, sellers and renters alike can all benefit profoundly from the Internet, since the real estate industry is large-scaled, regionally decentralized, and highly information-intensive. The Internet has undergone two periods of development since 1995.
- For most consumers, buying or selling a home is a daunting event involving a huge amount of money and complicated procedures. It is a highly information-intensive decision which relies heavily on accurate information. Unfortunately, such information is not easily accessible to consumers due to its complicacy, specialism and opacity.

The century-long history of the US brokerage industry has witnessed the centralization and integration of information matching media, a process that can be termed as "the rise of the market maker system". In a market where buyers and sellers are both highly decentralized, a market maker acts as a neural center, establishing the rules of the trade and integrating the decentralized information channels. For one thing, it can acquire listing information and control the supply; for another, it can attract buyers and control the demand, providing a highly centralized platform for buyers and sellers to find each other. In short, a market maker is a platform where buyer information and listing information are shared and correlated. In the pre-Internet days market makers were multiple listing services; now they are Internet platforms (Fig. 3.1).

S. Ba and X. Yang, *"Internet Plus" Pathways to the Transformation of China's Property Sector*, DOI 10.1007/978-981-10-1699-8_3

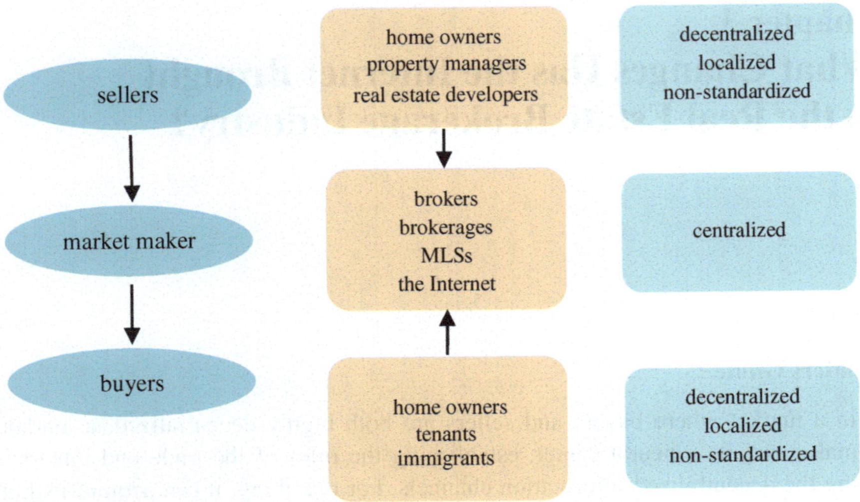

Fig. 3.1 The structure of the real estate brokerage industry. *Source* The Authors

3.1 The Driving Force Behind the Transformation of Information Media

3.1.1 The Three Periods in the Development of Information Media

There were three obvious periods in the development of information media in US brokerage industry.

The first period was from 1905 to 1995, which was the longest of the three. Agents, being both providers of listings information and the channels where information was disseminated, were the axis of the brokerage industry.

The second period was from 1995 to 2005. The biggest change in this period was that the Internet became popular and began to permeate into the brokerage industry. However, the Internet, as a replacement of print media, was simply a medium through which information was shared and disseminated, thus improving the efficiency of information dissemination and correlation. It had not fundamentally transformed the brokerage industry.

The third period started in 2005 and continues to this day. The change in the past decade equals the change over the hundred years before 2005. The application of map-based search in real estate industry, the fast popularization of smart phones, the outburst of user generated content, do not just increase the channels through which consumers acquire information, but involve them in the production and dissemination of information as well, thus reducing the information asymmetry between real estate agents and consumers (Figs. 3.2 and 3.3).

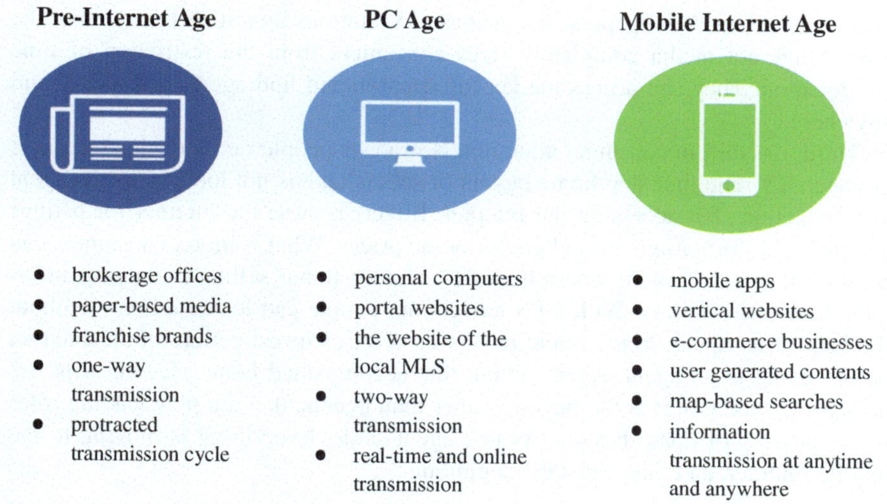

Fig. 3.2 The changes of information media in the real estate brokerage industry. *Source* The Authors

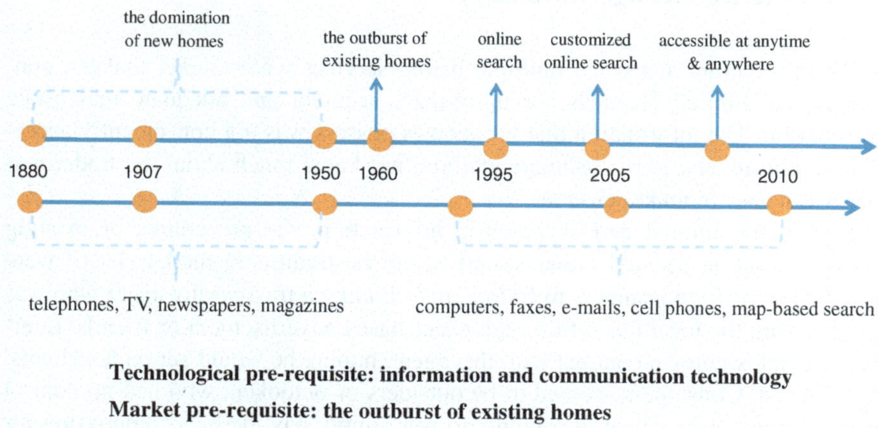

Fig. 3.3 The driving force behind the changes of information media: the shift of consumer attention. *Source* The Authors

3.2 The Driving Forces Behind the Transformation of Information Media

First, the market demand. The new technology related to the brokerage industry will not be developed or adopted without a large enough market.

Second, new technologies. Computers, fax machines and emails enable agents and consumers to contact more efficiently without the physical confinement of a brokerage office. Newspapers, magazines, TV stations advertise for agents. The rise of Internet media completely frees consumers from the restriction of time and location. They can access market information and find agents at anytime and anywhere.

Third, the shift in consumer attention. Nowadays people rarely read newspapers or watch TV. The first step home buyers or sellers take is not looking for an agent in a brokerage, but accessing the Internet. Buyers browse the Internet for listings and market information, and sellers for home prices. What is more, consumers can position themselves with smartphones to acquire home selling or buying information in their vicinity. With GPS navigation, people can locate a home without the help of an agent. Many home buyers do a lot of investigation on the Internet before going to an agent. Agents claim that accompanied home viewing trips are decreasing, and that it is the buyers, rather than agents, that are play leading roles in the process of home buying. As one agent said, "Everything is moving to the mobile Internet, and this is just the beginning."

3.3 What Changes Has the Internet Brought to the Real Estate Brokerage Industry?

In the pre-Internet age when multiple listing services were market makers, consumers had limited channels for up-to-date, accurate and adequate real estate information. The information that brokerages possess was not conveniently accessible to consumers. For consumers who did not know much about the trade, neither was it easy to make sense of.

Due to the limited and asymmetric information, the procedures of existing home transaction seemed rather simplistic in the traditional model. There were only two steps for consumers to follow: first, finding a trustworthy agent who was familiar with the local market through paper-based advertisement or friends' referrals; second, signing a contract with this agent, hoping he would act on his clients' best interest. Consumers seemed to be outsiders or onlookers who had no control over the transaction. What they could do was simply pay the 5 % commission for agents to make decisions for them.

Although brokerage offices and newspapers both collect and share information, the information held by brokerage offices was restricted to a limited area and newspapers released real estate information once a week only. Such information was not up-to-date, accurate or adequate, and therefore was of little value to consumers. Brokerage offices and print media are simply brokers' tools to attract consumer attention and get buyers and listing contracts.

Since 1995, the Internet has fundamentally changed people's ways of communicating, acquiring information and buying products or services. Buyers, sellers and renters alike can all benefit profoundly from the Internet, since the real estate industry is large-scaled, regionally decentralized, and highly information-intensive. The Internet has undergone two periods of development since 1995.

3.3.1 Web 1.0 (1995–2005): Listing-Centered B2C Platforms

In the pre-Internet age, multiple listing services (MLS) were closed systems open only to member agents. Buyers and sellers could not access multiple listing services. Their sources of information are traditional brokerage offices, print media or agents.

The US brokerage industry spent billions of US dollars each year to advertise on print media in order to attract consumers and get listing contracts. However, along with the rise of the Internet media, consumer's attention shifted to the Internet. Subsequently, Internet companies in the real estate sector began to flourish. They signed contracts with multiple listing services so that the formerly closely guarded data can be released to B2C online real estate information platforms (see Fig. 3.4).

The Internet has brought about three changes in this stage:

(1) The Internet has become the primary source of information for consumers since it replaced print media in 2001.
(2) Listing information, now pushing beyond the restriction of time and location, can be fully exposed to buyers.
(3) Consumers have begun to investigate and choose agents through the Internet.

The impact the Internet exerted on the brokerage industry was restricted to information search. People began to search for information on the internet rather than relying on print media. Statistically, there was a steep increase in the number of consumers searching for information on line. Only 2 % of the buyers searched for

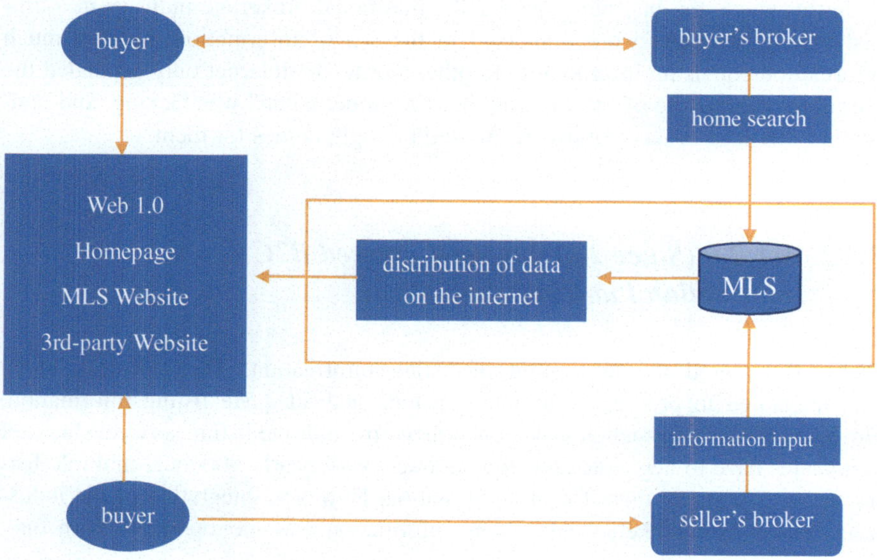

Fig. 3.4 B2C information platforms established in the age of Web 1.0. *Source* NAR (2013)

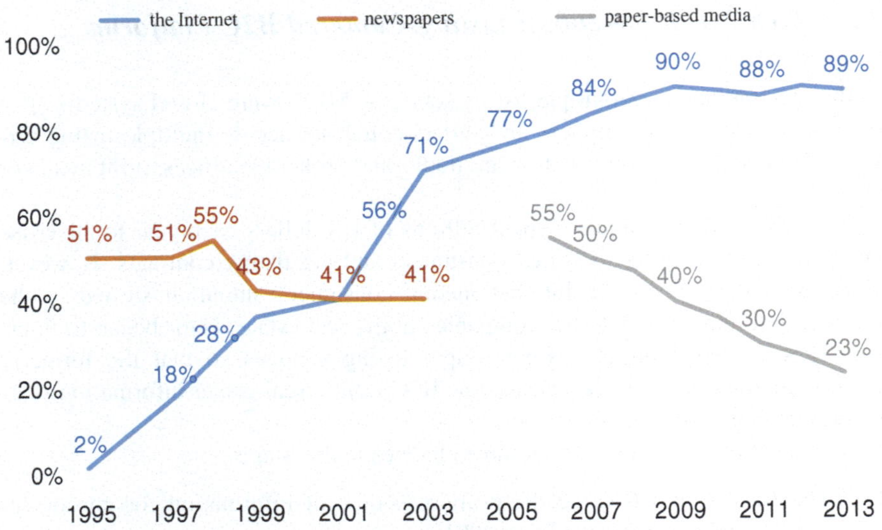

Fig. 3.5 An increasing percentage of people conducting home searches on the internet. *Sources* NAR (2013)

listings on the Internet in 1995, but this figure rose to 71 % in 2003 and 89 % in 2013 (see Fig. 3.5). However, besides being the new medium of information dissemination, the Internet did not play other significant roles. Internet companies assisted agents rather than threatening their business. Agents paid Internet companies so that they could release information to their websites.

In this stage, the Internet impacted the traditional brokerage industry in a limited way. Consumers were immersed in the sea of information, but too much information equals no information. In other words, the Internet only expanded the coverage or exposure of information, but "accurate match" was lacking, and consumers still need brokers' assistance to find the right homes for them.

3.3.2 Web 2.0 (Since 2005): User-Centered B2C Information Platforms

Web 1.0 featured the integration of listing information. The industrial chain was integrated to provide up-to-date, accurate and adequate listing information. However, listing information was monopolized by multiple listing services. Internet companies have to negotiate and sign contracts with nearly 900 local multiple listing services and pay them for the information. However, integration of the industrial chain was not likely when listing information was monopolized. With only incomplete listing information, online platforms could not attract users and therefore could not sell enough advertisements to remain solvent. Consequently they had no money to acquire more listing information or improve user experience. The several thousand online platforms set up after 1995 rarely survived after the Internet bubble around 2000. Most of them either closed down or were acquired.

By contrast, online platforms in the age of Web 2.0 are user-centered, relying on home valuation service, neighborhood information, search engines and user generated content to attract users. When the number of users reaches a critical point, listings will naturally follow and more agents will pay to use the online platforms, resulting in a "user-listing-broker" network effect. Integrating the industrial chain through users has proved to be easier than through information. Users' attention is indeed the real resource in the Internet age.

3.3.2.1 The Breakthrough Points in the Effort to Integrate the Industrial Chain in Web 2.0 Age

First, home valuation. With various home valuation models, Internet companies provide home price trends, prices of comparable homes in the area, rental prices, and the ratio of monthly rent and monthly mortgage payment. Users only need to enter information like the location or the square footage of the home to get a relatively accurate estimation. Internet platforms like Zillow can valuate almost every estate in America. The error rate of its valuation in 2013 was within 10 %.

In the US, there are two reasons why home valuation tools attract users. The first is that the potential users are numerous. Besides buyers, sellers and renters alike all need home valuation tools. Besides, every family wants to know how much their home is worth, especially during economic crisis. The second reason is that through home valuation buyers can get a good idea about what price to begin at when they put their homes on the market. An over-priced home is not likely to be sold and if the property has to be re-priced and put back on the market, it will be more difficult to sell. The longer the time on market, the lower the price, so pricing is very important to buyers.

Second, search engine. With the application of LBS (Location Based Search) technology and Google search algorithm in vertical real estate industry after 2005, Internet companies are not only able to show listings and home prices on the map, but also create mobile home search engines based on location, offering novel search experience for the users and change their ways of using the Internet from browsing to customized searching. On a mobile interface based on 3-D maps, users can not only view local school information and parents' comments on the schools, but also restaurants, convenient stores, service stations, banks and people's comments on the neighborhood, even the history of earthquake, fire and hurricane damages to the neighborhood (see Fig. 3.6). Home search engines have brought essential changes to real estate online service (Fig. 3.7).

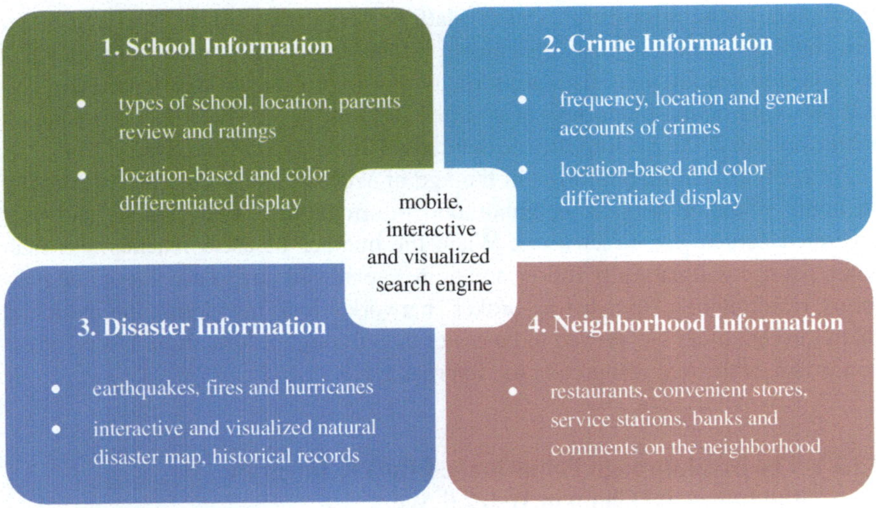

Fig. 3.6 Map-based home search. *Source* The Authors

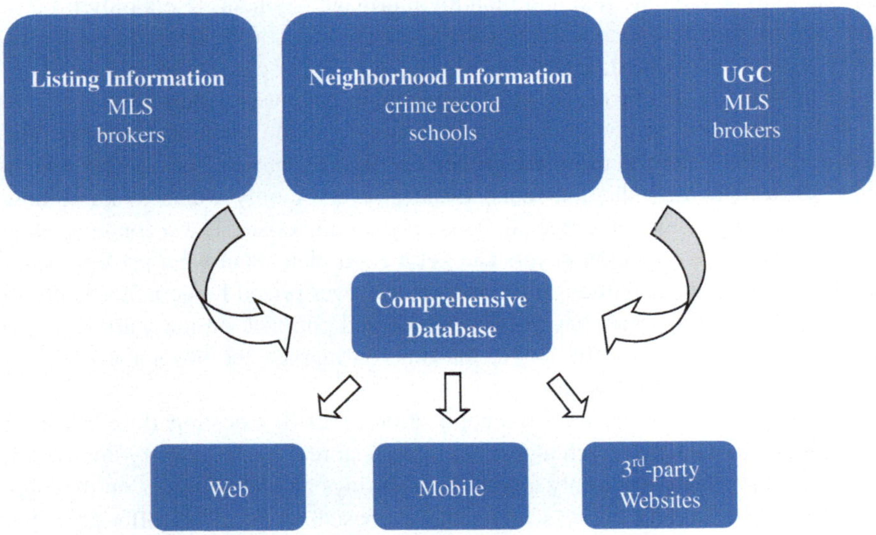

Fig. 3.7 More comprehensive contents on internet platforms. *Source* The Authors

Third, user generated contents and the evaluation of agents. The biggest change in the age of Web 2.0 is that users can input and update home information and neighborhood information and also comment on their brokers' service on Internet platforms. Because of the information asymmetry in the traditional model, consumers had no choice but follow their brokers' advice, but now through online platforms they have access to the information that was once carefully guarded by agents. Furthermore, one on one communication is made possible. Internet companies at this stage all provide online Q&A service, where users can communicate with other consumers, or agents and experts. Users can also share the homes that they are interested in on their Facebook and Twitter accounts, so that their friends can comment on the properties.

3.3.2.2 The Impact of Web 2.0 on the Brokerage Industry

After 2005, especially after 2010, with home valuation, neighborhood information, mobile search and user participation, the Internet began to permeate almost every step of home sales (see Fig. 3.8). The most greatly impacted step is the search for agents. Consumers can search for suitable homes through location based search engines, which makes home search more accurate and better-targeted. The ratio of successful home search through the Internet has risen to 43 %, while the ratio of home search through agents has decreased to 33 % (see Fig. 3.9).

As smart phones become prevalent, more and more home searches are conducted through cell phone terminals. In 2013, 30 % of internet users searched for

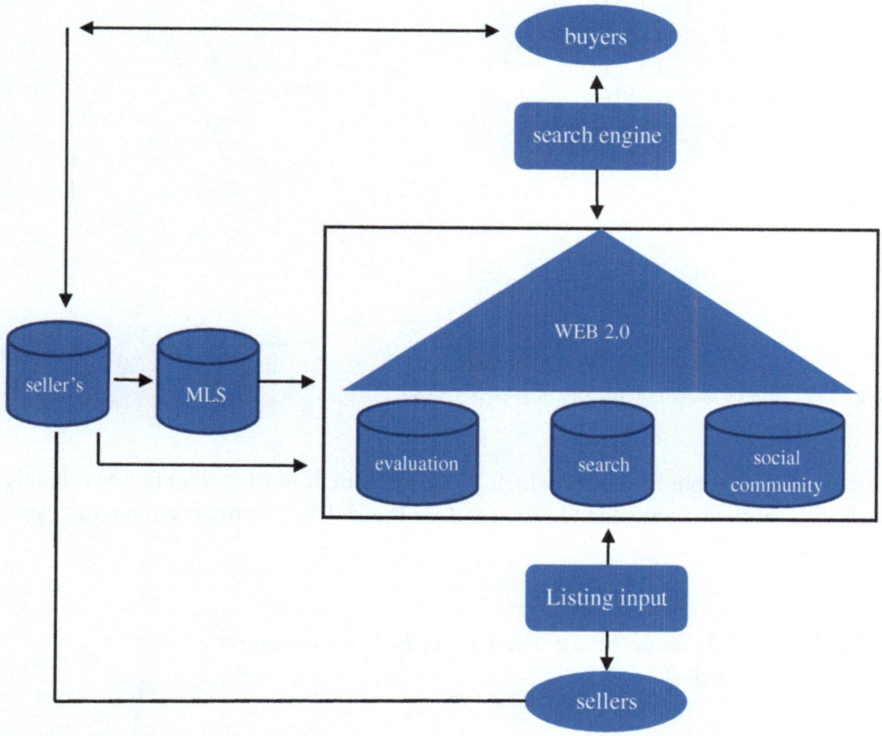

Fig. 3.8 User-centered platforms established in the age of WEB 2.0. *Source* The Authors

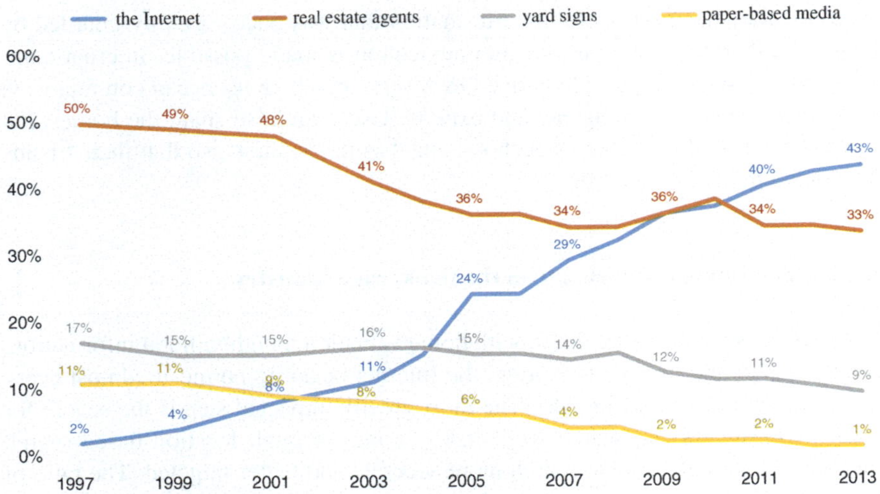

Fig. 3.9 The internet becoming the step of home search. *Source* NAR (2013)

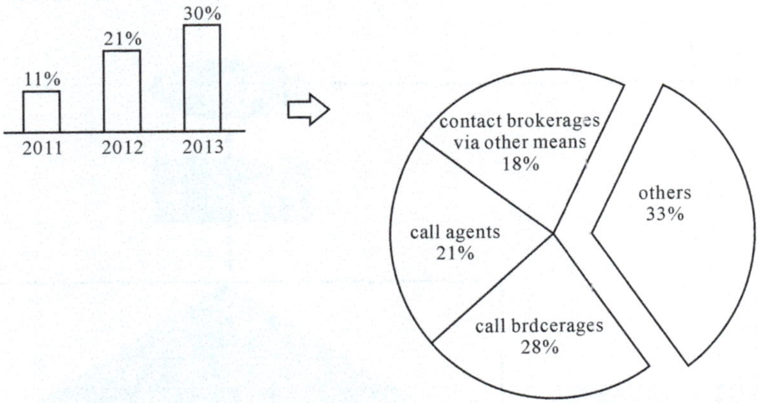

Fig. 3.10 Mobile search on the rise *Source* NAR (2013)

homes with cell phones, after which 21 % of them contacted agents immediately and 28 % of them contacted brokerages (see Fig. 3.10). The decision making cycle was shortened.

3.3.2.3 Web 3.0 (Since 2005): The Rise of E2E e-Commerce Companies

Around 2005, there were two attempts at reforming traditional brokerage, resulting in two different models. The first is online platform model represented by

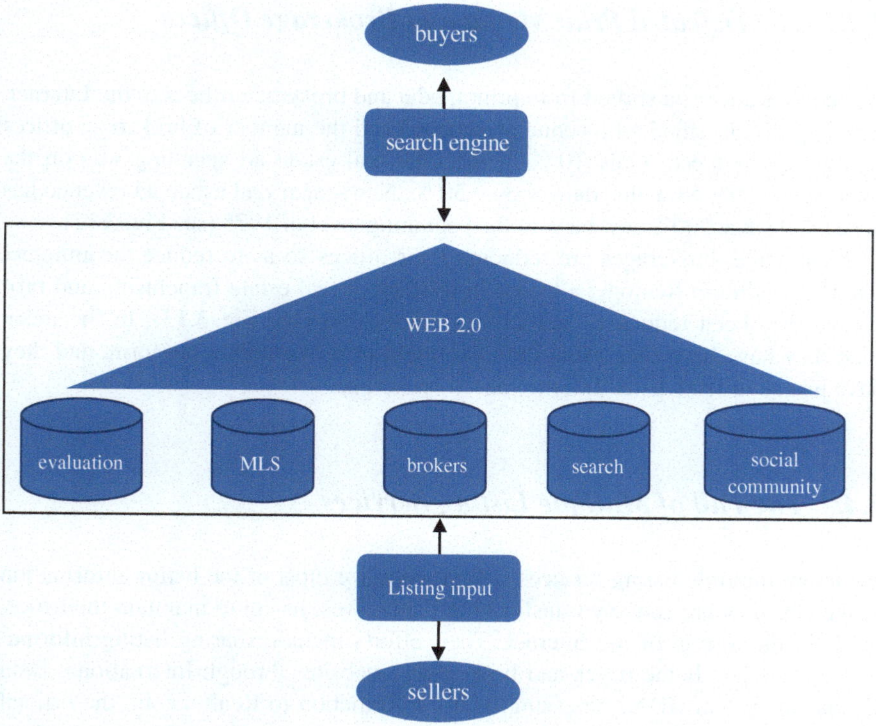

Fig. 3.11 E2E e-commerce businesses. *Source* NAR (2013)

Zillow and Trulia, providing excellent online search and correlation while traditional agents provide services in real life. The second is E2E model as represented by Redfin, who is an e-commerce company providing both online search and other services conducted by agents hired by the company.

In contrast to online media models, E2E e-commerce companies are by nature brokerages and MLS members, so they have free access to MLS data base for complete, up-to-date and accurate listing information. On the contrary, Zillow and Trulia can only acquire MLS data indirectly, through a third party, so their listing information is not complete, accounting for only 80 % of the total; not up-to-date, usually 7–9 days late; and not accurate, with mistaken listing status. (see Fig. 3.11).

3.4 Who Has Lost the Battle to the Internet?

Fundamental changes have taken place in US brokerage industry. The once strongly-held tradition has begun to crumble. Internet companies are reorganizing the traditional brokerage industry that has sustained over the hundred years. New business models are to be expected.

3.4.1 The Defeated Print Media and Brokerage Offices

As people's attention shifted from print media and brokerage offices to the Internet, newspaper's classified ad revenue avalanched and the number of brokerage offices was greatly reduced. Only 10 % of the total real estate ad spending was on the Internet in 2001. Now this ratio is over 50 %. Newspaper real estate ad revenue has nosedived since 2007, now back to the beginning level of 1975 (see Fig. 3.12).

Meanwhile, brokerages are reducing their offices so as to reduce meaningless fixed expenditure. Realogy, a leader in residential real estate franchising and brokerage, has been reducing their offices since 2006 (see Fig. 3.13). In the mean time they have been increasing the investment in their internet platform, and they have just acquired a listed Internet-based brokerage.

3.4.2 The Fall of Multiple Listing Services

Although multiple listing services still monopolize most of the listing information in the US, they are actively transforming themselves, trying to maintain their footholds in the torrent of the Internet. Their efforts include sharing listing information on brokers' home pages and brokerages' websites through International Data Exchange system (IDX); releasing listing information to Realtor.com, the official site of National Realtors Association, making it a website with the most complete, the most up-to-date and the most accurate listing information; releasing listing information to third-party websites like Zillow and Trulia through their own portal, Realtor.com.

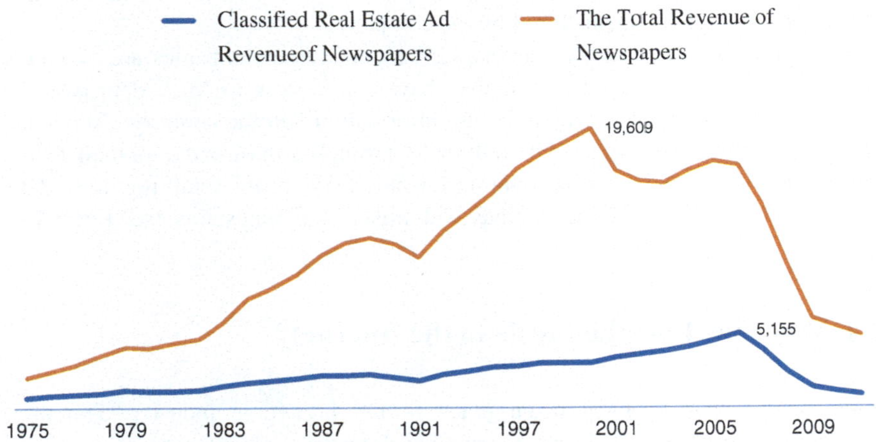

Fig. 3.12 The avalanche of classified real estate ad revenue of newspapers. *Source* NAR (2013)

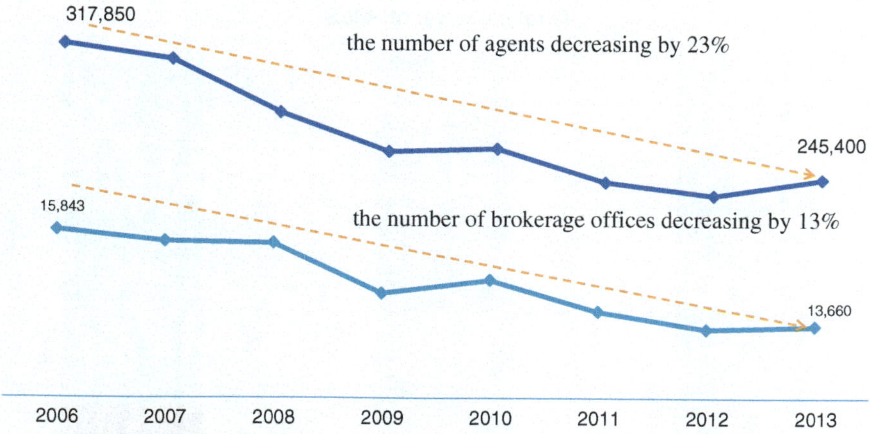

Fig. 3.13 Realogy reducing its offices. *Source* Realogy (2013)

However, these initiatives were not able to stop the decline of Multiple listing services' monopoly, which is aggravated by the growing practice of Pre-MLS and Off-MLS. Pre-MLS refers to agents posting listing information on the Internet before releasing it to MLS data base, while Off-MLS means the listing information is only posted on the internet (see Figs. 3.14 and 3.15).

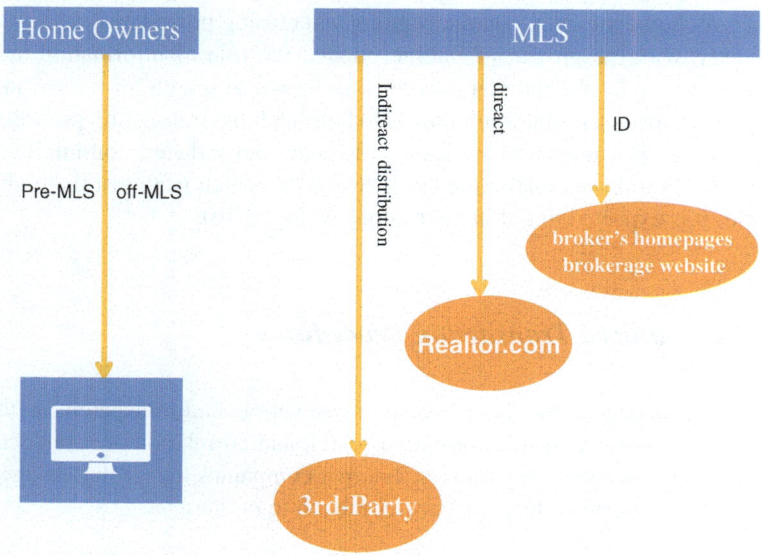

Fig. 3.14 MLS data's distribution on the internet. *Source* The Authors

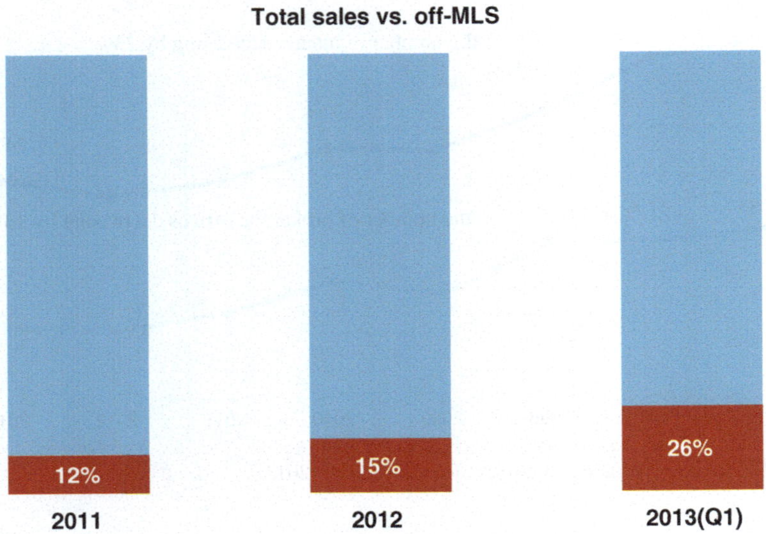

Fig. 3.15 The ratio of off-MLS sales. *Source* Counties of Monterey, San Benito, San Mateo, Santa Clara, Santa Cruz

3.4.3 The Brokers' Weakened Role as Information Channels

Traditionally, agents provide listing information and market information besides helping with home viewing, contract signing and closing procedures.

However, with the growth of Internet media, the role of information medium has been taken up by the Internet, where consumers can search for homes anytime and anywhere. Brokers' major job now is to help with the transaction procedures.

This change has improved brokers' efficiency and reduced commission rate. The present commission rate in the US is over 5 %, which is almost the highest in the world. It is expected to fall in the future (see Fig. 3.16).

3.4.4 Reorganized Transaction Procedures

Transaction procedures now have become more simple and transparent, with consumers having more control. Information search and correlation are conducted on the Internet by consumers themselves. Internet companies then will hire agents to take care of closing procedures or transfer the job to brokerages.

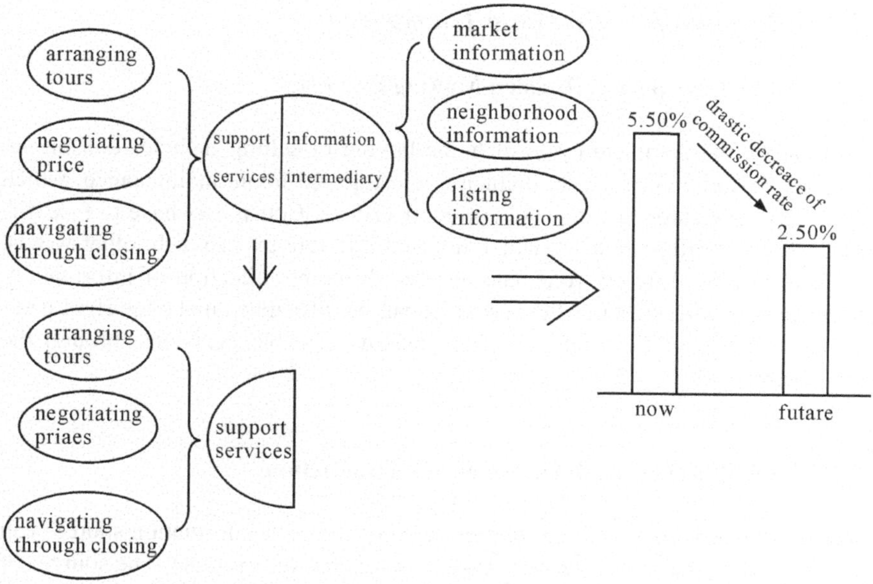

Fig. 3.16 The function of real estate agents to be transformed. *Source* The Authors

3.5 The Future: Smarter Users to Be Expected

For most consumers, buying or selling a home is a daunting event involving a huge amount of money and complicated procedures. It is a highly information-intensive decision which relies heavily on accurate information. Unfortunately, such information is not easily accessible to consumers due to its complicacy, specialism and opacity.

However, the Internet has fundamentally changed people's way of communicating, acquiring information and buying products and service. With its huge advantage in information presentation, information search and interpersonal communication, real estate websites have made home search and the communication between different parties of the transaction easier and more efficient. This has helped consumers make informed decisions. On the long run, while providing accurate home search and correlation, real estate websites are also training their users and changing their conventional practices in real estate business. Users are expected to shift from being the passive recipients of information to smart users who voice their demands on their own initiative.

3.5.1 *Information to Be Made Transparent*

3.5.1.1 More Transparent Decision Making Process

Traditionally, the complete cycle of home buying or selling includes consulting, information searching, pricing, financing, closing and home maintenance, which are all important steps that demand correct decisions. Consumers have to face different parties at different steps, which demand different expertise. In other words, they have to play different roles and analyze different collection of information. For consumers without related expertise, it can be difficult to make the right decision in even one of the steps, let alone making sensible decisions through the whole cycle.

3.5.1.2 User Presence in All Decisions of a Transaction

Users have to deal with different parties in every step, but information sources can be varied within the same one step. Take home search for example. The sources of information can be real estate websites, agents, brokerages, sellers and print media.

There are now a considerable number of market participants like excellent real estate agents, home appraisers and mortgage lenders for consumers to choose from. Their information has become accessible owing to the powerful search engines of the Internet. The difficulty on the consumers' part is how to find a good individual from such a multitude. Statics show that in the Internet age consumers spend 12 weeks searching for information, while in the past they spent only 8 weeks. Now the problem is no longer the lack of information, but rather the ability to make sensible choices in the sea of information.

3.5.1.3 More Professional User Decisions

The process of home buying or selling involves a large amount of varied professional information. Consumers are faced with two difficulties. The first is obtaining professional information that used to be in the custody of professionals only. The second is processing the information and making decisions accordingly. The skill of analyzing professional information is essential to consumers. Without it consumers will not be able to convert data into economic value and will still have to blindly rely on professionals.

Real estate websites have already changed the way consumers make decisions. Consumers can now browse real estate information without leaving their homes. However, if real estate websites simply display the information, they are not much different from traditional brokerages. What they do is simply changing the medium through which information is collected and disseminated. They are supposed to develop functionalities that enable users to generate information on their own rather than remaining passive receivers of information.

3.5.2 *Smarter Users to Be Expected*

The purpose of involving consumers in the generation of information is to bring their roles into full play. For one thing, consumers can directly voice their demands. For another, consumers, as participants in the real estate market and users of brokerage services, are important sources of feedback. Their active participation in the market makes them less reliant on real estate professionals and thus leads to more transparent and autonomous decision making.

Therefore, real estate websites should not identify themselves simply as platforms to collect and disseminate information. Instead, they should focus on consumers and try to engage them in the generation of information. The once one-way flow of information from suppliers to demanders should be replaced by two-way communication between the two parties.

3.5.2.1 Users as the Providers of Content

As direct participators in the real estate market and users of brokerage service, consumers are in the best position to evaluate brokers' service, especially when word-of-mouth marketing plays essential roles in the brokerage industry. Take Zillow, the leading real estate website in the US, for example. In Dec 2010, Zillow developed a rating system via which consumers can rate and review agents. The ratings and the comments will be collected and made accessible to future users, who may choose their agents accordingly. This has changed the consumers' conventional ways of dealing with real estate business. In the past, consumers did not have many choices over agents because of the scarcity of information. Information search actually started from home search and consumers' decisions were heavily reliant on brokers' information and expertise. With this online rating system, the first step of information search becomes searching for agents, rather than searching for homes. This helps avoid the risks caused by brokers' mistakes. Consumers are put in the driver's seat from the very beginning.

Real estate websites do not only collect information from both buyers and sellers, but also provide easy-to-use and self-conducted professional tools. For example, Zillow launched a home value estimator called Zestimate at the very beginning of its establishment in 2006. Users can simply enter facts like the location and square footage of their houses to get an estimation of the houses' value. In addition to giving value estimates of homes, it offers several features including value changes of each home in a given time frame, and prices of comparable homes in the area. The errors of the estimated value against the actual price paid are measured at 5, 10 and 20 %, respectively accounting for 32, 54 and 77 % of the total cases. These online home valuation tools are not just convenient, but also quite accurate. Besides Zestimate, Zillow launched a mortgage platform, Mortgage Marketplace, in 2008. Borrowers can provide home facts and personal credit status to lenders anonymously to request quotes on terms for home loans.

In 2012 over 14.5 million borrowers submitted such requests, each receiving 25 mortgage plans and quotes in average. The similarity between Zestimate and Mortgage Market Place is that they simplify complicated and professional process into a self-conducted functionality. Users only need to enter some facts to get high quality feedback. Users can thus take charge of their own business, without having to rely on professionals.

3.5.2.2 Customized Home Search to Guarantee Complete and Effective Information

As the whole is greater than the sum of parts, the integration of information improves efficiency. Customized search integrates home sales with rentals, users' pSource:s with home facts and home search with home viewing.

Both homes for sale and homes for rent will appear in the search results, with monthly mortgage payments automatically calculated to be compared against monthly rents. The sales market and rental market can be complementary, as they both offer people a place to live. Zillow gives a clear-cut answer with figures when users are contemplating whether it is more cost effective to rent a home or to buy one.

The integration of users' personal pSource:s and home facts relies on an important functionality: information filtering. There are literally dozens of filters that Zillow users can attach to their real estate searches to find exactly what they are looking for. And users themselves can do all that in order to make efficient and informed decisions, without help from any professionals.

Facts like location and square footage are not the only things consumers care. Statistics show that they care more about neighborhood conditions. Therefore, another leading real estate website, Trulia, provides information on local crime rate, natural disasters, local schools and amenities for each listed property. This, together with Google street view maps, gives users a realistic idea of what it is like to live in this neighborhood. In other words, besides improving home search efficiency, Trulia makes online home viewing possible.

3.5.2.3 Community Discussions and Q&A to Make Users More Well-Informed

In the traditional model, consumers had to rely on professionals or experts due to the asymmetry of information. While in a community platform the information is on fast flow and person to person communication is convenient. Both Trulia and Zillow offered online Q&A, where users can communicate with other consumers, agents and experts about real estate issues. Users can also share their favorite homes on their Facebook or Twitter accounts to get advice from their friends.

With this free and interactive flow of information, the knowledge that used to be exclusive to professionals and experts is now demystified and made easily accessible to the general public. Users, while receiving information from different sources, are also information generators. This virtuous interaction helps generate more valuable information and empower consumers in the process of decision making.

Chapter 4
The Impossible Trinity

Readers Guide

- The real estate brokerage industry has always been confronted with three tricky issues related to information asymmetry. The various business models adopted in different parts of the world at different periods in the history of real estate brokerage could only solve two of the issues at the most. This is the so-called "the impossible trinity" in the real estate brokerage industry.
- Simply put, the three conundrums in the Real Estate Brokerage Industry are maximizing exposure of listing information, safeguarding real estate agents' interests and safeguarding consumers' interests.
- The advent of the mobile Internet age and the infusion of venture capital have equipped China for the "impossible trinity", the ultimate solution of which relies on the following four practices: monopolizing the listings, sharing the listings without revealing client information, enforcing stricter control and regulation, developing a business ecosystem.

The real estate brokerage industry has always been confronted with three tricky issues related to information asymmetry. The various business models adopted in different parts of the world at different period in the history of real estate brokerage could only solve two of the issues at the most. This is the so-called "the impossible trinity" in the real estate brokerage industry.

4.1 The Three Tricky Issues in the Real Estate Brokerage Industry

The first of the tricky issues is the exposure of listings. Basically, the job of the real estate brokerages is to bring together sellers and buyers who do not have information about each other. Sellers wish to maximize the visibility of their homes so that they can find the highest bidders in the shortest time. How can real estate brokers or brokerages attract enough buyers? The key lies in a huge

S. Ba and X. Yang, *"Internet Plus" Pathways to the Transformation of China's Property Sector*, DOI 10.1007/978-981-10-1699-8_4

database of listings. Only with enough listings can they increase the odds of finding the most suitable one. However, as traditional real estate brokerages are small-sized and decentralized, listings are widely scattered. That is, every brokerage owns only a small proportion of the listings and therefore cannot attract enough buyers, resulting in the increasing cost of home search.

The second tricky issue is the so called "hitchhiking" in brokerage practice, which severely undermines real estate agent's interests. This problem arises from the high production cost and low dissemination cost of information products. Although maximizing the dissemination of information will consequently maximize scale effect in the whole real estate industry, it may not be such a good thing for individual information producers, such as real estate agents or brokerages who have invested time and money to acquire the listings. Once such information is made public, buyers and sellers can bypass real estate agents and contact each other, or the information can be used for free to the advantage of other brokers. As a result, information producers will not be paid any commission. This is called "hitchhiking". To compensate for all the initial costs of collecting information and avoid "hitchhiking", brokers will have to limit the access to the information, which in return limits the exposure of listings and makes it harder to match buyers and sellers.

The third tricky issue is one of ethics, which concerns the choice and evaluation of real estate agents. It is difficult to monitor and evaluate real estate agents' conducts. For instance, if commission is calculated on the basis of a fixed percentage of home prices, chances are that real estate agents will go to great lengths to pursue the highest selling prices possible in order to obtain higher commissions. In this case it will take longer to sell a home. Certainly, the opposite might hold true as well. Real estate agents may try to sell as many homes as possible because more transactions means more commissions. In this case, homes might be underpriced. Even if real estate agents do act in the best interest of their clients, as professional competence varies greatly from one broker to another and is hard to evaluate in advance, it is still difficult for consumers, who are the disadvantaged party in the information asymmetry, to judge which agent is the most experienced and trustworthy. As is often the case, even the worst real estate agents get clients, but some good ones can be pushed out of the market.

4.2 The Impossible Trinity in the Real Estate Brokerage Industry

Simply put, the three conundrums in the Real Estate Brokerage Industry are maximizing listing exposure, safeguarding real estate agents' interests and safeguarding consumers' interests.

The various business models adopted at different times and in different countries could only manage to tackle two of the problems. No matter which country

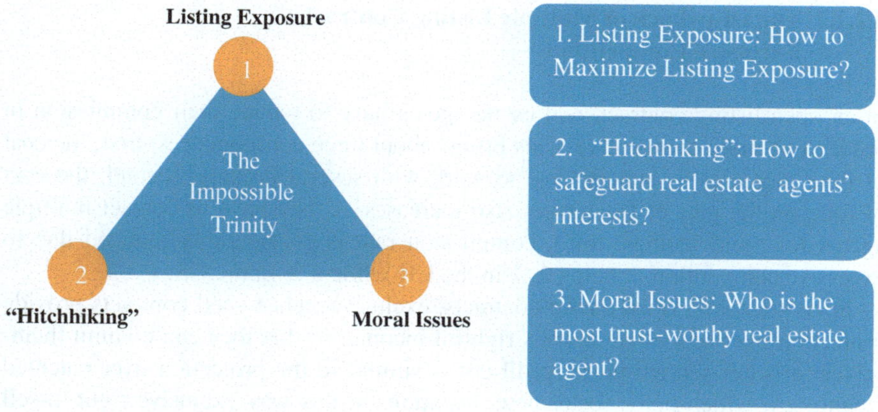

Fig. 4.1 "The impossible trinity" in the real estate brokerage industry. *Source* The Authors

you examine, be it the US, the UK, Australia or China, these "trilemmas" have never been solved concurrently, even in today's age of the Internet. Let's examine this "impossible trinity" by looking at the examples from the UK and the US (see Fig. 4.1).

4.2.1 The UK Scenario: Open Listing Without Multiple Listing Services

Open listing was the most widely used listing contract in the US from 1930 to 1960, in the UK from 1960 to 1990 and in today's China. The seller is allowed to list his house for sale with several real estate agents, but only the one that finds the buyer and eventually helps close the deal collects the commission. The seller himself is also allowed to sell his own home. If he finds a buyer himself, none of the agents will be able to get the commission.

4.2.1.1 Tackling Moral Issues While Increasing Listing Exposure

Open listing is a counter measure against ethical risks. It creates the competition between agents and reduces the risks on the seller's part. Both theoretical and empirical researches have proven that in a market with both open listing and exclusive right-to-sell contracts, open listing contracts bring about faster sale and higher price. In addition, as a home is listed with multiple agents, its exposure to the market is increased.

On the contrary, exclusive right-to-sell contracts provide maximum protection over agent's commission, and in combination with multiple listing services they maximize the exposure of listing information, but they are powerless against ethical problems.

4.2.1.2 The Drawback of Multiple Listing Contracts: Excessive Competition

In an open listing contract, real estate agents have to reduce their commission in order to be more competitive. This brings about three consequences: first, the cost of time increases as sellers have to work with several brokers; second, the cost of time on the part of the buyers also increases as they have to contact multiple agents for more listings; third, commission rate is considerably reduced due to excessive competition, it being 2 % in the UK while 6 % in the US.

In contrast with open listing contracts, exclusive right-to-sell contracts provide protection over real estate agent's rightful income, so that they can commit themselves to better service more readily. It is similar to the protection over patented technology, which helps foster new invention. In this way exclusive right-to-sell contracts help maintain an orderly market. It is evident that different listing contracts offer different incentives and lead to different behaviors.

4.2.2 The US Scenario: Exclusive Right-to-Sell in Combination with Multiple Listing Services

The most widely adopted listing contract in the US is exclusive right-to-sell listing, which gives the listing agent an exclusive right to sell the client's property. It stipulates that the seller must pay the commission as long as the listing agent finds a buyer who will agree to the selling terms.

4.2.2.1 Minimizing Information Leak While Maximizing Listing Exposure

While exclusive right-to-sell listing protects agent's benefits, multiple listing services maximize listing exposure and gather the once scattered listings and agents on a unified information platform. Supposing all selling agents release their listings to MLS database for all buying agents to see, then the job of multiple listing services is to increase the exposure of listed properties by displaying them to a greater number of buying agents. This reduces buying agent's home search cost. In theory, buyers only need one single buying agent to access all market information.

In this way, each of the "part of the market" that individual agents have access to are connected to form "the whole market", and a seller or a buyer needs only one agent to disseminate his supply or demand information to the whole market. With more extensive dissemination and exposure of listing information, buyers and sellers can find each other with more precision and efficiency.

4.2.2.2 Powerless Against Ethical Problems

Since home sales are infrequent events and it is difficult to monitor the brokerage industry, although there have been several attempts at handling ethical issues, the problem has never been solved.

There have been two attempts to tackle this problem in the history of US brokerage industry. The first is licensing, started in 1913, as an entry barrier to guarantee the quality of service. The second is franchising. Brokers raise their profile through franchising with a well-known brand. However, they are futile attempts to solve the ethical problems. People still have to rely on referrals from friends to find good agents. According to a survey made in 1983, 54 % of the home sellers found their agents through their friends' referrals.

4.3 The Chinese Version of the Impossible Trinity

China's brokerage industry has had a history of 20 years and is long past its infancy. However, one cannot find any trade so chaotic and disorderly, with new problems on top of old ones. There are long standing problems, including illegal brokerages, brokerages holding buyer's down payment to earn the interest, brokerages ripping consumers off by getting buyers to pay a higher amount than sellers actually agree on, consumers bypassing brokerages to close the deal without paying the agents their due commission, agents bypassing or stealing information from their brokerages and secretly working with other brokerages for better commission splits. Then in 2014 brokerages rallied a boycott against online platforms like anjuke.com and fang.com, who had been marking up charges drastically. Qfang.com launched "partner-broker program", offering favorable commission splits to "super brokers" who worked as its partners rather than employees. Homelink launched an "open platform", recruiting brokers with tempting commission splits. Brokerages and Internet companies are competing for clients by discounting the commission. At the same time they also compete for experienced brokers by offering favorable commission splits. China's brokerage industry, already ridden with misconducts of all sorts, has suddenly become a bloody and chaotic battle field between traditions and innovations, and the battle has just started.

Why, then, is China's brokerage trade so disorderly and notorious? When and how will this mayhem stop? The answer lies in the solution of the "impossible trinity" in the brokerage industry, and the same is even truer of China.

Today's China, like the US from 1930 to 1960 and the UK from 1960 to 1990, is confronted with the "impossible trinity" caused by the practice of open listing contract, and the situation is made worse by the lack of proper legal protection. Real estate gents in China are actually mediators with "split responsibility", who, while looking after their clients' interests, often have to betray their interests in order to facilitate the deal and get the commission. No matter how hard they try, they cannot gain trust from either the sellers or the buyers. In the UK or the US, open listing contract at least solves two of the tricky issues by reducing ethical risks and increasing listing exposure, but in China, this practice only helps increase listing exposure while remaining powerless in dealing with ethical risks and "hitch-hiking". With two of the major problems remaining unsolved, the chaos in China's brokerage is but a matter of course.

Open listing, being the most widely adopted listing contract in China, makes real estate agents mediators between the buyers and the sellers. This model, which is the source of all the problems in China's brokerage industry, has three characteristics:

First, densely deployed brokerage offices are the major means of attracting listings and buyers and ultimately snatching market shares.

Second, "sharing listings without revealing client information" is the way to correlate buyers and listings. This practice can effectively increase listing exposure while preventing information leak. In other words, open listing plus "shared listings without client information" can be the solution to China's "impossible trinity", at least within a brokerage or a local market. However, not many brokerages truly understand this practice. Only a few take it seriously, the most successful of which are Centaline, HK and Homelink, Beijing.

Third, real estate agents are not independent contractors, but employees working on meager commission splits of 20–30 %. The result is that agents hop from brokerage to brokerage, or even from profession to profession, making it impossible to build a professional and well regulated talent pool of real estate agents.

4.4 Can the Impossible Trinity Be Solved in China?

Is it possible, then, to solve the impossible trinity in open listing and agents-as-mediators model? Is it possible to end this mayhem and bring this trade into sunlight, so that real estate broker can be a decent job that is worth doing for a life time?

The answer is yes. In fact this goal is now rapidly drawing closer to us. The reasons lie in two areas:

First, the advent of the mobile Internet spurs the transformation of the brokerage industry. 2014 ushered in a whole new age of the mobile Internet, marking the beginning of the transformation in China's brokerage industry. It is not just transference from computers to mobile phones. The formerly impossible service scenario becomes common practices, buyer-seller match becomes more efficient and user experience is improved.

Second, venture capital is forcing its way into the market. China is now a hotbed for capital. Entrepreneurs' trial-and-error efforts are constantly fueled by venture capital. Entrepreneurs from the traditional brokerage industry are launching new start-ups, while Internet entrepreneurs are trying to break the old order and establish a new world. Whatever their purposes, dreams are more important than "genes", and capital is more important than dreams. In today's China, it seems that entrepreneurs are supposed to feel ashamed if they do not have "Internet genes", but our research shows that entrepreneur's dreams, or visions are vital to the development of an enterprise. The dream of Zillow's founders directed them to break into the market through home valuation and build the most complete and lively database. The dream of Trulia's founders is to change Americans' home search experience, so Trulia is committed to creating a powerful home search engine. The dream of Redfin's founders is to overthrow the traditional brokerage industry, so he chose to build his own brokerage team and is still holding on to this dream today. Whether an enterprise carries "Internet genes" may be important, but more important is the founder's dreams, as dreams are the beginning of all success stories. An entrepreneur's dream is the ceiling of his enterprise's development.

Entrepreneurs, inspired by their dreams and fueled by venture capital, will be constantly transforming China's brokerage industry. More internet companies will enter the brokerage industry while traditional brokerage companies will quickly transform themselves into internet based companies.

But the winners will be few. The sizzling scene will have cooled down and the cast of characters will have been set by 2016. Many companies will be pushed aside by the current of reform, but the world will have been changed because of them. To make it or blow it through trial and error is an entrepreneur's portion. Our respect goes to those who are going to perish from this adventurer's playground.

4.5 What Must Be Done to Solve the Impossible Trinity in China?

The advent of the mobile Internet age and the infusion of venture capital have equipped China for the "impossible trinity", the ultimate solution of which relies on the following four practices: monopolizing the listings, sharing the listings without revealing client information, enforcing stricter control and regulation, developing a business ecosystem.

4.5.1 *Monopolizing the Listings*

As China does not have multiple listing services, a massive monopoly of listings is the only way brokerages attract buyers. When more buyers come, more listings follow and listing exposure increases. This naturally brings about a positive feedback loop.

Strategies for the monopoly are legion. Increasing the number of brokerage offices and agents, enlisting the Internet techniques, building up an encyclopedic knowledge of the local homes, and marking off spheres of influence with other brokerages, all of which are for one purpose only—maximizing the control over listings in a locality, like the control Centaline holds over Hong Kong's listings and Homelink holds over Beijing's listings.

Only with exclusive information of a considerable number of listings in a locality, including sellers' expectations and contact details, can brokerages create a complete, up-to-date and accurate database to speed up the information matching process.

It is said that in the age of the Internet, brokerages are not supposed to profit from information asymmetry. This is true of the situation between brokerages and consumers, but not so between brokerages. The key to the competition between brokerage companies lies in the monopoly of listing information. If Homelink does not have control of over 80 % of the listings in Beijing, how can she maintain a truly complete, up-to-date and accurate information store, and how can she effectively correlate buyers and listings?

4.5.2 Sharing the Listings Without Revealing Client Information

The practice of sharing listings and while concealing client information means that all the agents in a company have access to the listings while clients' contact details are exclusive to individual agents. Shared listings are still individually owned information, the protection over which relies on laws and multiple listing services in the US. In China, the brokerage companies themselves have to protection such information through effective management.

However, many companies do not understand the value of this practice, or do not have effective protection over private information property. This may have several consequences. First, due to the lack of protection, few agents are willing to share their listings. Second, the information on Internet platforms is inaccurate, because its source, the information in the company's ERP (Enterprise Resource Planning) is inaccurate. That explains why there are many repeated listings on both anjuke.com and fang.com, despite the two companies' efforts to keep their database true. Third, the correlation between listings and buyers is very inefficient. Agents do not trust each other.

In order to bring the practice of shared listings and individually owned client information into full play in this unique land of China, there is only one way, which is to strengthen control and regulation and maintain powerful protection over share listings.

4.5.3 Enforcing Stricter Control and Regulation

Why can agents act as independent contractors in the US, while in China, they have to be controlled and regulated?

The reason is that in the US the market is provided by multiple listing services, market makers that set and enforce the rules and punish the violators. Every broker is in fact a company who makes its own advertising budget and determines his own working hours.

However, in China, with no market rules to speak of, brokerage companies have to set the rules themselves and develop incentives and deterrents to guarantee the enforcement of these rules. This can be done more efficiently and flexibly in the context of the mobile Internet. Without such control and regulation, it is impossible for a company to monopolize the local listings and give all agents free access to the listings while keeping the contact details exclusive to individual agents.

4.5.4 Developing a Business Ecosystem

The business ecosystem in question does not simply refer to the mutually supportive online and offline sectors of the brokerage industry. It comprises three areas. The first is the ecosystem of rules. If it is possible to maintain the monopoly of listings, free access to listings without contact details and stricter control and regulation, the awareness of rules and work ethics will develop. If these rules and work ethics can be duplicated, companies will become markets or platforms. The second is the ecosystem of data. The future winner in China's brokerage industry will surely be a data company. A huge database, with scale effect and accumulative efficiency, is the most valuable asset of a company. The third is closed loop business model. In fact, the source of revenue is the least important part in a business ecosystem. If a company or a platform can establish and maintain rules, take control over transactions and accumulate data, a closed loop business model can be duly expected.

Chapter 5
Why Does the Internet Impact China More Tremendously?

Readers Guide

- In present day China, listings are not monopolized by traditional brokerages, and most real estate agents are not competent enough to provide quality offline services. The brokerage industry defined by open listing contracts is chaotic and inefficient. Therefore, Internet companies can penetrate into this market more quickly and reorganize the industrial chain to a greater extent than they can possibly do in the US.
- At present, 50 % of the existing home sales take place in first-tier cities and a few second-tier cities. This enables agents to serve more people at the same time, and the company's investment in fixed assets and research and development can be more cost effective. Due to the network effect of online platforms and scale effect in offline services, Internet companies can engage more in both online and offline services at a lower cost and with higher efficiency.

The US has a very strong tradition of non-Internet brokerage. While multiple listing services monopolize the listings, a large number of professional agents provide offline services. Traditional brokerages, franchises or independent businesses, efficiently integrate such support services as financing, title insurance, home inspection and moving, which limited the incremental value that an Internet based company may create. Internet companies, most of which online media companies, largely serve as advertising platforms for traditional agents and brokerages. They exert strong impact on print media and brokerage offices, while the foundation of the traditional brokerage industry remains intact.

The situation in China is the contrary. Listings are not monopolized by traditional brokerages, and most real estate agents are not competent enough to provide quality offline services. The brokerage industry defined by open listing contracts is chaotic and inefficient (see Fig. 5.1). Therefore, Internet companies can penetrate into this market more quickly and reorganize the industrial chain to a greater extent than they can possibly do in the US.

The situations in China and the US are contrasted as follows.

S. Ba and X. Yang, *"Internet Plus" Pathways to the Transformation of China's Property Sector*, DOI 10.1007/978-981-10-1699-8_5

	the US	China
type of homes	90% being single-family homes, non-standardized	90% being apartments, highly standardized
distribution of homes	highly scattered	centralized in major cities
basic real estate information	comprehensive and accurate basic information and historical records	basic real estate information either lacking or scattered in real estate brokerages
listing information	gathered in local MLSs	scattered in real estate brokerages
listing contract	exclusive right-to-sell	open listing
real estate agents	professional, many years of work experience in the trade, low job-to-job mobility	unprofessional, limited work experience in the trade, high job-to-job mobility
the real estate brokerage industry	with strong management administered by NAR	no trade association to set codes of conduct, full of vicious competition

Fig. 5.1 The structural differences of the real estate brokerages in China and the US. *Source* Huachuang securities

5.1 Monopoly Over Active Listings

As a "members club" for agents over the century, Multiple listing services have control of the most complete, up-to-date and accurate listing information in almost the whole country. Although Zillow and Trulia thoughtfully provide home valuation services and neighborhood information search, they have to resort to multiple listing services for listing information, most of which is distributed by the official site of National Association of Realtors. The information is not just incomplete, but also inaccurate and behind time, being 7–9 days late, with an error rate over 30 %.

China's real estate platforms like fang.com and anjuke.com have similar problems, but the nature of the problems is not quite the same. The problem in the US is multiple listing services' monopoly over listings, while China's problem is that neither Internet media companies like fang.com nor traditional brokerages have the motivation to provide accurate information for users. As internet companies are by nature media companies whose profit comes from online advertisement, listing information is only their tool to attract users.

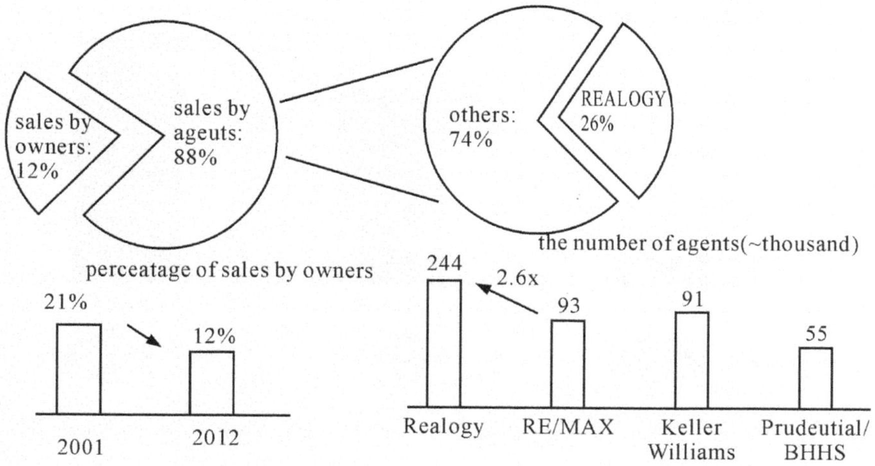

Fig. 5.2 The top ten franchisors taking the lion's share. *Source* Realogy (2013)

5.2 Traditional Brokerages' Market Share and Their Capacity to Handle Offline Procedures

Traditional brokerages still hold the lion's share of the market in the US. The top five franchisors in the US, including Realogy and Re/Max, occupy over 50 % of the market, with Realogy alone holding 25 % (see Fig. 5.2). These franchisor brands have long history and well-established reputation. With strong offline networks they can provide almost all the follow-up services like title insurance, financing and moving, offering the so-called "one-stop" service.

5.3 The Size and Professionalism of the Brokerage Talent Pool

In the US, real estate brokers are not employed by brokerages. They are independent contractors who work on with clients independently, while brokerages provide them a work place and office supplies like computers and fax machines. They work on a commission split of 70/30, getting the larger share because they do almost all the work. Moreover, multiple listing services help maintain a cooperative relationship between real estate agents, who work more efficiently when the market is free of distorted competition. Because of the low entry barrier, which is usually real estate agent exam, the size of the brokerage personnel is huge, including one million realtors, who are members of National Association of Realtors and another one million non-realtors (see Fig. 5.3). Because agents are easily available, most Internet companies choose to advertise for these agents, rather than participating in offline services themselves.

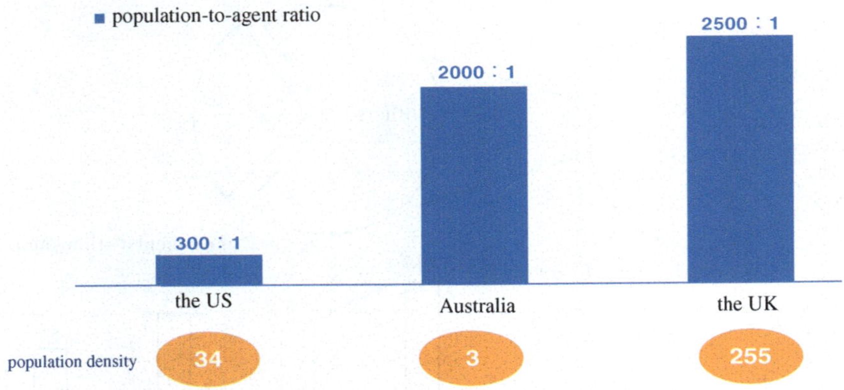

Fig. 5.3 The great number of real estate agents as against the population in the US. *Source* NAR (2013)

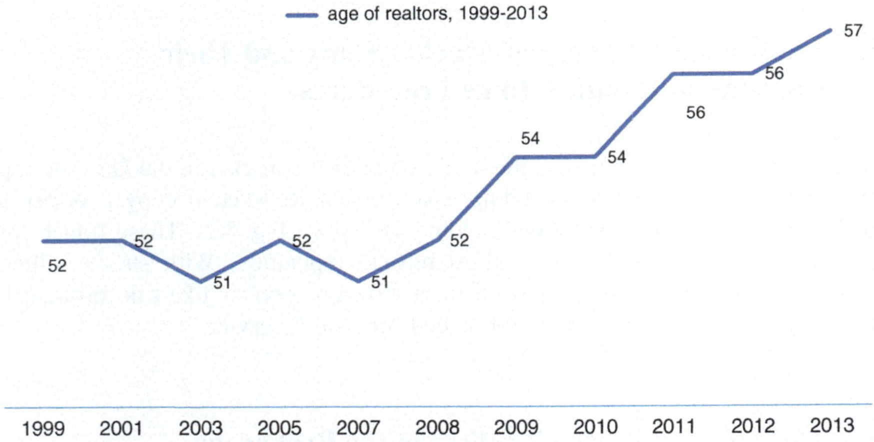

Fig. 5.4 The median age of American real estate agents being over 50. *Source* NAR (2013)

Many American real estate agents have been in the trade for long years, with median age at 57 (see Fig. 5.4). They are very familiar with the local market. Therefore, even when the world is well into the Internet age, people still rely on word of mouth or friend's referrals to hire agents. Only a small number of people find agents on line.

By contrast, Chinese real estate agents are employed by brokerages and they earn a small percentage of the commission, even though they do most of the job. There is no entry barrier to speak of. Most agents are very young and are not experienced or professional. Their greatest skill seems to be deceiving consumers and ripping them off. There is little prospect of developing a professional talent pool of the brokerage industry. Given this chaotic and inefficient offline service, Internet companies will eventually take care of offline services as well.

5.4 Centralization and Standardization of Homes

In the US, 90 % of homes are single family homes and town houses, while in China, 90 % of them are apartments. Homes in the US are scattered, while homes in China are centralized.

Consequently, it costs Internet companies in China much less to acquire home information than their counterparts in the US. The centralization of listings in China increases the scale effect in offline procedures. Therefore it is possible to greatly improve the efficiency in China's real estate brokerage industry, while in the US there is not much room for improvement.

At present, 50 % of the existing home sales take place in first-tier cities and a few second-tier cities. This enables agents to serve more people at the same time, and the company's investment in fixed assets and research and development can be more cost effective. Due to the network effect of online platforms and scale effect in offline services, Internet companies can engage more in both online and offline services at a lower cost and with higher efficiency.

5.5 The Speed of Mobile Internet Penetration

Statistical Report on Internet Development in China released by China's Internet Network Information Center in January, 2014 revealed that by the end of December 2013, China's Internet penetration rate has reached 45.8 % (see Fig. 5.5), with 618 million Internet users, among which 500 million were mobile Internet users, a growth of 20 % compared with that at the end of 2012. Among all the Internet users, the proportion of those using mobile phones to access the Internet was 80 %, way higher than America's 51 % (see Fig. 5.6). The penetration of mobile Internet has great impact on real estate brokerage, which is a highly localized business. With access to mobile Internet, users can conduct online home search wherever they are and whenever they want to. This will be a fundamental impact on the operation of the whole trade.

The value chain in the real estate brokerage industry is bound to be integrated and reorganized, as people are now swarming to the Internet. This integration will be faster, more extensive and more intensive in China than in the US.

There are three types of real estate websites in China's real estate industry. The first is vertical websites represented by fang.com, anjuke.com and leju.com. They are media companies that make money through online advertising. The second is the official websites of traditional brokerages. These websites attract consumers

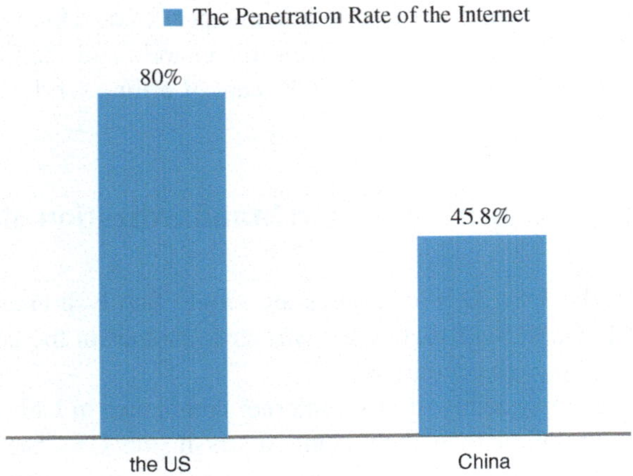

Fig. 5.5 The penetration rate of the internet. *Source* The Authors

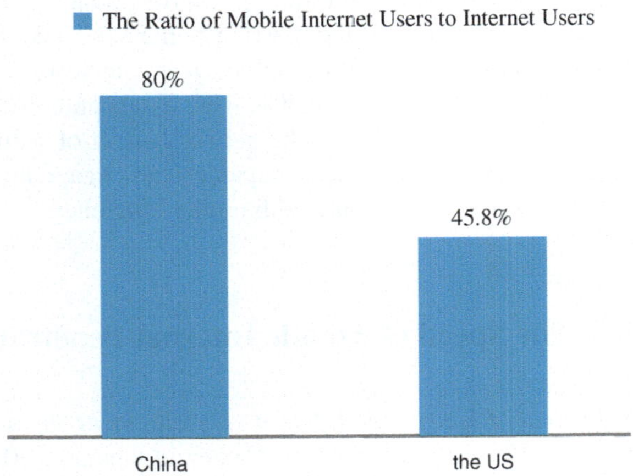

Fig. 5.6 The ratio of mobile internet users to internet users. *Source* The Authors

online, as a supplement to their offline operations. The third is venture companies, whose business models are distinctly different from others, a significant presence that deserves our attention.

However, none of the above has sufficiently participated in real estate brokerage and none has truly taken care of consumer complaints. Internet media companies rely heavily on advertising to remain solvent. There are many repetitions in their listings, but they have not made any effective efforts to improve the situation. Traditional brokerages now have their own websites, but the websites are only supplement to their offline service. Their goal is still maximizing commission. Venture companies are still in their infancy, and it is still unclear whether they will stand the test of time. On the whole, the Internet has not yet penetrated into the core of the real estate brokerage industry.

Chapter 6
Zillow—Online Media Tycoon in US Real Estate Brokerage Industry

Readers Guide

- After 2005, America's century-old traditional real estate brokerage industry began to undergo a fundamental transformation due to the fast penetration of location based search (LBS) technology, mobile Internet terminals and user generated content (UGC). Consumers can now acquire information in multiple ways. With mobile Internet terminals, they can search for listings, acquire market information and contact real estate agents in their bath robes. A more disruptive change is that consumers are not simply the recipients of information, but producers and disseminators as well. This has significantly reduced the asymmetry and opaqueness of information.
- Zillow is the biggest real estate information website in the US. It makes home buying and selling cheaper and more efficient by aggregating buyer information and seller information on the information platform. With America's most authoritative real estate database, Zillow provides information products and services concerning home sales, rentals, loans and remodeling, and therefore helps consumers to make informed decisions.

After 2005, America's century-old traditional real estate brokerage industry began to undergo a fundamental transformation due to the fast penetration of location based search (LBS) technology, mobile Internet terminals and user generated content (UGC). Consumers can now acquire information in multiple ways. With mobile Internet terminals, they can even search for listings, acquire market information and contact real estate agents in their bath robes (see Fig. 6.1). A more disruptive change is that consumers are not simply the recipients of information, but producers and disseminators as well. This has significantly reduced the asymmetry and opaqueness of information.

There were two trends of reforms among online vertical companies in the real estate brokerage industry around 2005, both aiming at transforming the traditional business models, but following different paths:

The first trend is building online platforms like Zillow and Trulia, who are by nature Internet media companies that generate revenue by selling advertising. Their goal is to provide consumers with excellent information platforms and

S. Ba and X. Yang, *"Internet Plus" Pathways to the Transformation of China's Property Sector*, DOI 10.1007/978-981-10-1699-8_6

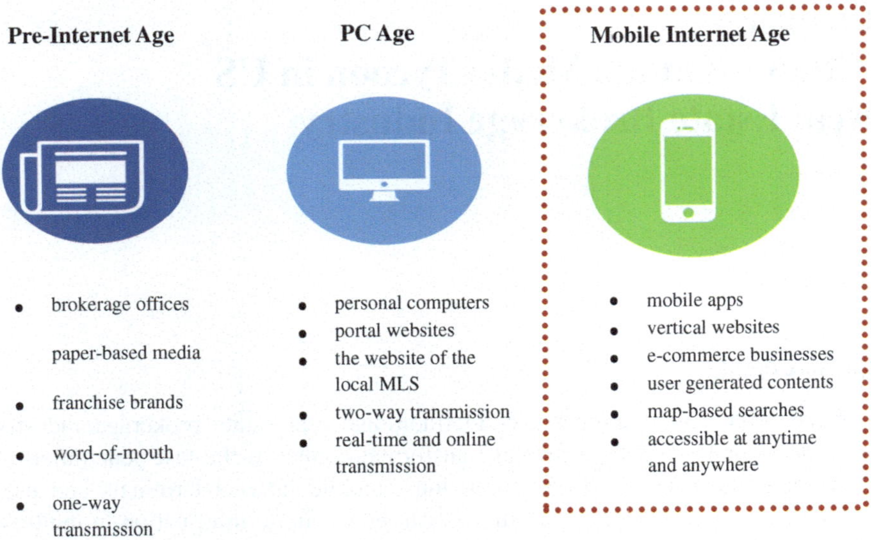

Fig. 6.1 The changes of in the real estate brokerage industry in the US after 2005. *Source* The Authors

search experience. They identify themselves as media companies rather than brokerages, claiming that they sell advertising rather than houses, trying to picture themselves as the friends, rather than enemies of real estate brokers.

The second trend is building E2E models like Redfin, who are by nature E-commerce businesses aiming at handling all the online and offline jobs in a home buying or selling process. They do not just provide information on their online platforms, but also hire real estate agents to do offline work. In contrast with media companies, Redfin's goal is more disruptive in nature, which is hinted by its name Redfin, an assonant of "redefine". Redfin's grand vision is to redefine the real estate brokerage industry and build a closed loop, controlling all the procedures in home sales. Redfin's understanding of the Internet is simple: you cannot revolutionize the real estate brokerage industry by selling advertising to brokerages. Therefore, Redfin chose the difficult path of disrupting the traditional model. After ten years of endeavor it has now grown into a considerable force in the real estate brokerage industry. Redfin and its followers will blow up a greater storm of change in the next few years.

6.1 Zillow—The Largest Online Information Platform in US Real Estate Brokerage Industry

Zillow is the biggest real estate information website in the US. It makes home buying and selling cheaper and more efficient by aggregating buyer information and seller information on the information platform. With America's most authoritative real estate database, Zillow provides information products and services concerning home sales, rentals, loans and remodeling, and therefore helps consumers to make informed decisions.

6.1.1 The "Genes" that Zillow Carries

Zillow is a genetically pure Internet company. It was created by Rich Barton and Lloyd Frink, former Microsoft executives and founders of Microsoft spin-off, the first online travel company in the world, Expedia. Top Zillow executives are an impressive cast of Internet experts from online media companies, portals, online payment companies, e-commerce giants and search engine advertising companies (see Fig. 6.2).

The mother of Zillow's current CEO, Spencer Rascoff, used to be a real estate broker and was acutely aware of the problems in the real estate brokerage industry. The name "Zillow" is a combination of the "zillions" of data factors involved in making complex real estate decisions and the idea of a house being a place to lay your head, aka a "pillow". "Zillions" and "pillow" make "Zillow".

According to our research on the most influential businesses in the real estate brokerage industry, an entrepreneur's dreams, or visions are vital to the development of an enterprise. The dream of Zillow's founders directed them to break into the market through home valuation and build the most complete and active database. The dream of Trulia's founder is to change Americans' home search experience, so Trulia is committed to creating a powerful home search engine. The

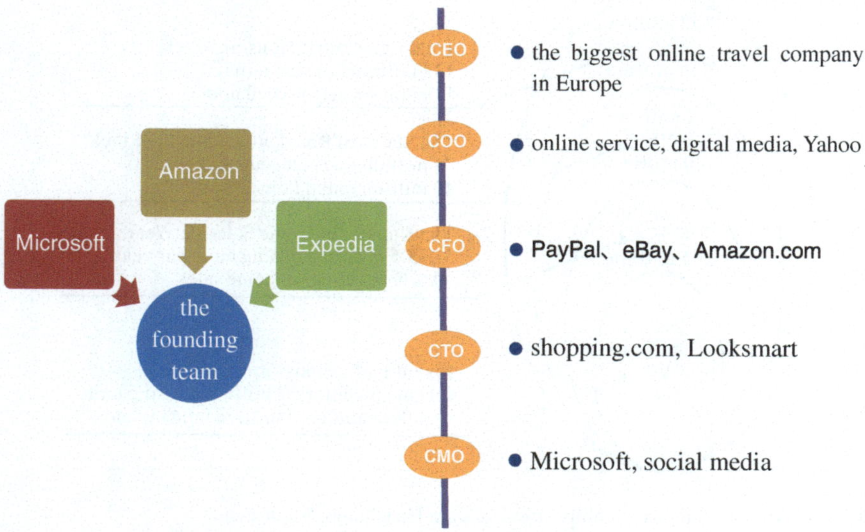

Fig. 6.2 The background of Zillow's founders and top executives. *Source* Huachuang Securities

dream of Redfin's founder is to overthrow the traditional brokerage industry, so he chose to build his own brokerage team and is still holding on to this dream today.

Perhaps it is the "dreams" that really define a company. Whether a company carries "Internet genes" may be important, but more important is the founder's dreams, as dreams are the beginning of all success stories. Since 1995 when the Internet began to transform the traditional brokerage industry, thousands of internet companies have sprouted like mushrooms, only to perish in the subsequent dot-com collapse, leaving little traces of what they had been. However, it is the passion and dreams, fueled by the capital from Silicon Valley, that are constantly pushing the real estate business forward.

6.1.2 The Market Zillow Has to Deal with

6.1.2.1 The Huge Market Size and Long Industrial Chain

Real estate is the largest sector in the US economy, covering existing home sale, rental, remodeling and new construction, generating a GDP of approximately 2000 billion US dollars. The huge market and the long industrial chain together build the foundation of America's home circulation sector, creating huge margins for traditional brokerages, traditional media companies and Internet media companies. 5.3–5.5 million housing units are sold in the US each year, 90 % of which are existing home sales (see Fig. 6.3). Existing home sales involves many complicated procedures, each generating certain costs.

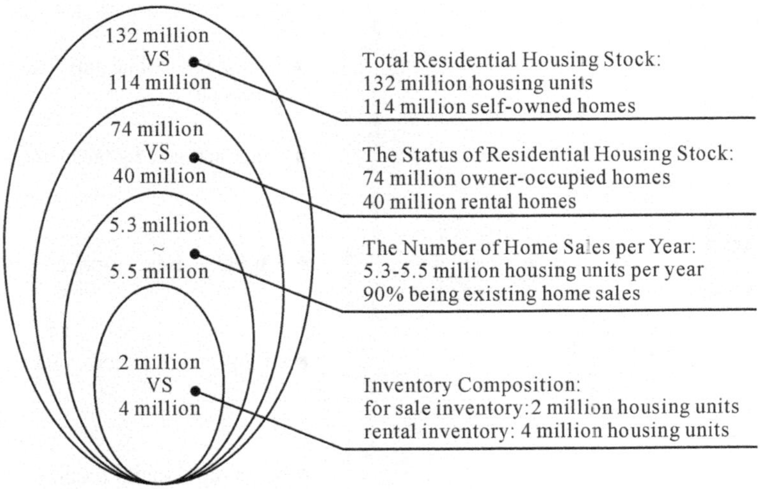

Fig. 6.3 America's housing composition. *Source* Huachuang Securities

6.1.2.2 Localized, Unstandardized and Information-Intensive Existing Home Transactions

Real estate transactions are highly localized, non-standardized and information intensive, but the information is opaque and asymmetrical. In the past, there were hardly any sources from which consumers could get complete, accurate and up-to-date information. This had prepared the stage for the birth and boom of Zillow, whose trove of proprietary information were extremely valuable to the disadvantaged consumers.

First, buying or selling a home is an important commitment, and usually the biggest and most important assets deployment in a family life cycle. People need information to help them make such big decisions.

Second, real estate transactions involve a series of important steps, including consulting, home search, home viewing, contract signing, financing, settlement, moving and insurance, all of which can be excruciating for buyers with no expertise in real estate. They often vacillate between listings, finding it hard to make a decision. Buying a home in the US is as stressful and dramatic as taking a roller coaster ride. Statistics show that in average buyers spend 2 weeks in looking for a real estate agent, 12 weeks in home search, and view 10 homes before the final buy.

Third, homes in the US are highly non-standardized. Professional knowledge is badly needed to deal with the diversified information in the process of home buying and selling. During the past 30 years, the number of single family housing starts was three times that of multiple family homes. Every home is different, and home information changes over history and has to be constantly updated. In the past 40 years, single family homes accounted for 70 % of annual housing completions. The footage area of each year's housing completions is on the rise, and the layouts are also different from before.

6.1.2.3 A Highly Decentralized Market that Calls for a Centralized Information Platform

First, buyers and sellers are decentralized. There are 74 million home owners and 40 million tenants in the US. Each year about 5 % of US families sell their homes. Many home owners become tenants and tenants become home owners. People's housing needs are constantly changing.

Second, the sources of information are decentralized. The sources of information in the US are traditionally real estate brokers and brokerages. Due to the low entry barrier to this trade, the number of real estate agents, brokers and brokerages is huge. However, most of the brokerages are small and locally based brokerages. According to recent statistics, over 90 % of the brokerages have less than 10 brokers. Two thirds of the brokerages have only one office. The top ten brokerages in the US occupy only less than 10 % of the market, the top 500 occupying merely a quarter (see Fig. 6.4).

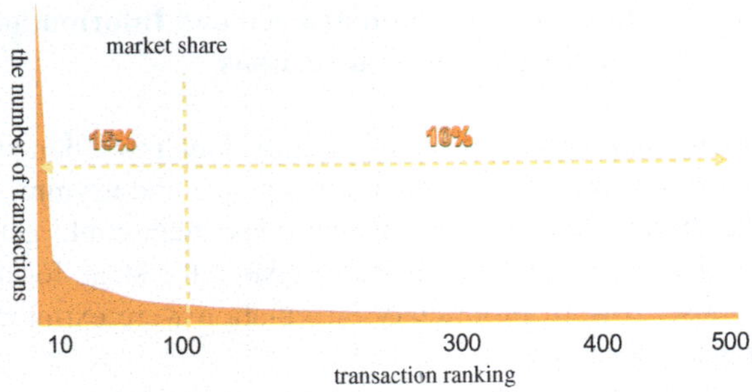

Fig. 6.4 Market share of US real estate brokerages. *Source* Real trends (2013)

Third, consumer attention is highly decentralized. The Internet has taken the place of print media and has become the most important source of information. However, the information on the Internet is still decentralized, with online platforms like Yahoo Real Estate and AOL (America Online) Real Estate; search engines and social websites like Google and Facebook; websites of traditional brokerages and local multiple listing services. The emergence of a centralized information presentation and correlation platform is therefore inevitable and most welcome. Zillow's acquisition of Trulia in 2014 accelerated the integration of online information platforms, making Zillow an online media giant.

6.1.3 The Nature of Zillow: The Biggest Real Estate Media Company in the US

Zillow generates revenue by selling advertisements to brokers, real estate developers, mortgage lenders, property management companies and home remodeling companies. Its competitors are traditional media companies and other internet media companies.

Having a huge audience is critical to an advertising provider. It is what enables Zillow to monetize its website. ComScore data shows that Zillow attracted 45 million unique visitors in April, 2014 while Trulia attracted 20 million. After the acquisition Zillow's unduplicated audience mounted to 65 million, accounting for more than 70 % of the total traffic, cementing Zillow's position as the biggest real estate media company.

In 2013, 67 % of Zillow's revenue came from real estate agents' subscription, 11 % from mortgage brokers' subscription and 22 % from cost per million (CPM) advertisements of real estate developers and home remodeling companies. The revenue from CPM advertisements has fallen from 99 % in 2008 to 22 % in 2013 (see Fig. 6.5).

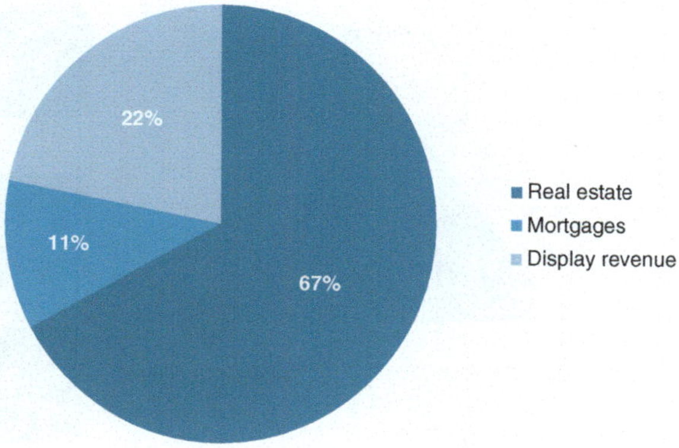

Fig. 6.5 Zillow's revenue composition. *Source* Zillow (2013)

6.2 How Does Zillow Reorganize the Industrial Chain of the Real Estate Brokerage Industry?

Research on the development of the real estate brokerage industry shows that in a market where buyers and sellers are both highly decentralized, a true Internet platform has to integrate the decentralized information channels, so that it can acquire listing information and control the supply while at the same time attract buyers and control the demand, providing a highly centralized platform for buyers and sellers to find each other while letting real estate agents provide offline support services. In short, an Internet company has to be a platform where buyer information and listing information are shared and correlated.

Therefore, there are basically three ways for an Internet company to integrate the industrial chain of real estate brokerage industry.

The first is to have a considerable database of listings, so that the website attracts buyers and subsequently real estate agents, to whom the company sells advertisements. Move, the first real estate information website in the US and the world at large, is a typical company of this kind. The limitation of this model is that as listings are monopolized by multiple listing services, Internet companies have to pay for the listing information.

The second is to use buyers to attract listings and subsequently real estate agents, who will pay for their subscription to the website. Zillow and Trulia are typical companies of this model. They attract users with home valuation tool and powerful search engine respectively. Users include both buyers and sellers. When the number of users reaches a critical point, listings will naturally follow and more agents will pay to use the online platforms, resulting in a "user-listing-broker" network effect (see Fig. 6.6). Integrating the industrial chain through users has proved to be easier than through information. User attention is indeed the real resource in the Internet age and the wind vane in the development of real estate brokerage industry.

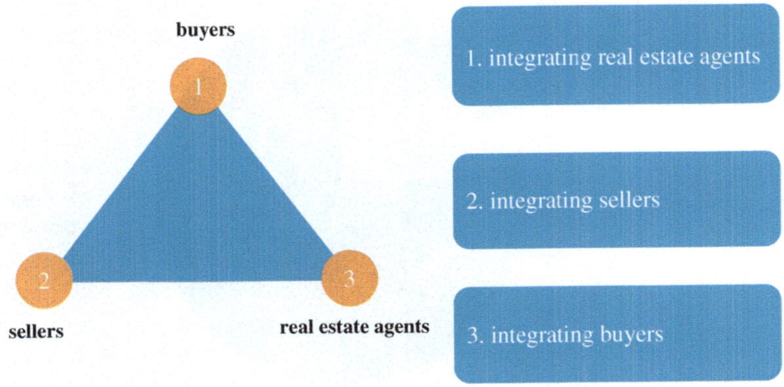

Fig. 6.6 The resources that real estate brokerages are to integrate: buyers, sellers and real estate agents. *Source* Huachuang Securities

The third is attracting real estate agents, who usually bring with them listings and buyers. This is rather common in the US. Some traditional real estate brokerages build online user platforms on the basis of their offline real estate agent platforms. Internet companies, however, attract real estate agents by franchising their businesses and then aggregate users through the agents. A typical example is ZipRealty, a listed real estate brokerage that was bought by real estate franchise and brokerage giant Realogy.

6.2.1 Dual Strategy: Free Access for Users + Subscription for Paying Real Estate Agents

Zillow integrates the industrial chain through a user-centered dual strategy (see Fig. 6.7). The first step was attracting users with home valuation service. When users grow to a considerable number they began attracting real estate agents. Agents choose Zillow because Zillow's users are potential home sellers and buyers, from whom agents can get listings and buyer leads. Zillow offers an interactive communication platform for users and real estate agents.

6.2.2 Home Valuation—A Path Way to an Active Database

6.2.2.1 An Active Database

It is the active database based on home valuation service that distinguishes Zillow from other Internet media companies. Zillow's home valuation service, Zestimate, user generated content (UGC) and Zillow Advice have help maintain

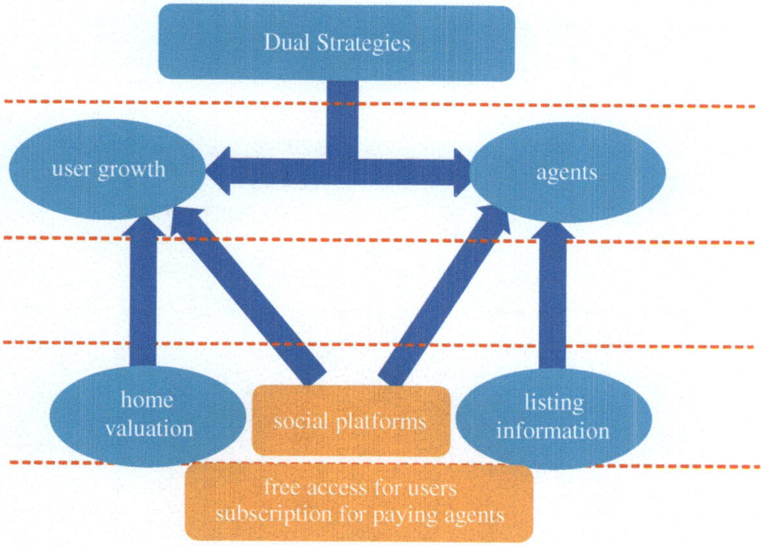

Fig. 6.7 Zillow's dual strategy. *Source* Huachuang Securities

an active database. The Zestimate home value is Zillow's estimated market value for an individual home and is calculated for about 100 million homes nationwide. Users can enter details like the location, layout and condition of the home to get an estimation computed using a proprietary formula. Zillow lets you see historical Zestimates over the past 10 years, and now the new Zestimate forecast provides the projected value up to 12 months out. User generated content is what brings life to Zillow's database. Zillow's users have made 35 million updates by the end of 2013, with a monthly addition of 1 million updates and 200 million pictures. Zillow Advice is a place where consumers and real estate professionals gather to ask and answer questions about real estate. It also offers a platform for consumers to rate and comment on real estate agents. Over 800,000 questions have been asked and answered so far and 460,000 comments have been filed.

6.2.2.2 The Huge Number of Users that Zestimate Attracts

When talking about home valuation, most people focus on its accuracy. They think zestimate's estimation of home value is not accurate enough to be of help and ultimately consumers have to rely on real estate agents for pricing and negotiating price.

Zesitmate's error rate has dropped to 7 %, down from 30 % in 2006 when it was first launched (see Fig. 6.8). However, the true value of Zestimate does not lie in its accuracy. Home valuation attracts not just buyers and sellers, but all who want to know how much their homes worth. That is how Zillow attracts a huge

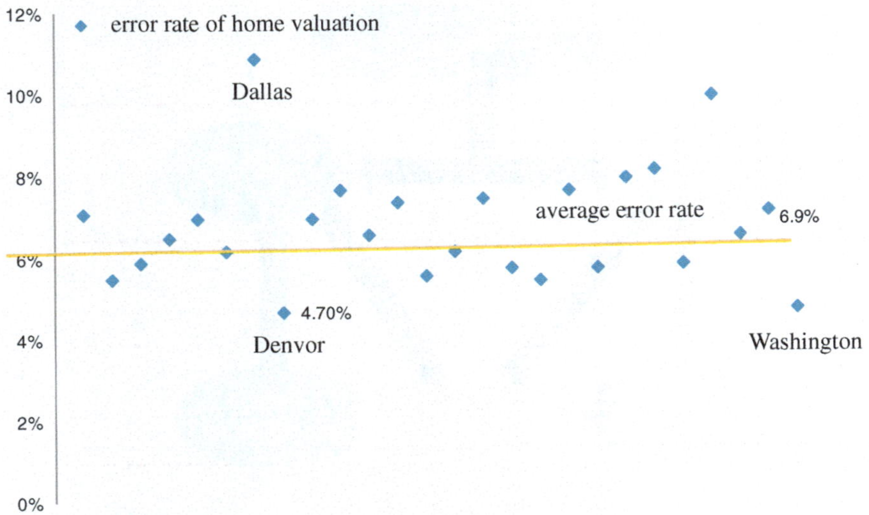

Fig. 6.8 Zestimate's error rate. *Source* Zillow (2014)

number of users in a short time. Price trend is more significant to users than estimation of current home value. For most people, buying or selling a home is the biggest expenditure or investment in life. It takes a long time to make the decision. People usually spend 12–18 months watching home price fluctuations and trends, so that they can choose the right time to enter the market. These people are frequent users of Zestimate during this period. Users are attracted to Zillow because of the transparency of home prices more than the accuracy of the estimation. Consumers have always wanted to access home price information themselves rather than relying on real estate agents' advice alone, but they are given the cold shoulder by traditional brokerages. Now Zestimate makes home buying and selling more transparent and consumers more resourceful. This is important to consumers, even though professionals may snort on its inaccuracy. Although Zestimate's estimated home value may not be the actual selling price, it offers a reasonable price range for both buyers and sellers. Buyers need this information to avoid buying an overpriced home, and sellers need it to price their homes at an appropriate level, because overpriced homes may have to stay on market for a long time without attracting any inquiries.

6.2.2.3 The Multitude of Listings that Users Bring with Them

Following the release of Zestimate, Zillow continued to launch a series of functionalities, including Mortgage Marketplace, Zillow Rentals, Zillow Digs as well as the Zillow Mobile App. The number of users keeps soaring.

Zillow Mortgage Marketplace disrupts the traditional lending market by completely changing the way consumers apply for loans and the way the loans are priced. Borrowers can provide home facts and personal credit status to lenders anonymously to request quotes on terms for home loans. Then they will receive mortgage plans and quotes from various lenders and choose the best offer. It is up to the borrower to reach out and contact those lenders, not the other way around. The main advantage of this marketplace lies in protecting borrowers' identities and tipping the balance of power into their favor.

Zillow Rentals targets landlords and tenants. Users can easily compare monthly rent and monthly mortgage payment on Zillow rentals. It is a frequently used functionality, because home rental may happen every few years, while home buying or selling usually happen only three of four times in a family life cycle. Home buyers sometimes change their minds and decide to rent homes. And a large number of immigrants are moving into the US every year. Most of them will choose to rent homes when they arrive. So Zillow Rentals help attract a great number of users.

Zillow Digs targets home remodelers. Zillow has culled tens of thousands of images from homes it has listed for sale across the country. Home owners can peruse remodeling projects, choose a remodeling plan or change it to suit their own pSource and get estimates on how much each project will cost.

Zillow was totally aware of consumers' shift of attention from computers to mobile devices. Zillow had developed 27 mobile apps by the end of 2013. This strategy is highly successful if one looks at Zillow's traffic composition, with 65 % of visits from mobile devices. This figure can rise to 70 % during weekends (see Fig. 6.9).

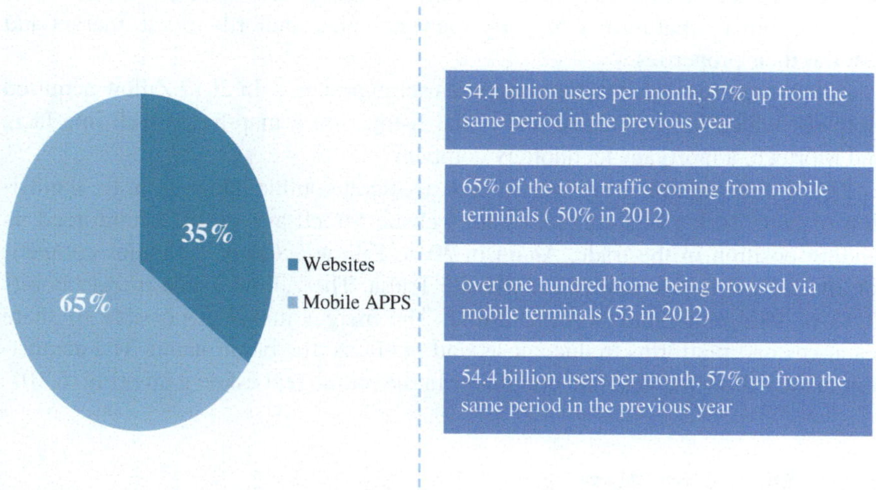

Fig. 6.9 The rapid growth of mobile APP users. *Source* Zillow (2014)

Since its founding in 2006, Zillow has developed a series of cost estimation products that provide suggested home price, loan quotes, rents and remodeling costs respectively: Zestimate, Zillow Mortgage Marketplace, Zillow Rentals and Zillow Digs. This helps put consumers in the driver's seat, with more information and therefore more control over the transaction. The number of unique visitors has been increasing by 50 % since 2009.

Because of network effect, success will bring even greater success, and one step ahead of others will establish one's leading position throughout the rest of the race. As the first real estate website to offer home valuation tool and as the dominant real estate player on the mobile Internet, Zillow has left his competitors far behind.

Zillow, with its huge number of users, is like a magnet to real estate agents. Listings find their ways to Zillow as well. Traditional real estate agents, brokerages, local multiple listing services and even portal websites like Yahoo sign contracts with Zillow to have their listings presented. Users and listings combined enable Zillow to gradually monetize the traffic.

6.2.2.4 More Control Over the Business Cycle Through Acquisitions

Zillow's strategy has always been building user base. For this purpose, besides riveting its effort on R&D and marketing, Zillow has had its fair share of acquisitions.

Zillow acquires companies that provide service to real estate agents. In 2011, Zillow acquired Postlets, an online real estate listing creation and distribution platform, and then Diverse Solutions, which helps real estate professionals manage their brands and businesses. In 2012 Zillow acquired Rentjuice, a software-as-service company that allows property managers and landlords to list, market and rent out their properties.

Zillow acquires websites that improve user experience. In 2012 Zillow acquired Hotpads, which list real estate and rental listings on a map-based web interface, and Mortech, a mortgage technology company.

Zillow also acquires its competitors to accelerate online integration. Its acquisition of New York's biggest real estate website StreetEasy in 2013 reinforced its leading position in the trade. Again in 2014, Zillow acquired its major competitor, the second largest real estate website Trulia. The Zillow-Trulia merger boasts 70 % of total real estate website traffic. The merger makes it possible to share resources and platforms, reduce costs and publicize the brand name. The acquisition made Zillow the absolute dominator in the online real estate game (Fig. 6.10).

6.2.2.5 Zillow's Next Move

Zillow's acquisition of Trulia is a monumental event marking the end of user-centered integration on the Internet. If Zillow continues to identify itself as a

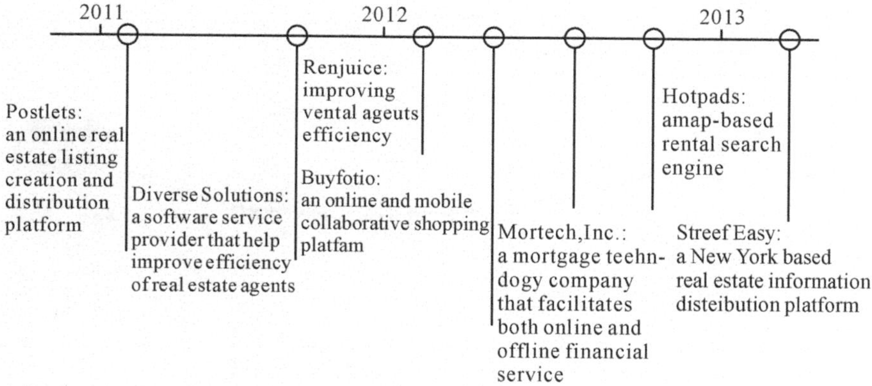

Fig. 6.10 Zillow perfecting the composition of its products through acquisition. *Source* Zillow

media company, its next step will be building a complete, up-to-date and accurate database.

Presently most of Zillow's listings come from the official site of National Association of Realtors, Realtor.com. The listing information is incomplete, outdated and inaccurate. According to a survey made in 2013, Zillow had only 81 % of the listings in the market. It took seven days for active listings to enter multiple listing services and then be distributed to Zillow. Over 30 % of the listings on Zillow are inaccurate.

Zillow's solutions to these problems are three folds. First, Zillow tries to maintain a good relationship with traditional brokerages, because multiple listing services (MLS) actually monopolize the listings. That's why Zillow declares that it sells advertisements, not houses. Second, Zillow endeavors to gain more listings from Off-MLS and Pre-MLS sources. Third, Zillow also targets for-sale-by-owner listings.

6.3 What Is the Potential for Zillow?

As a media company, Zillow generates profit by selling advertising on its website. Zillow's potential revenue growth is determined by two factors: the first is the percentage of online advertising in the total advertising business, which is 50 %, up from 10 % ten years ago; the second is Zillow's share of the online advertising market.

Zillow's revenue in 2013 was less than 200 million USD, accounting for a very small share in the market. As presently there is no dominant player in the rapidly growing online advertising market, Zillow enjoys great market potential (see Fig. 6.11).

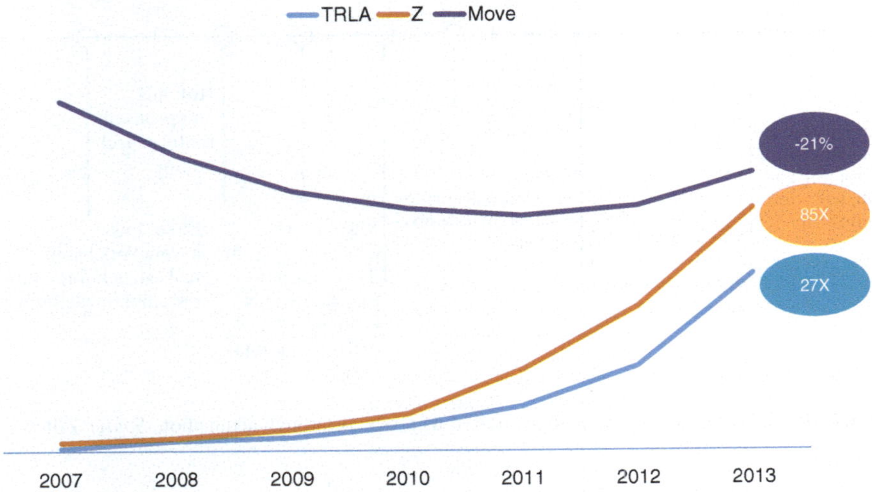

Fig. 6.11 Zillow's revenue growth since 2007. *Source* Zillow

6.3.1 A Popular Belief: Zillow with Huge Potential

6.3.1.1 Online Advertising on the Rise

America's annual home transaction volume averages at 1, 200 billion US dollars, which, at the rate of 5.2 %, generates 62.4 billion USD of commission. 10 % of the commission, which is 6.24 billion USD, is spent on marketing. If online advertising is to occupy 70 % of the total advertising market, then 4.368 billion USD will be spent on online advertising.

Zillow's revenue from real estate agents' subscription was only 132 million in 2013, accounting for merely 3 % of the market (see Fig. 6.12).

6.3.1.2 The Seemingly Great Potential for Subscription from Real Estate Agents

Only less than 50 thousand (see Fig. 6.13) real estate agents subscribed to Zillow in 2013. Even with Trulia's subscriptions added, Zillow's subscribers account for only 9 % of the total one million members of National Association of Realtors.

However, in Australia, 95 % of the real estate agents advertise on online media giant, REA; in the UK, 75 % of the agents advertise on RMV (see Fig. 6.14). These are typical cases of "winner takes all".

Following these analogies, one can naturally come to the conclusion that there is great potential in Zillow's paying agent growth. Zillow's CEO voiced this opinion many times in telephone meetings. That is also the reason why Zillow is overvalued, with P/S ratio as high as 20.

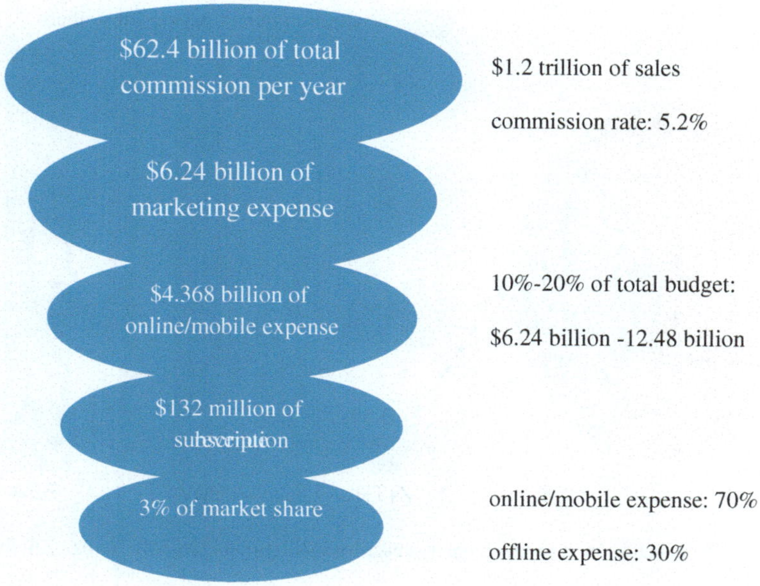

Fig. 6.12 The huge potential of real estate online advertising. *Source* Zillow

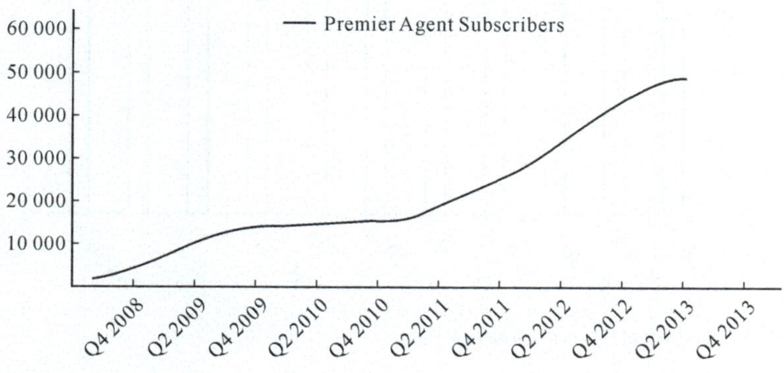

Fig. 6.13 The number of premier agent subscribers. *Source* Zillow

6.3.1.3 The Seemingly Great ARPU Potential

Zillow's current ARPU (Average Revenue per User) stands at less than 300 USD, with limited growth over the past three years (see Fig. 6.15). Foreign capital banks in China also project Zillow's potential ARPU growth on the basis of an analogy between Zillow and REA and RMV. REA's paying agents spend 7 times as much as Zillow's paying agents do on subscription, and RMV's paying agents spend 3 times as much as Zillow's agents do (see Fig. 6.16). That Zillow can mark up its charge and increase ARPU seems to be a matter of course.

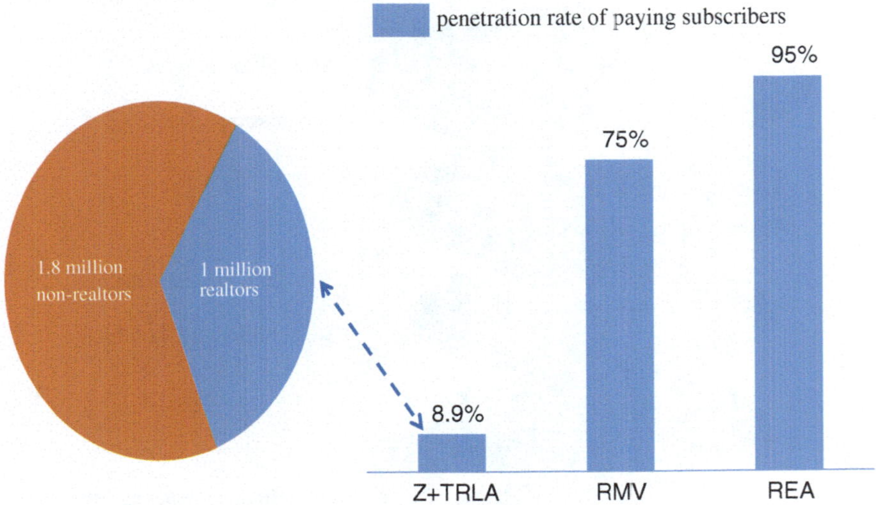

Fig. 6.14 The penetration of premier agent subscribers still growing rapidly. *Source* Zillow

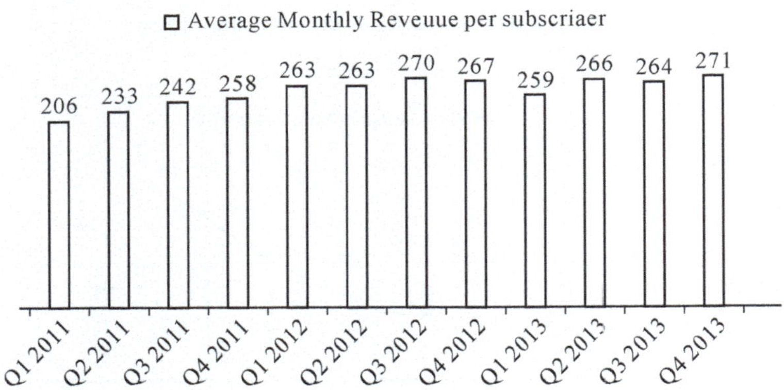

Fig. 6.15 Limited ARPU growth. *Source* REA

6.3.2 Popular Belief Debunked: Zillow's Potential not as Great as It Seems

Zilllow's stock price has grown by 8 times since it went public. Zillow indeed has a bright future, but it is just not as glorious as what most people believe.

6.3.2.1 Commission Rate Bound to Fall

The present commission rate in US existing home market is 5.2 %, down 30 % in the past 10 years, but it is still the highest among developed countries.

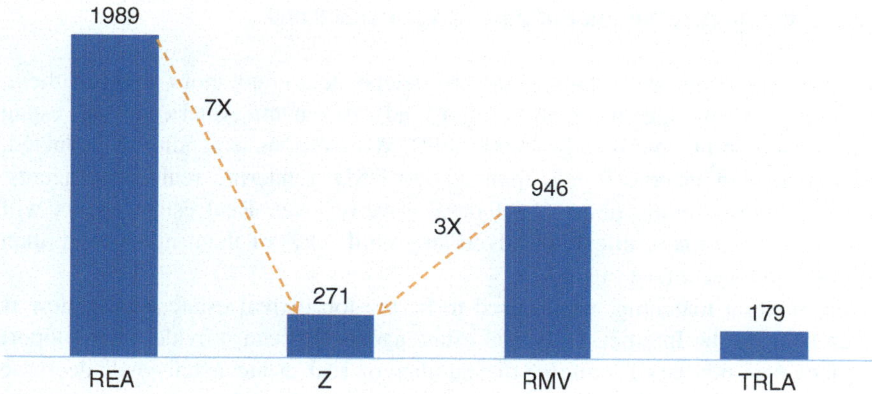

Fig. 6.16 Zillow's ARPU in comparison with Rea's and RMV's. *Source* REA

The commission rate is only around 2 % in the UK and Australia. America's high commission rate is due to MLS pricing and protective mechanism. With the rise of Internet media companies, the gradual shrinkage of MLSs and the emergence of discount real estate agents, the decrease in America's commission rate is but inevitable.

The Internet age is bound to end the traditional high commission rate, which is based on information asymmetry. As the Internet minimizes this information asymmetry and probably changes America's traditional practice of dual agency to single agency, the commission rate will fall considerably.

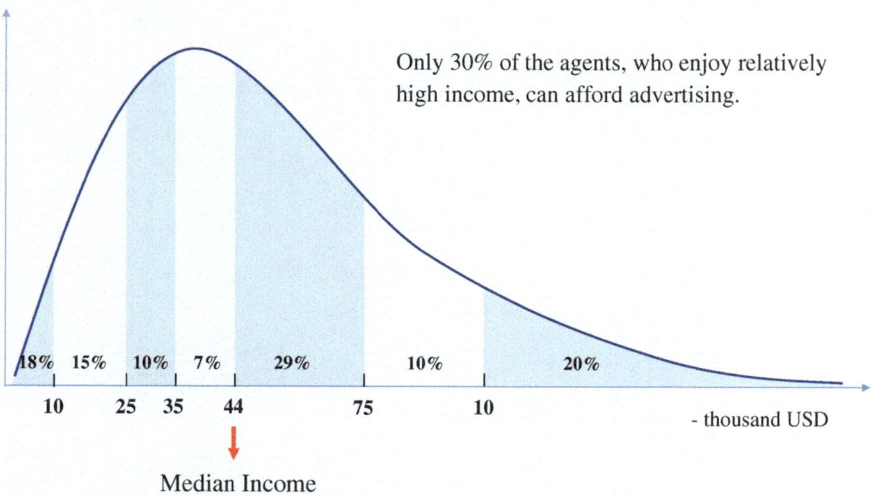

Fig. 6.17 The distribution of American real estate agents' income. *Source* Huachuang Securities

6.3.2.2 Prospective Number of Paying Agents: 300,000

Because America's real estate agents are independent contractors, most of them, especial part-time agents, cannot afford advertisement. American real estate agents' median income is only 44,000 USD. With various expenditures deducted, the net median income is less than 30,000 USD, rendering real estate agents' families living slightly above the federal poverty level. Real estate agents will not become the major clients of advertising until 30 % of them make more than 75,000 USD a year (see Fig. 6.17).

Information matching, which used to be the job of real estate agents, now is taken over by the Internet. Only real estate agents that can provide other support services can survive. Therefore, the number of real estate agents will decrease drastically, significantly hampering the growth of potential average revenue per user.

Chapter 7
Redfin—A Developing Vertical e-Commerce Model

Readers Guide

- The whole division between e-commerce pure-plays and media pure-plays is a canard. Media companies have to participate in transactions if they want to maximize revenue generated from traffic. And e-commerce companies have to stop buying traffic and start making their own if they want to increase their margins. Redfin, a perfect amalgamation of a media company and an e-commerce company, sets a good example for all those in the trade.
- Redfin agents are six times as efficient as traditional real estate agents. The scale effect in real estate agents' service is achieved through division of labor and the streamlining of work flow. Redfin agents work in a team to provide full service to individual consumers. On a typical team there will usually be multiple agents each specializing in one or two things. The team leader is usually an experienced broker who is directly responsible to the consumer, helping consumers with home search and purchase offers. There are coordinating agents that arrange home tours, home inspections and home appraisals, as well as getting documents in order. Then there are junior agents that accompany consumers on their home tours. Each agent may accompany over 50 showings a week in average.

Redfin is an E2E (End to End) e-commerce company by nature, a true disrupter of the traditional real estate brokerage industry. It is the seamless amalgamation of an online media and a brokerage, a beast with double faces.

Redfin employs its agents and pays them a salary, and it ties bonuses to customer satisfaction, rather than sales volume. This is different from the commission-based compensation model adopted by most traditional brokerages, e.g. Realogy and RE/MAX.

Unlike other major real estate web portals like Zillow or Trulia, which make the majority of their earnings from advertising and lead generation, Redfin operates as a brokerage and collects commission when users buy or sell homes through its real estate agents. It offers one-stop shopping for homes by providing services every step of the way of buying or selling a home, with online platform acting as a control center and real estate agents providing full service (see Fig. 7.1).

S. Ba and X. Yang, *"Internet Plus" Pathways to the Transformation of China's Property Sector*, DOI 10.1007/978-981-10-1699-8_7

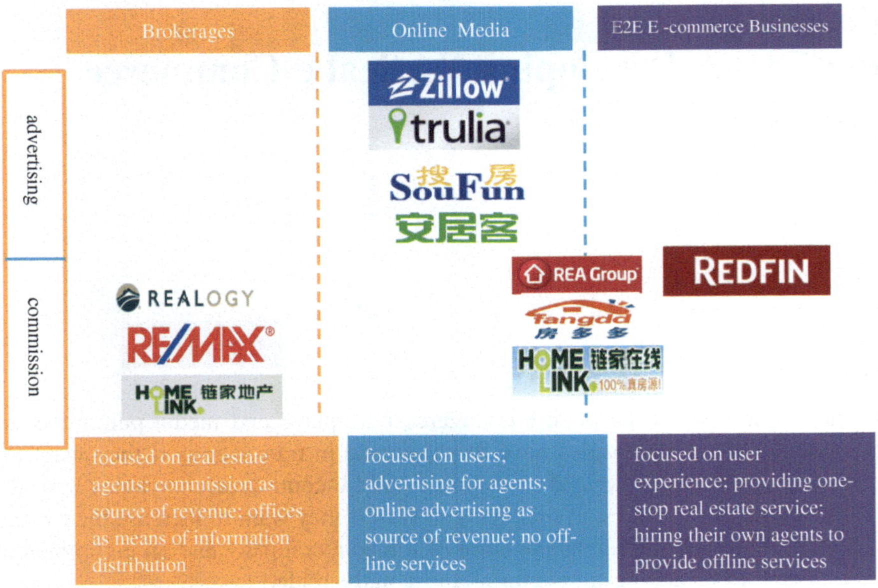

Fig. 7.1 Different business models compared. *Source* The Authors

A large number of E2E startups like Redfin are blowing up a storm of reform in the US.

In Australia, online media giant REA is also testing waters in the transaction process, in an attempt to transform itself into an e-commerce company.

In China, Anjuke and Fang's experience and lessons have proved that online platforms alone, without connection with the real world, are by no means adequate. These two industry leaders will inevitably participate in more transaction proceedings and address consumer needs. They will grow into E2E e-commerce companies and merge online and offline, virtual world and real world services. Ambitious, well-financed startups are not to concern themselves with such questions as "what is more important, online service or offline service" or "which one will kill the other". They must put themselves in users' shoes and think about how to provide practical service and better user experience.

In the Internet Age algorithms become outdated and patents expire faster than ever. Good consumer experience and word-of-month are truly lasting advantages. A recent survey shows that 94 % of the mobile apps are uninstalled by consumers six months after they are installed, which means that if a user installed your app a month ago, the probability of his still using it after five months is only 6 %. A great number of O2O (online to offline) companies are sprouting like mushrooms in China, a hot bed with abundant supply of venture capital. The same is true of the real estate brokerage industry, but who will win in the end?

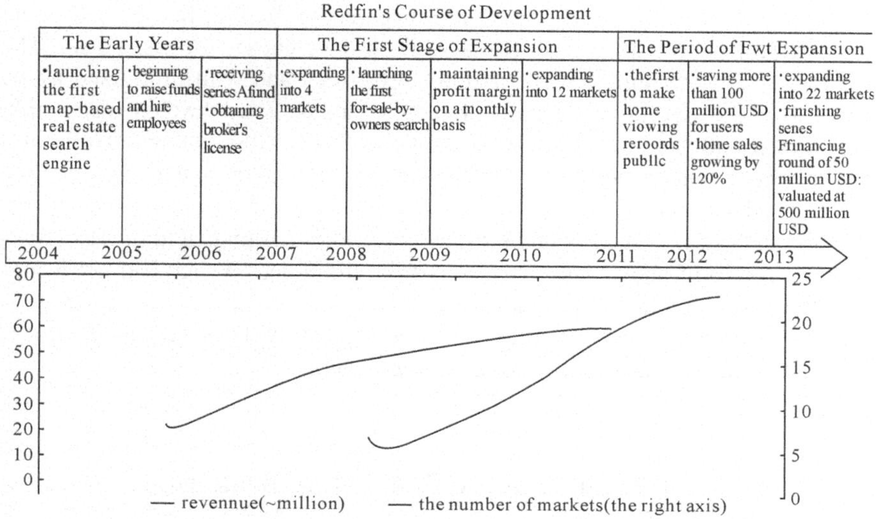

Fig. 7.2 Redfin's course of development. *Source* Redfin; The Authors

We can find the answer by examining Redfin's story.

Redfin is the first residential real estate company that provides web-based home search in the US, preceding Zillow and Trulia. The founders of the three companies used to exchange opinions when they were brewing a change in the real estate brokerage industry, but Redfin chose a bumpier and more tortuous path.

In 2002, David Eraker, who had dropped out of University of Washington's medical school, and Michael Dougherty, an electrical engineer with a degree from Yale decided to overthrow the brokerage industry. They believed that consumers, while paying excessive commission at the rate of 6 %, did not get good service. They believed they can upend the traditional brokerage model. First, they decided to display real estate information on satellite maps, so that users could conveniently browse homes on any particular locations on the map. This was before the introduction of Google Maps or Microsoft's Bing Maps, so they had to spend much time and money to obtain data authorization. Second, they employed their own real estate agents who worked on salaries rather than commissions to navigate consumers through transaction procedures. Traditionally, real estate agents are independent contractors who can practice independently with a license. Redfin's ways are disruptive to the traditional business model, bringing rather significant consequences to the firm. These strategies were extremely innovative at that time.

Redfin's online map-based real estate search was launched in 2004, the first of its kind in the US (see Fig. 7.2). Prior to launching their first product, Eraker discussed the business model with one of his neighbors, Sami Inkinen, who later launched Trulia in the library of Stanford University after he obtained his MBA degree. Almost at the same time, Rich Barton, the founder of the first online travelling company in the world, launched Zillow after his failed attempt at acquiring Redfin.

Although both Zillow and Trulia were inspired by Redfin, the three of them took different paths. Zillow and Trulia seem to have chosen an easier path. The easy money is in running ads for traditional brokers, and with little fixed assets of their own they are favored targets of venture capital. They developed smoothly over the ten odd years and both went public in 2011. Zillow bought Trulia in a stock-for-stock transaction in 2014 and ended the competition in the field of online real estate advertising.

While Zillow and Trulia's stock prices were skyrocketing, Redfin was struggling to keep itself above water. Investors from the Silicon Valley had not recognized Redfin's potential until recently.

In 2013, Redfin raised $50 million in a round led by Tiger Global. Redfin is now driving on a fast lane and is expected to go public.

7.1 Redfin—A Disruptor of the Real Estate Brokerage Industry in the US

7.1.1 A Media Company Mating with an e-Commerce Company

Redfin is a media company mating with an e-commerce company.

As a media company and an information platform, Redfin generates its own traffic instead of buying traffic. It creates online community, publishes unique content, offers unique inventory and provides perfect search experience. In this way Redfin functions as a destination site for users to browse and search for homes and acquire market information and neighborhood information.

As ane-commerce business, Redfin facilitates and closes transactions. To make this happen, Redfin builds a complete, up-to-date and accurate database of historical transaction information and active listing information and hires real estate agents to navigate consumers through the procedures of pricing, negotiation, viewing, financing, home inspection, insurance and settlement. Redfingets firsthand information on price fluctuation and consumer needs from its full participation in the home buying and selling process. Redfin is in the game as a dominant player, while other real estate websites seem to be watching the game on tape delay.

The whole division between e-commerce pure-plays and media pure-plays is a canard. Media companies have to participate in transactions if they want to maximize revenue generated from traffic. And e-commerce companies have to stop buying traffic and start making their own if they want to increase their margins. Redfin, a perfect amalgamation of a media company and an e-commerce company, sets a good example for all those in the trade.

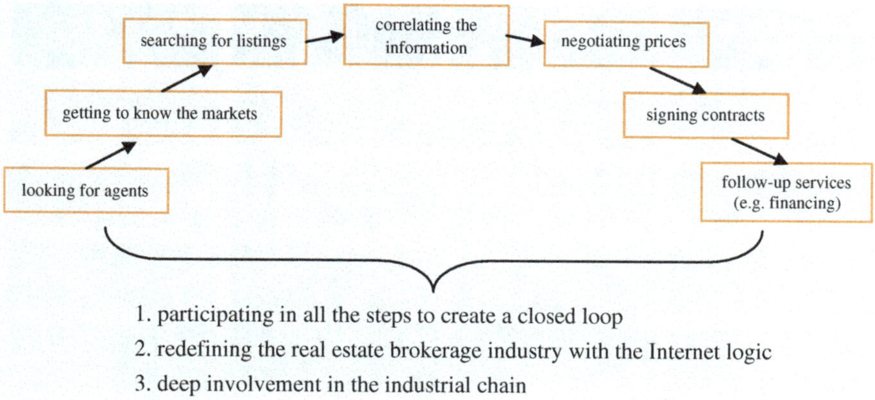

Fig. 7.3 Participating in all the steps in a transaction cycle. *Source* The Authors

7.1.2 Redfin: An E2E e-Commerce Focusing on User Experience

Unlike other real estate websites, Redfin employs its own real estate agents and builds a closed loop encompassing all the online and offline procedures of a home transaction cycle (see Fig. 7.3). This is the key to Redfin's higher consumer satisfaction over traditional brokerage companies.

A company's control over all the steps in a home buying or selling cycle (see Fig. 7.4) is the prerequisite for good consumer satisfaction. However, having control of the whole cycle does not mean they have to employ all the service providers involved in the saling or buying cycle. First, in major metropolitan areas that Redfin serves, it employs salaried agents. But for homes outside their direct service area, Redfin will refer them to their partner agents on some referral fee. Although these partner agents are not Redfin employees, they have to meet Redfin's standards and adhere to the same principles that guide Redfin agents. Second, although Redfin does not own insurance companies, financial companies or moving companies, they can provide insurance, financing and moving services through their own platforms.

Redfin builds the E2E (End-to-End) closed loop on the basis of Internet technologies. Redfin streamlines the business process through the Internet and maximize real estate agents' efficiency and therefore saves time for consumers. This is similar to a popular concept in China: O2O, meaning online to offline, but in fact there is no clear distinction between online and offline activities in a real estate business chain (see Fig. 7.5). For example, home viewing is often seen as an offline, but in fact it can be virtualized. Redfin's information platform does not just offer complete, up-to-date and accurate listing information, but also innumerous pictures and videos of homes, as well as a panorama of map-based neighborhood information. These virtual home tours greatly reduce real estate agents'

Fig. 7.4 Controlling all the steps from information search to closing. *Source* The Authors

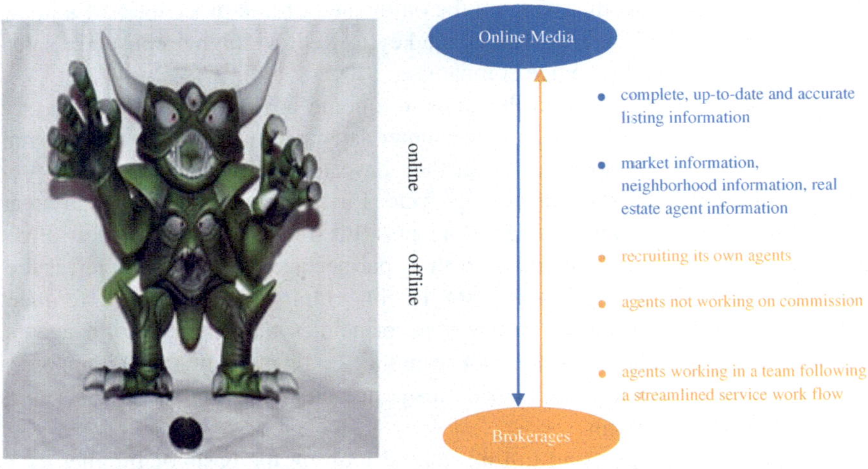

Fig. 7.5 Redfin: A double-faced beast. *Source* The Authors

workload as well as saving consumers' time. Besides, online offer and online mortgage application also save a lot of time and makes home buying and selling more efficient.

Redfin's online platform acts as a control center that manages all the steps from home search to closing and provides on-demand service. A user can view listing information of a certain area by entering query words in Redfin's powerful

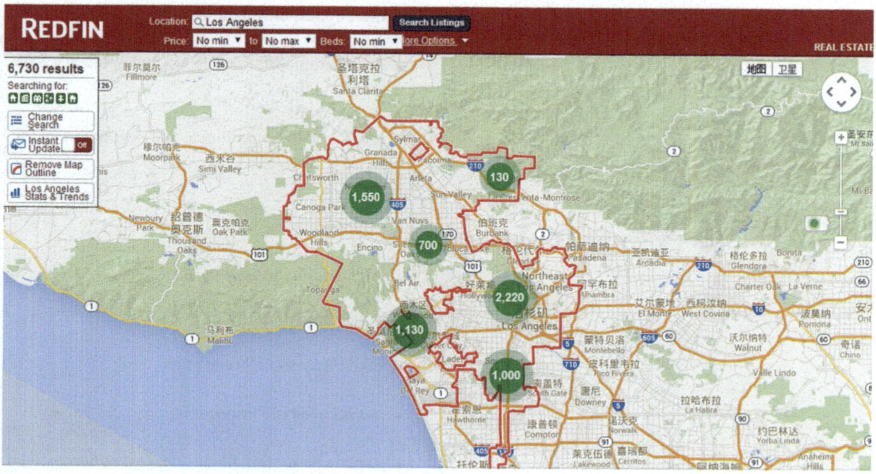

Fig. 7.6 Redfin's powerful map-based search engine supporting huge amount of traffic. *Source* Redfin

map-based home search engine (see Fig. 7.6). If he wants to see any of the homes in person he can request home tours online or via telephone, and then a Redfin tour coordinator will call the user to confirm the details and help finalize the overall schedule. Redfin agents will then follow up with procedures like making offers, signing contracts, financing, home inspection and title insurance. When the deal is closed, the user will receive a commission rebate and will be requested to review the agents' service (see Fig. 7.7).

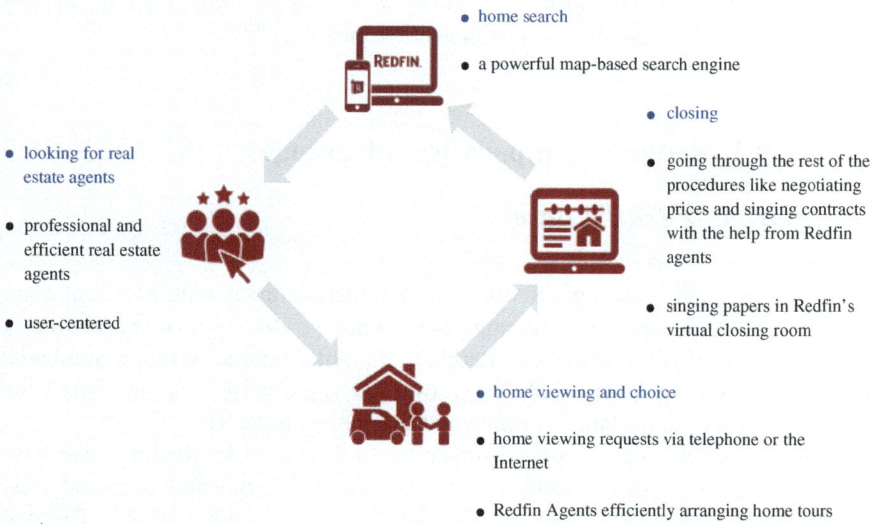

Fig. 7.7 Redfin's business model. *Source* Redfin; The Authors

Fig. 7.8 Professional division of labor. *Source* Redfin; The Authors

Redfin agents are six times as efficient as traditional real estate agents. The scale effect in real estate agents' service is achieved through division of labor and the streamlining of work flow. Redfin agents work in a team to provide full service to individual consumers. On a typical team there will usually be multiple agents each specializing in one or two things. The team leader is usually an experienced broker who is directly responsible to consumers, helping them with home choice and purchase offers. There are coordinating agents that arrange home tours, home inspection and home appraisal, as well as getting documents in order. Then there are junior agents that accompany consumers on their home tours. Each agent may accompany over 50 showings a week in average (see Fig. 7.8).

7.2 What Is Redfin's Comparative Advantage?

7.2.1 Adequate Traffic Base

Unlike a traditional brokerage, Redfin is an Internet company with powerful map-based home search capacity, generating considerable traffic on its own. According to a recent third-party statistics, Redfin's monthly unique visitors numbered around 6 million, an increase of 220 % over the same period the previous year. Redfin is now the fourth largest online media company in the US.

Although franchising or owner-as-operator brokerages like Realogy also have their own websites, their traffic is very limited. Realogy itself attracted only 500,000 unique visitors, accounting for only 25 % of its total traffic. The rest 1.5 million came from third-party websites like Zillow.

ZipRealty identified itself as an Internet-based real estate brokerage company; however, it did not generate its own traffic, but had to pay an average traffic fee of $500 per transaction. Consequently, its revenue in 2013 was 40 % down from 2009. It was not doing very well when it was bought by the traditional brokerage giant, Realogy, in mid-2014.

7.2.2 *Complete, Up-to-Date and Accurate Listing Information*

As a brokerage firm, Redfin works with several local multiple listing services (MLS) to ensure data is updated and accurate (see Fig. 7.9), and it lists all the agent-listed homes out there (see Fig. 7.10). On the other hand, Zillow's listings mostly come from Realtor.com, the official website of National Association of Realtors. The information is not complete, timely or accurate. A 2013 survey showed that Zillow only list 81 % of the listings on the market, and as it took 7 days for active listings to enter MLS's database and then be distributed to Zillow, over 30 % listings were inaccurate.

7.2.3 *More Efficiency with Lower Commission*

Redfin charges a 1.5 % commission from home sellers, which is only half of the traditional 3 % commission. This results in a $ 7500 save on each transaction in average.

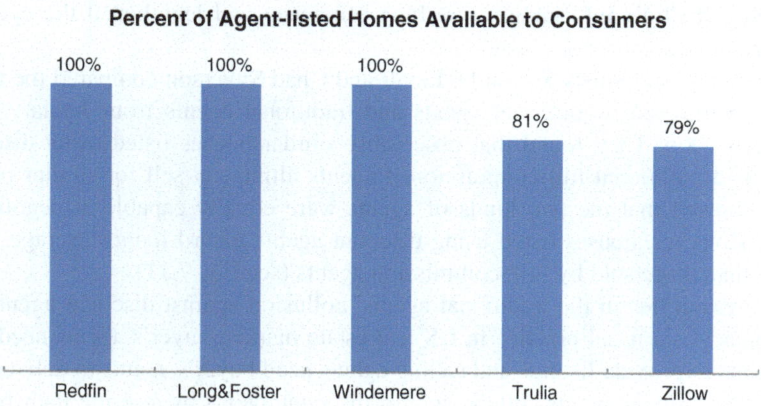

Fig. 7.9 100% of agent-listed homes available to Redfin consumers. *Source* Redfin (2013)

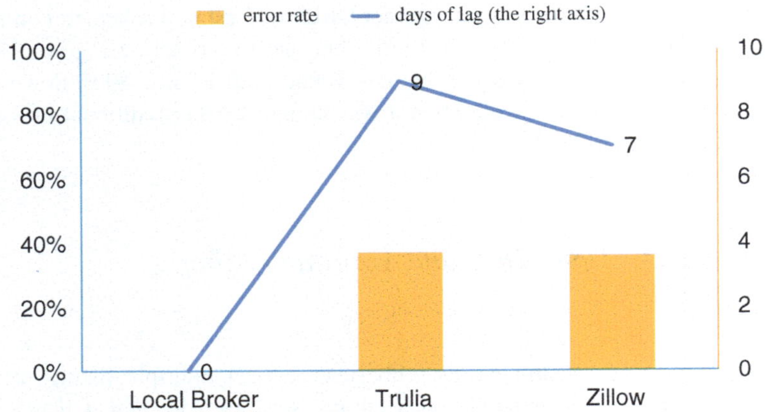

Fig. 7.10 Redfin's listing information more timely and accurate. *Source* Redfin (2013)

7.3 Why Does Redfin Develop Relatively Slowly?

Due to its limited financing and the strong opposition from traditional real estate agents, Redfin's revenue grows more slowly than Zillow and Trulia.

7.3.1 The Strong Opposition from Traditional Real Estate Agents

Redfin had a rather difficult time during its early years, because the flaming opposition from traditional agents ever since the company's establishment had hampered Redfin's information matching efficiency and lengthened the cycle of transactions.

American economists Steven D. Levitt and Chad Syverson compared the transactions completed by discount agents and traditional agents from January 2004 to March 2006. They found that observably similar houses listed using discount agents and traditional full-commissioned agents ultimately sell for similar prices, which showed that the two kinds of agents were equally capable at negotiating prices. However, houses listed using discount agents record longer average time-to-sale than those sold by full–commission agents (see Fig. 7.11).

The reason lies in the traditional agents' collusion against discount agents. As dual agency is a usual practice in US real estate market, buyer's agents need selling agents to provide listings and selling agents need buyer's agents to deliver customers. Traditional agents collude against discount agents by steering their buyers away from such listings, and this has caused significantly longer average time-to-sale on discount agents' part.

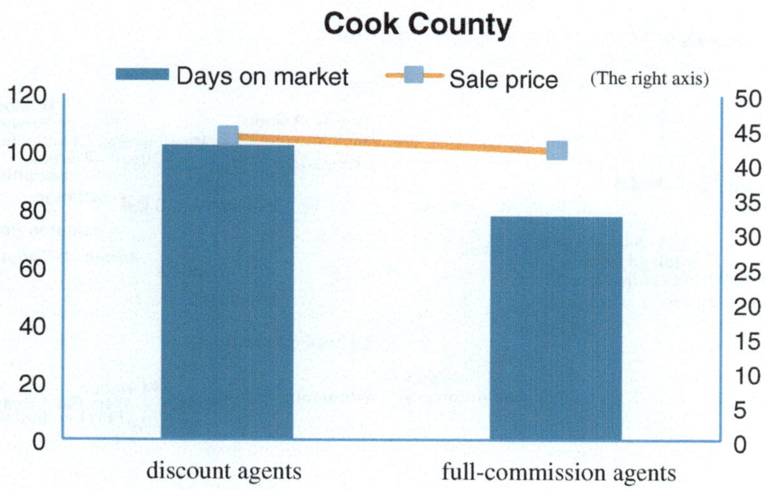

Fig. 7.11 Days on market of homes listed by discount agents and full-commission agents (cook county as an example). *Source* The Authors

7.3.2 *Inadequate Financing*

Redfin has had a hard time in financing ever since its founding. Venture capitalists generally prefer asset light business models. Online advertising model like Zillow's has always been in the spotlight, so it is rather easy for Zillow to attract venture capital and use it on R&D and promotion. On the other hand, asset heavy business models like Redfin's have never been investors' favorites. It is not easy to explain to them why E2E model leads to scale effect, and why Redfin agents are six times as efficient as traditional agents.

By 2011, Redfin had raised a total of only $ 4600 through its several financing rounds (see Table 7.1). Redfin's expansion did not pick up until it raised $50 million from Tiger Global (see Fig. 7.12).

Table 7.1 Redfin's financing rounds

Rounds	Time	Amount of each round (million USD)	Accumulated fund (million USD)	Lead investor
Series F	2013	50	96	Tiger global management
Series E	2011	14.8	46	Globespan capital partners
Series D	2009	10	31.2	Greylock partners
Series C	2007	12	21.2	Draper fisher jurvetson
Series B	2006	8	9.2	Paul allen's vulcan capital, BEV capital, The Hillman company
Series A	2006	1.2	1.2	Madrona venture group

Source Redfin; The Authors

Fig. 7.12 Redfin well into most of the expensive markets. *Source* Redfin; The Authors

7.4 Why Will Redfin Eventually Move into a Fast Lane?

Redfin's development is now gaining momentum. Redfin will snatch greater market share and grow into a significant force in the market if this momentum is maintained.

First, the opposition from traditional real estate agents is abating and discount agents' share is growing. Traditional agents' advantage lies in its greater efficiency in facilitating sales, which attributes heavily to their collusion. However, this collusion is gradually losing its influence as discount agents' share grows, and the discrepancy between their transaction efficiency narrows, rendering discount agents a more compelling choice. This virtuous cycle will contribute to the steady growth of discount agents' market share.

Table 7.2 Higher value for money with discount agents

	Using traditional agents (million USD)	Using discount agents (million USD)
Average price	4500	4500
Commission rate (%)	5	2.5
Commission expense	225	112.5
Extra days-on-market		0.26
Cost of time		26
Extra cost of time (-h)		0.5
General cost of work		15
Extra marketing cost		10
Total cost	225	16.35

Source Antitrust implications of home seller outcomes

Second, Redfin is expected to gain more listings in the future, because it charges only half of the traditional commission rate, and even if the expected time-to-sale is a bit longer (see Table 7.2), it is still very compelling to consumers.

Third, Redfin' successful financing rounds in recent years add fuel to its development.

7.5 Why Will the Chinese Version of Redfin Rise and Thrive?

Our elaboration on the history of US real estate brokerage industry and the development of Internet firms like Zillow and Redfin offers insights into the driving force behind the development of an industry and a company. With this insight we can perhaps find signs of China's Internet brokerage giants.

We have come to the conclusion that the most promising business model for China is an E2E e-commerce model like Redfin's, but why?

7.5.1 E2E: The Key to Better User Experience

For one thing, China's online media companies cannot offer valuable information to its users the same way Redfin does. Since there is no complete, up-to-date and accurate listing information, fairly accurate home valuation or market information, not to mention map-based interactive real estate search, correlation of information is unlikely via Internet media companies. For another, China's offline brokerage is a chaotic industry featuring open listing contracts and vicious competition. The sole purpose of real estate agents is to facilitate sales, totally disregarding consumer satisfaction. Therefore traditional brokerages are not likely to provide satisfactory offline support services. Moreover, presently China's Internet media companies and traditional brokerages seem to be independent of and even conflicting to each other. Their cooperation is rather improbable.

Therefore, E2E e-commerce model remains the only way to address both online and offline consumer needs. First, only online information platforms that do not rely on advertising to generate revenue can provide accurate information, and only accurate information can attract users and form positive feedback loop between users and content, which ultimately results in network effect. Second, only active participation in offline transaction procedures can provide valuable data for the complete online real estate information base and accurate home valuation. Besides, when a company participate in all the home buying and selling steps, including home viewing, deciding on which home to buy, paper work, financing and insurance, it is possible to coordinate the different steps and divide the work among the agents. Without such coordination and division of labor, there will be no "central coordination plus on-demand service" to speak of, and therefore no scale effect. To conclude, E2E model makes it possible for e-commerce firms to achieve network effect and scale effect, which is essential to the survival of asset heavy Internet companies.

7.5.2 E2E: The Only Business Model that Generates the Last-Second Economy

In an era of the mobile Internet, consumers expect immediate service at the touch of a button on their phones, a phenomenon called "the last-second economy" or "same-day service". With this on-demand service, consumers act more spontaneously with compressed planning cycles. They expect to get instant response when they submit a request. For example, a person using Uber to request a car expects the car to turn up in a few minutes, rather than waiting helplessly on the roadside, depending on sheer luck for a vacant taxi to drive by. Similarly, if a home buyer browses listings on Redfin and wishes to see one of them, he expects to contact an agent and arrange a home tour on the spot, without the uncertainty of waiting to be contacted (see Fig. 7.13).

Without up-to-date listing information, manageable personnel of agents, central coordination supported by transaction data, there will not be "the last-second economy". The last-second economy can be additive to users who have the chance

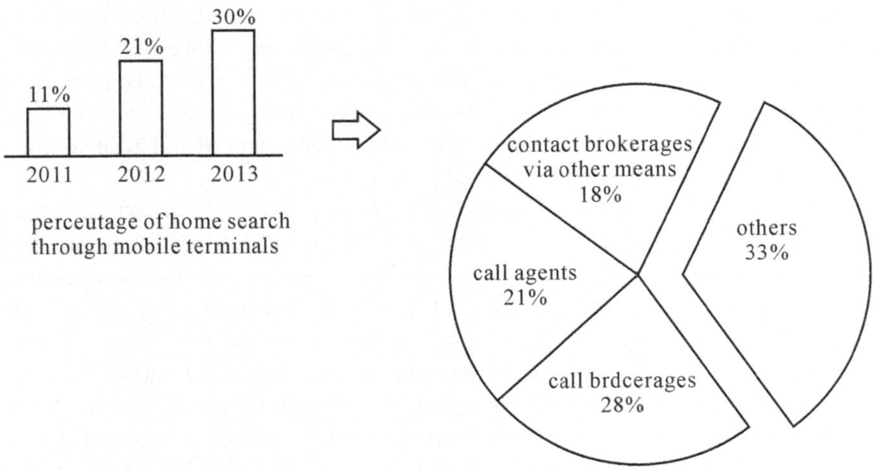

Fig. 7.13 The last-second economy in real estate business. *Source* NAR (2013)

to enjoy service with such ease and convenience. Uber's competitive advantage over its rivals lies in its one-stop transport solution with typical E2E car service. The same is true of Redfin, whose advantage comes from its full participation in the whole process of a service, having control over agents the way Uber has control over drivers.

So the only way out for a Chinese enterprise, be it a forerunner in the industry or an entrant, is building an E2E closed loop, having control over the whole business process and acting on consumers demand.

7.5.3 A Revelation to Investors: Good User Experience Over Good Business

Quite unlike Redfin, who had a difficult time raising fund during its early years, China's startups are not short of money. A considerable number of startups, like Fangdd and Haowu, have been generously financed. In recent years, Apple beat Microsoft; Amazon pulverized Ebay; 360 buy went public. Venture investors are constantly learning lessons from these events. They have come to realize that asset light business model is not all that good and good consumer experience is more important than rapid growth. It is the best age than ever for China's startups because financing has been easier than ever before.

7.6 Is It Possible for Real Estate Brokerages to Transform into E2E e-Commerce Companies?

It is possible for traditional real estate brokerages to transform into E2E e-commerce companies, but the chance is slim. The reasons do not lie in their lack of the so-called Internet genes or their lack of innovation, but rather their long-term neglect of consumer needs and wrong focus of innovation.

Traditional brokerages have always been indifferent to consumer needs. As strong fortresses are more likely to be captured from within rather than via open assailment, the fall of the traditional brokerage industry does not result from an external impact, but rather its long-standing negligence of consumer needs. For so many years traditional brokerages have been pursuing more listings, more business leads and more money. This pursuit of maximum profit rather than best consumer experience has percolated through every aspects of the industry, including the recruitment and training of real estate agents and the establishment of business models. Traditional brokerages address their own needs rather consumer needs.

Innovation is not absent or disregarded in traditional brokerages, it is just wrongly focused. 90 % of innovations in traditional brokerages are targeted at new methods to increase listings and sales, with the rest 10 % at commission split models or pay policies. Now the market is glutted with various innovative ideas and so-called new models. The numerous websites and apps, Internet franchises, everyone-as-agent program and all sorts of promotion campaigns all fall into these categories. None of them is worthy of note.

7.7 Is It Possible for Online Media Companies to Transform into E2EE-Commerce Businesses?

One has to examine three questions before drawing a conclusion. What motivates the transformation? How eager are they for the transformation? Are they advantaged in such transformation?

Some media companies declare that they will participate in transaction procedures and transform themselves into transaction platforms. But this transformation is focused on sales rather than consumer experience. It is only a transformation of monetizing model, because the information is still as incomplete and inaccurate as before, and there is not much improvement in offline service either.

While online media companies are fast growing and highly profitable businesses, there is no easy money for E2E companies. Online media companies have to compromise their present revenue if the transformation is to happen, like amputating one's unsalvageable arm to save his life, quite a reasonable decision, but by no means an easy one.

Online media companies do have some advantages in the transformation. They have a large number of users. However, this audience base does not seem as impressive if we take into consideration the enormity of China's potential users, and their websites are not very sticky to users.

Chapter 8
The Falls and Turns of Real Estate Media

Readers Guide

- Most real estate websites in the early stage of the Internet age focus on grabbing consumers' eyeballs through gathering and distributing listing information. Once the websites have aggregated a large enough user base, they can monetize the traffic in two ways: providing traffic or business leads to real estate agents and helping them build their professional profiles so that they can acquire more listings.
- As the first real estate website in the world, Move provides a trading platform that connects consumers with listing information and real estate agents. Its business model is a consumer-connection-customer (3C) model.
- Users are important to Move, but more important are real estate agents, because they provide listings and pay subscription fee to Move. Most of Move's products and services are about providing valuable traffic to real estate agents and facilitating sales for them. Move advertises for real estate agents, real estate brokerages and non-real-estate advertisers.

Move, Inc. (Move) is the first vertical real estate website in the US and the world at large. It is a typical Internet company in the first stage of the Internet Age, or the PC age, and also the only listed Internet company in the real estate brokerage industry that has survived the dot-com bubble. As Wall Street's former all-star stock, Move's stock price once hiked to over 400 USD, but now 96 % of it is gone. Although Move's revenue is about the same as the up-and-coming Zillow, its market value is only 11 % of Zillow's.

After Zillow's acquisition of Trulia, Zillow is without doubt the flagship of the industry and Move is significantly threatened. However, the case of Move falling from the leading position offers valuable lessons to China's start-ups and industrial leaders.

S. Ba and X. Yang, *"Internet Plus" Pathways to the Transformation of China's Property Sector*, DOI 10.1007/978-981-10-1699-8_8

8.1 The Rise of Real Estate Portals in the Personal Computer Age

Move is born against the background of two major trends: the first is consumer attention moving from the real world to the online world; the second is real estate advertising moving from paper-based media to online media.

8.1.1 Two Structural Shifts: Eyeballs and Advertising

8.1.1.1 The Traditional Transaction Process

The traditional home buying and selling process was facilitated by real estate agents, who held real estate information close to their chest and acted as information media between buyers and sellers. Before the Internet Age, potential buyers and sellers gathered information through their agents, word-of-mouth, local newspapers and brokerage offices. The information distributed through these traditional media was limited, usually only a few pictures with simple description.

In order to acquire comprehensive information, potential buyers had to work with a trustworthy broker, who then accessed the local MLS for matching for-sale listings. As consumers had no access to MLS data, the information search and matching process was in fact controlled by real estate professionals. Without complete information, consumers had to spend a lot of time viewing homes on their brokers' recommendation, which was rather inefficient. If this information asymmetry could be removed, consumers would be able to work more efficiently, filtering out inappropriate listings and focusing their time and energy on the most matching listings.

Similarly, without comprehensive market information, sellers were not able to reasonably price their homes. They had no channels to advertise their listings, either. Like buyers, they had to work with a local broker, who will give them advice and help them price their homes and publicize their homes through the local MLS, so as to find the highest bidding buyer in the shortest time. Sellers had to sign an exclusive-right-to-sell agreement with the broker and promise a 5 % to 6 % commission rate.

8.1.1.2 Eyeballs Moving Online

Since the Internet disrupted the above mentioned tradition in 1995, it has become the first stop for home buyers and sellers. The proportion of buyers searching for online for-sale listings soared. In 1995, only 5 % of the buyers searched for listings online, but the proportion rose to 71 % in 2003 and 92 % in 2013

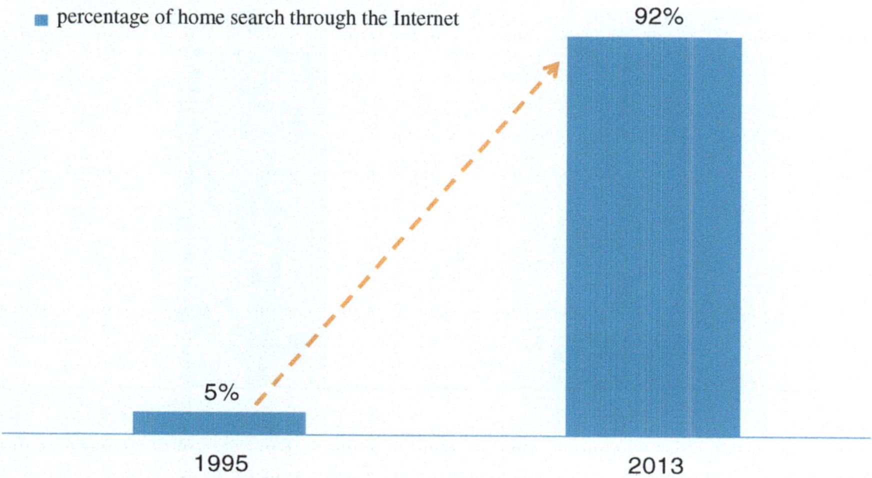

Fig. 8.1 Consumer eyeballs moving online. *Source* NAR (2013)

(see Fig. 8.1). Consumers can easily enter a street name or a zip code and search for homes in the designated area. They can also download pictures and layout plans, and email real estate agents for the constantly updated active listings. Information correlation has become much more efficient than before.

8.1.1.3 Advertising Moving Online

In the pre-Internet age, the real estate brokerage industry spent billions of dollars each year advertising on print media like newspapers and magazines to attract consumer attention and acquire listings. As consumer's eyeballs move online, real estate advertising follows suit. Although real estate agents are reluctant to immediately cut down on their conventional ad spending on local newspapers, they are no longer the dominant media for advertising.

Online advertising accounts for only 9 % of the total in 2003. Now it has reached 53 %, and the figure is still on the rise (see Fig. 8.2). During the financial crisis, the real estate section of classified ads plummeted, but online real estate advertising grew by 30 %.

According to an advertising research and consulting firm, Borrell Associate, online advertising in the real estate industry was projected at 4.7 billion USD in 2014 and then all the way to 7.6 billion USD in 2018. The projected growth is sustained by the augment in the online category itself as well as the industry's shift from traditional (offline) marketing to online marketing (see Fig. 8.3).

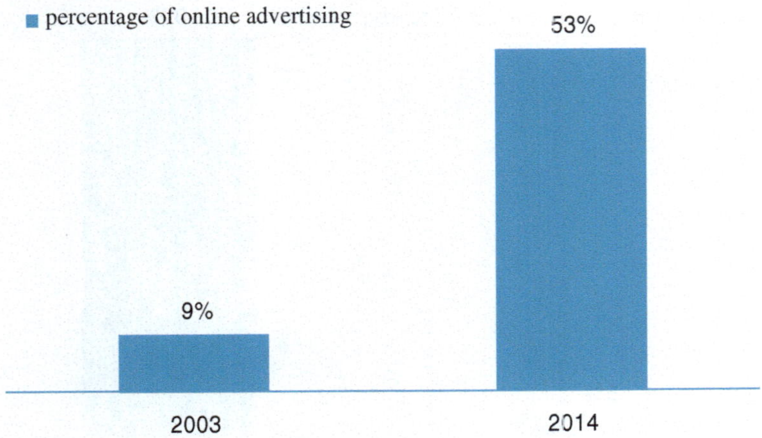

Fig. 8.2 Real estate advertising moving online. *Source* Market leader (2013)

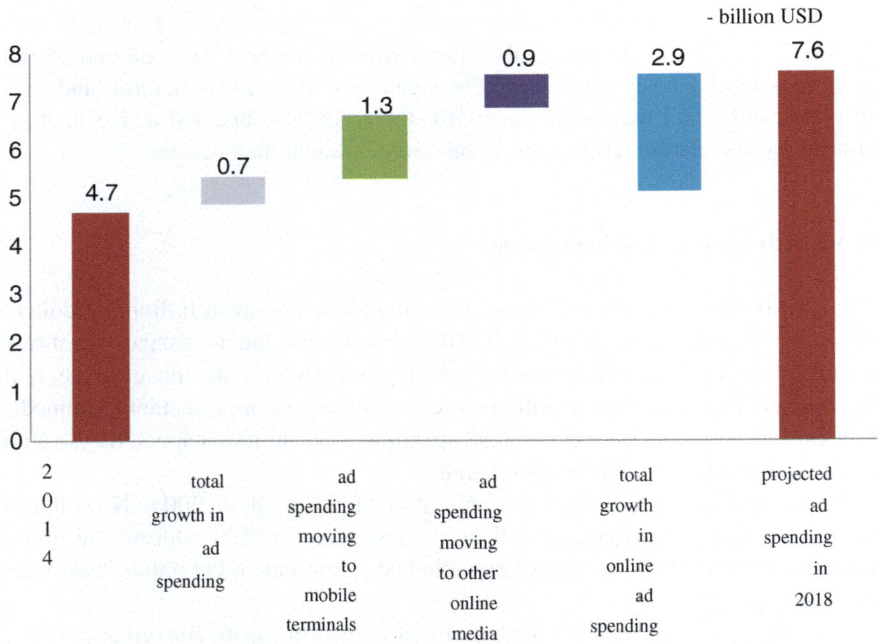

Fig. 8.3 Projected online ad spending of brokers and brokerages. *Source* Borrell (2013)

8.1.2 Revenue Source of Real Estate Websites: Providing Traffic and Building Professional Profiles

Most real estate websites in the early stage of the Internet age focus on grabbing consumers' eyeballs through gathering and distributing listing information. Once the websites have aggregated a large enough user base, they can monetize the traffic in two ways: providing traffic or business leads to real estate agents and helping them build their professional profiles so that they can acquire more listings.

8.1.2.1 Traffic

Traffic is the major source of revenue for a real estate website. Home buying or selling is usually the biggest decision one ever makes in a family life cycle. It involves a large sum of money and happens rather infrequently. Since impulse buying usually does not happen in such cases, the key to effective advertising is to constantly engage and secure the "eyeballs" of the most probable buyers.

Home buyers expect to acquire complete, timely and accurate information so as to find the property that best matches their preferences. In most cases, it is the properties themselves that determine the volume of traffic and transaction, not the real estate agents. As buyers are not likely to have any "brand loyalty" for their agents, the motivation for agents' advertising is to acquire listings, rather than to attract buyer clients.

Before the Internet age, the first stop for home buyers was real estate brokerage offices and local newspapers. The greater office coverage, the more advertising pages in newspapers, the more likely agents got valuable leads. Now that the Internet has become the source of information for buyers, real estate websites are capable of charging real estate agents, property developers, mortgage lenders and other participants in the industrial chain for advertising fee.

8.1.2.2 Professional Profile Building

Most real estate agents' ad spending focuses on profile building so as to increase their chances of acquiring listings rather than attracting buyers. Anyway, as an agent, he has to have listings on hand before he sets out to look for buyers.

While buyers pay more attention to listings, sellers are more concerned with real estate agents' brand name, word-of mouth and historical sales. They hope to work with an excellent agent to maximize the visibility of their listings and find a high-bidding buyer in a short time. This is actually what real estate agents do for the commission they charge; therefore, agents are more concerned with their business profile rather than traffic.

8.1.2.3 Sources of Revenue: Subscription Fee and Accessorial Service Fee

The first is subscription fee. Real estate websites usually charge a flat fee for the display of a listing or a broker office. They may even offer such service for free in order to encourage real estate agents to use the Internet media.

The second is fee based on traffic or business leads.

The third is extra fee from agents or sellers for increased visibility of listings in search engine results.

The fourth is data service fee. Mortgage lenders, real estate developers, home remodelers are all potential users of market data and transaction data, the part of real estate websites' information asset that has not yet been fully utilized.

8.2 Move—The First Real Estate Portal in the US and the World at Large

As the first real estate website in the world, Move provides a trading platform that connects consumers with listing information and real estate agents. Its business model is a consumer-connection-customer (3C) model (see Fig. 8.4).

The 3C model is firstly built on the connection between consumers and listing information. With adequate listing information, consumers will be able to make wiser selling, buying, financing or rental decisions.

The second foundation of the 3C model is the connection between consumers and real estate agents. Move has declared that attracting consumers is an important

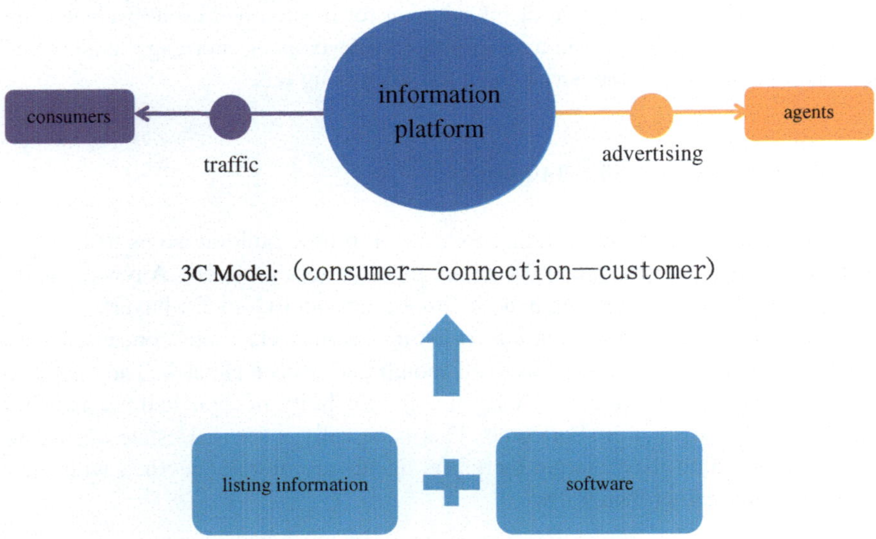

Fig. 8.4 The 3C model. *Source* The Authors

part of its business. However, attracting real estate professionals is by no means less important. They are both users and content providers. Move promises to respect all real estate agents, real estate brokers, MLSs and other listing information providers.

8.2.1 *The 3C Model: Listing Information as the Cutting Edge*

As an online platform, Move itself does not generate information. All the listings are from traditional sources. Listings of existing homes are from MLSs, National Association of Realtors (NAR), brokers and brokerages, while listings of new homes are from National Association of Home Builders (NAHB) and land developers (see Fig. 8.5).

Move signs contracts with traditional listing providers and pays them for a direct feeding of their listings. It works with National Association of Realtors (NAR) and operates its official website, Realtor.com. This has made Move the only website in the US that is capable of providing complete, up-to-date and accurate listings.

Realtor.com is the official website of the National Association of Realtors, the trade association in the US, with more than one million members including real estate brokers, salespeople, property managers and counselors. Because of its permanent and exclusive access to listings on Realtor.com, Move is able to display nearly all listings from MLSs for free on their website and mobile apps.

Move therefore enjoys incomparable advantage over its competitors, for example, Zillow. It boasts information of over 100 million existing homes in the US and for-sale properties in over 36 countries. Move's business covers existing homes,

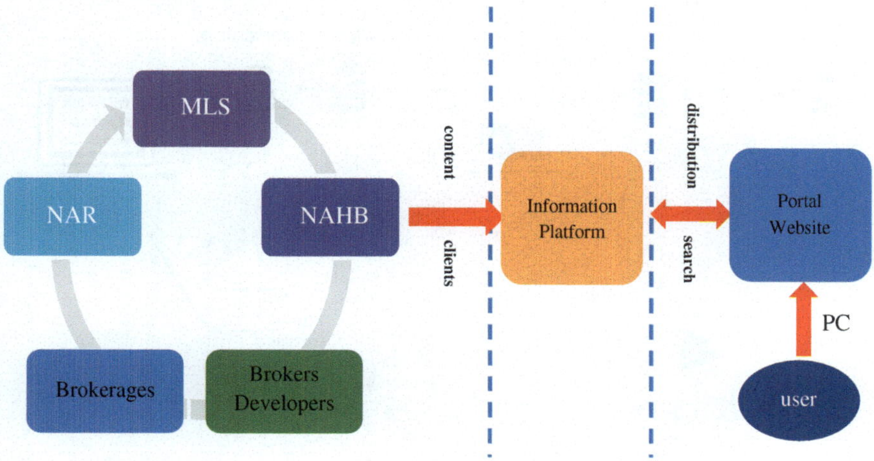

Fig. 8.5 Sources of website contents. *Source* The Authors

Fig. 8.6 Listings: the real competitive edge. *Source* The Authors

new homes, multiple family homes, posh neighborhoods as well as rentals. Its four million for-sale listings, which accounts for 98 % of America's on-sale properties, are displayed in 11 languages on their websites and mobile apps. Move leverages its relationships with more than 800 MLSs and displays almost all of the MLS-listed for-sale properties. More than 90 % of the active listings are updated every 15 min, and inactive listings are updated every day (see Fig. 8.6). Move has the most comprehensive, timely and accurate information.

Moreover, because it manages NAR's official site, Realtor.com, Move actually controls the distribution of information to third-party websites. Move is where information comes from (see Fig. 8.7).

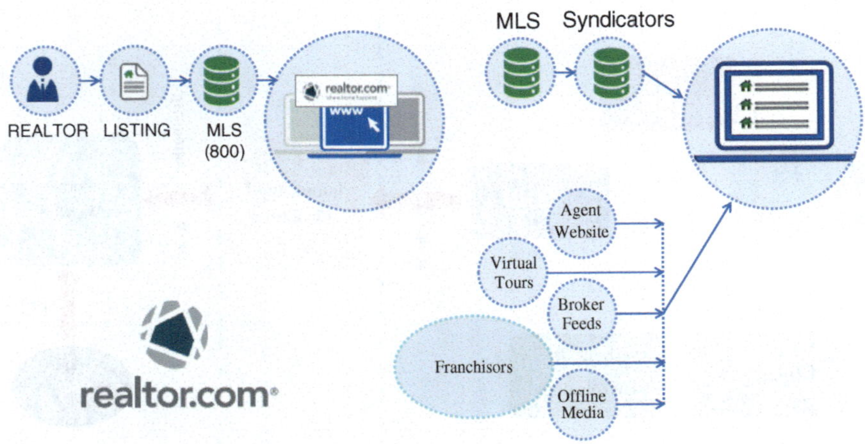

Fig. 8.7 Move controlling the distribution of listing information. *Source* The Authors

8.2.2 The 3C Model: Supporting Real Estate Agents

Users are important to Move, but more important are real estate agents, who provide listings and pay subscription fee to Move. Most of Move's products and services are about providing valuable traffic to real estate agents and facilitating transactions for them. The advertisements Move provides for real estate agents, real estate brokerages and non-real-estate advertisers are as follows.

First, display advertising for listings. This includes increasing visibility of listings in search engine results pages, with more images, videos and virtual experience. Move also enables real estate agents to advertise themselves and their professional profiles. Advertising rates are determined according to the local markets, historical prices and user coverage.

Second, display advertising for non-real-estate content. This includes sponsorship, images, text links and link units. Other participators in the industrial chain who wish to access Move's audience, including insurers, home remodelers, movers and loaners are all their potential advertisers. Display advertising is sold at CPM (Cost per Thousand Impressions), CPC (Cost per Click) or a subscription fee.

Third, software and services (see Fig. 8.8). Move provides software-as-a-service Customer Relationship Management (SaaS CRM) products, including Top Producer, TigerLead and Fivestreet, which are lead generation and management and CRM tools for real estate professionals who pay a subscription price to use them. Top Producer provides both computer-based software and mobile apps as well as personal webpages. TigerLead provides an Internet data exchange (IDX) platform that enables real estate agents to access background data, for example, the number of visits. FiveStreet allows real estate professionals to manage a high

Fig. 8.8 Move's products and services. *Source* Move (2013)

volume of leads from over 60 third-party sources and then efficiently route and distribute those leads to real estate agents, without missing or repeating any of the leads. Move also optimizes search engines by classifying and rating leads according to users' keywords so that it can provide real estate agents with high-quality leads. ListHub is a digital platform that aggregates and syndicates MLS data to online publishers, reaching approximately 900 websites. ListHub compiles the traffic metrics it collects into performance reports that provide real estate brokers, venders and MLSs with market intelligence. Users pay a flat fee or a fee based on the number of listings.

8.3 Move—A Fallen All-Star Stock

Move enjoys incomparable advantage of comprehensive and timely listing information in the industry. Due to network effect in this Internet Age, an industrial leader is likely to snatch 80 % of the advertising market share. However, judging from Move's performance and its stock price, this industrial leader does not seem to have a very promising future. Wall Street analysts believed its best outcome was to be acquired by Zillow.

8.3.1 From Success to Failure

In spite of its position in the industry, Move's business performance is rather gloomy. It reported continuous loss for 14 years in a run. Its losses from 1996 to 2013 reached 2 billion USD (see Fig. 8.9). In 2013, Move reported 227 million USD in revenues, still lower than its historical peak in 2001, 292 million USD (see Fig. 8.10).

Fig. 8.9 The growth rates of move's revenue and cost over the years. *Source* Move (2013)

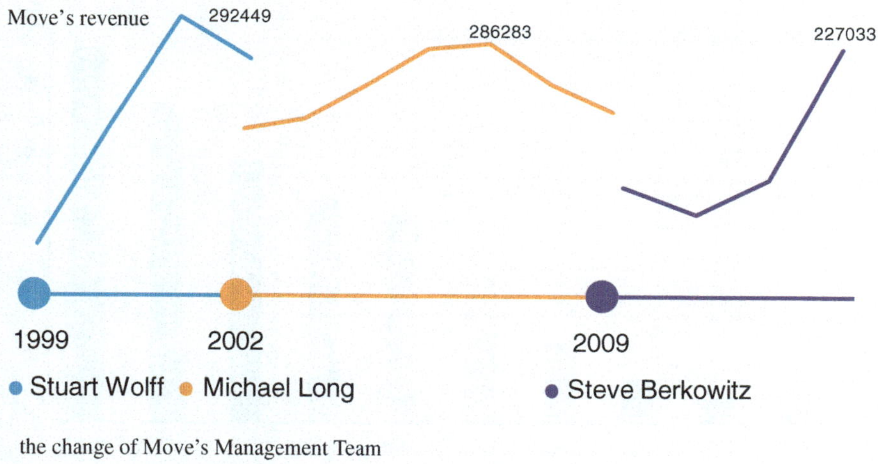

Fig. 8.10 The change of move's management team in relation with move's revenue. *Source* Move

Move's management team had falsified the company books for many years in order to keep up the inflated stock price before the dot-com bubble, resulting in the conviction of almost all the members of its founding team. Move's management team was involved in multiple lawsuits from 2002 to 2009, and was not able to focus on the company's business. Things did not change for the better until 2010 when the new CEO came into office, but by then Zillow and Trulia had already grown substantially and had surpassed Move. Since 2014, quite a few Move's top executives have left Move to join Zillow.

8.3.2 Internal Reason: Slow Growth of User Base

The success of such portal websites as REA and RMV shows that the ability of monetizing the website's traffic relies on a huge and stable audience. REA's revenue did not skyrocket until its user penetration reached 30 %. The company began to profit in 2005, eight years after its founding, while the first few years were all spent in R&D and user accumulation (see Fig. 8.11).

However, Move's number of users was only 10 million in 2009, penetration rate only 5 %. The number of users did not grow significantly during the ten years before 2010. And the growth after 2010 largely attributes to the company's reform and the shift of focus to mobile devices. Because of its own inadequacy of users, Move has to pay Google, AOL, Yahoo and MSN a large sum for their traffic (see Fig. 8.12). The growth of users remains stagnant because of the lack of investment in R&D. Consequently the company is not able to maintain a premium pricing strategy on real estate agents. The company has to buy both content and traffic, with no control over the business cycle.

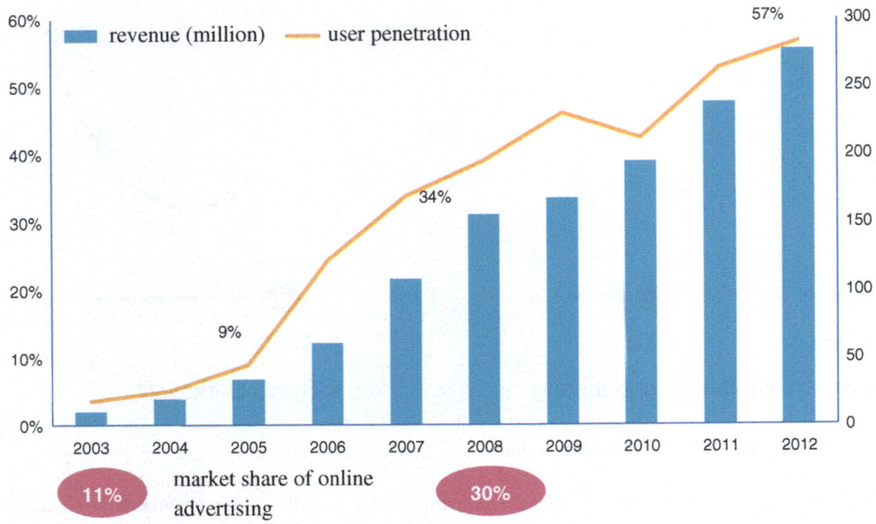

Fig. 8.11 REA's revenue and user penetration. *Source* Move

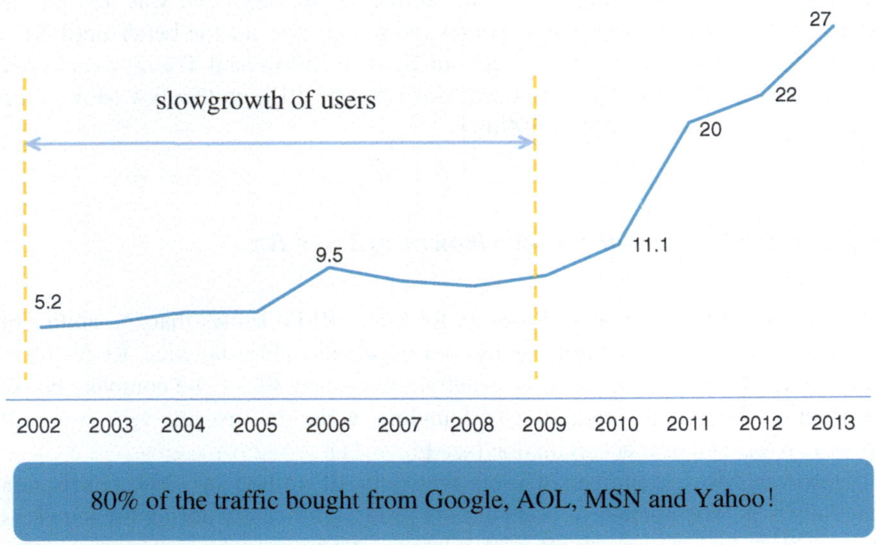

Fig. 8.12 Move's limited users. *Source* Move

8.4 External Reason 1: The Highly Competitive and Decentralized Online Advertising Market

The US real estate advertising market is highly decentralized. Move's competitors in the traditional advertising market are paper-based media, TV and outdoor advertising. The competition from the online sector includes display advertising on portal websites, search engines, videos and emails. The dual pressure weighs down not only Move's monetization capabilities, but also Zillow's. The latest statistics show that although the top three portal websites have occupied 70 % of the UV market share, online advertising accounts for only 20 % of the total advertising market (see Fig. 8.13).

8.4.1 External Reason 2: The Strong Community of American Real Estate Agents

Unlike real estate agents in the UK, Australia and China, American real estate agents have more than ten years of professional experience in average behind them. They have developed a stable social network with the locals. American home buyers and sellers still rely on traditional word-of-mouth and referrals from friends to find real estate agents. In most cases, they sign contracts with agents on their first meeting. This means that portal websites' contribution in building an agent's profile is negligible. According to surveys made in 2013, only 4 % of the home sellers and 9 % of the home buyers find agents on line. The Internet cannot take the place of traditional social network.

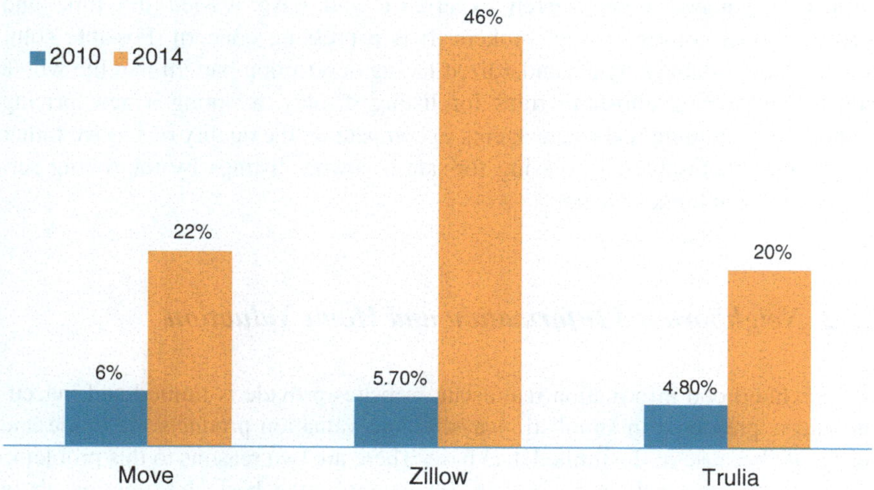

Fig. 8.13 UV market share. *Source* Move

8.5 How Should China's Real Estate Media Transform Themselves?

At present, consumer experience in China's real estate brokerage industry is not satisfactory. The worst consumer complaints center around these areas: listing information; neighborhood information and home evaluation; evaluation systems for real estate agents; financial services.

8.5.1 Listing Information

The problem with listing information lies in inaccurate and repeated listings, which attribute to three reasons. The first is the lack of a basic information database. China does not have a complete and accurate existing home data base. Some estate complexes have more than one name, resulting in repetition of listings. The second is the excessive competition between real estate agents. In order to increase their own visibility and attract buyers, real estate agents make their listings more appealing by providing false information, like false pictures or prices. The third is the inappropriate pricing methodology. Real estate agents have to pay for an account on the website so that they can display listings. The account fee is based on the number of listings displayed and the frequency of automatic clicks—the more frequently a listing is clicked, the more visible it is to visitors because each click will bring the viewed listing to the top. Real estate websites are not interested in displaying accurate listing information and deleting repeated listings, because their revenue does not rely on accurate information.

The inaccurate and repeated listings on real estate websites have severely harmed consumers' home search experience and have wasted the time and energy of both consumers and brokers. It is a pressing concern. Possible solutions include: establishing a standardized listing description pattern that the whole industry follows, establishing rules for listing display, adopting a new pricing methodology, guiding real estate agents to compete on the quality of service rather than listings themselves, increasing for-sale-by-owner listings by improving services targeted at home owners.

8.5.2 Neighborhood Information and Home Valuation

The neighborhood information real estate websites provide is limited and inaccurate and is presented in simplistic ways. Home valuation products are crude and inaccurate because of the limited data base. There are two reasons to this problem:

The first is the lack of basic data, for example, the basic information about schools, hospitals, stores, transportation, natural disasters and crimes. Building such a database is supposed to be the government's responsibility, but in China this will probably be jointly undertaken by both the government and enterprises, funded by corporate capital.

The second is the lack of historical transaction data. Accurate and complete historical transaction data is essential to home valuation. However, the prices recorded in housing authorities are not consistent with actual selling prices. The true transaction data is scattered among various brokerages, who do not share a unified data base. Building a complete and accurate data base of historical transactions will be an exhausting job, as transaction information has to be collected from various brokerages.

8.5.3 Evaluation System for Real Estate Agents

China presently does not have a strong pool of real estate agents. The whole industry is ridden with vicious competition. There are even cases of threats or revenge against clients. Consumers generally do not trust real estate agents. A reliable evaluation system for real estate agents is a pressing consumer demand. Given their considerable traffic, online real estate service providers are in the best position to create an evaluation system. The evaluation system has to strike a balance between the websites' short-term benefit and long-term benefit, ensuring objective, truthful and reliable evaluation. Otherwise it will soon be rejected by users.

8.5.4 Financial Services

Financing difficulty has been the No. 1 consumer complaint. The real estate financial market is in fact a gold mine.

Online real estate service providers can engage themselves in financial services in a variety of ways. The American model is to create a marketplace for real estate financial products, but it is not viable in China, given China's shortage of financial supply. Online service providers can also cooperate with traditional financial institutions and customize financial products that target home buyers. Another option is to integrate online payment systems and insurance institutions to create P2P (Person to Person) financial platforms for the real estate market. This seems to be the most reasonable model for present time China.

The key to the last two solutions is risk control, which is vital to online real estate finance. Due to the limited dimensions in the user data that online real estate service providers possess, and the limited coverage of the user information that traditional brokerages possess, the reasonable solution seems to be cooperating with Internet giants who possess the big data.

8.6 The Pathway to the Rise of China's Online Real Estate Tycoons

The future of China's real estate brokerage market is still foggy. It is not easy to identify the final winner among the many players, but we can map out online real estate giants' courses of development and predict their probability of the final win.

The ultimate form of online real estate service is a platform connecting buyers and sellers. Real estate agents will be affiliated to online platforms, acting as support service providers rather than information intermediaries.

8.6.1 The Courses of Development

All online real estate service providers are supposed to grow in these two ways: improving the quality of information, including listing information, neighborhood information and home valuation information and improving information matching efficiency by cutting the intermediary steps. The guarantee to this C2C (Consumer-to-Consumer) model is an adequate control of listing information.

The competition for the quality of information largely happens between online platforms, targeting at buyers, while the competition for listings takes place between online platforms and traditional brokerages, targeting at sellers.

First, online real estate companies needs to fully participate in the home buying and selling process so as to have more control over listings and improve the quality of listing information. Second, they have to build a database of existing homes, and provide high quality neighborhood information and home valuation.

Active listings, the basis of all real estate information, are the most pressing concern of most real estate platforms. They are also the targets of most industry entrants. There are basically two ways to acquire listings. The first is to create a platform for real estate agents, who will display their listings on the platform. The second is to acquire listings directly from sellers.

The key to the future competition is sufficient neighborhood information and accurate home valuation, which are presently hampered by the lack of a complete and accurate basic data base of existing homes in China. The basic data base of existing homes includes the structure, location, layout, remodeling records and transaction records of a home. This information is severely lacking in China. The housing registrations in Housing Administration Bureaus only cover 70 % of the local existing homes, with inaccurate information and nonstandard format of registration. The majority of the homes built before 2000 were not registered. Collecting basic existing home data is in fact the responsibility of government housing authorities, but it seems that this job will be supported by corporate capital. A complete and accurate data base of existing homes is a huge asset, the foundation of all effort aiming at creating effective real estate content. The enterprises that invest in this area deserve our attention.

8.6.2 Business Models

It is very difficult for Internet media companies to improve the quality of listing information, if the disorderly and vicious competition in China's brokerage industry continues.

Firstly, real estate websites that operate as Internet media do not have the motivation to eliminate repeated listings and improve the accuracy of information, because that will reduce the number of listings displayed on their platforms and subsequently reduce their revenue.

Secondly, they are not capable of providing complete, accurate and up-to-date information even if they are fully motivated, because listings are in the possession of real estate agents rather than Internet companies. Internet companies do not have any control over the content displayed on their websites.

The only solution lies in Internet companies' full participation in the home selling and buying process. There are two areas they can work on. The first is to provide more services for home sellers so that they can conveniently list their own homes for sale on the Internet platforms. In this way the Internet companies will have more control over listings. The second is to provide brokerage service by employing or working with real estate agents and participating in the whole transaction process.

But how can Internet companies provide better services for home sellers and increase their penetration?

There are two obstacles in the way of increasing for-sale-by-owner listings. First, listing own house for sale is an overwhelming task for sellers. Like ordinary products, homes need to be properly "packaged" before they go on the market, but the pictures and descriptions home owners provide are too simplistic. This reduces the chances of buyer-seller matching. Second, it is still difficult for home owners to bypass real estate agents. Online platforms treat for-sale-by-owner listings in a simplistic way, so that once home owners display their home information on the internet, they will be approached, or even harassed by real estate agents clamoring to represent them, and the rest is not much different from the traditional way. Therefore, home owners would rather work with a real estate agent in the beginning instead of listing their homes for sale themselves.

These two obstacles have to be removed if Internet companies expect to control listings and increase their penetration among home owners. First, they must help home owners with the presentation of their homes by optimizing the software and providing offline, real-world assistance, making the process simpler and more efficient. Second, they can optimize and streamline the selling process for home owners. Internet companies have to participate in the selling process that follows the display of listings, including the choice of real estate agents, home showing arrangements and closing procedures, so that the selling process is cost effective in terms of both time and money.

Chapter 9
How Should China's Real Estate Brokerages Transform Themselves?

Readers Guide

- 2007 was a watershed year in the real estate market. First, private-ownership housing was beginning to take the place of former public housing and dominate the market. Former public housing still accounted for 60–70 % of the total transactions. The figure fell moderately from 2008 to 2009, until private-ownership housing's market share exceeded 50 % in 2010 and then 80 % in 2014. Second, the industry went through a shakeup during the 2007 financial crisis. Zdhouse fell from its height; 5i5j expanded slowly and cautiously, Centaline remained tepid, Homelink developed rapidly in spite of the global recession, the number of offices growing from 300 offices in 2007 to 500 in 2010.
- Homelink is 6 times as efficient as its peers. Its success can be attributed to two factors. The first is information system. This is the solution to a labor-intensive industry. Replacement of human labor with powerful information system is consistent with the efficiency-based logic of the industrial revolution. The second is powerful management that is in line with the industrial management. Therefore, Homelink before 2014 was not much different from a traditional industrialized enterprise, with workflow restructured in an industrialized model, pursuing efficiency and market share.

According to Darwin's theory of evolution, it is the best-adapted, rather than the strongest or the most intelligent species that survive natural selection, but who will survive the present ecological shakeup in China's real estate brokerage industry? What will the present benchmark brand Homelink evolve into?

9.1 The Former Homelink—A Brokerage Based on Information System

The Homelink before 2014 was a brokerage company based on information system.

S. Ba and X. Yang, *"Internet Plus" Pathways to the Transformation of China's Property Sector*, DOI 10.1007/978-981-10-1699-8_9

9.1.1 Homelink as a Brokerage

The success of Homelink boils down to one point: doing the right thing at the right time. This involves some luck and hard work. In fact success is a matter of luck and hard work combined.

9.1.1.1 Riding the Tide of the Market at the Right Time

This particular time refers to the shift of Beijing's real estate market.

Beijing's existing home transactions began during the commercialization of public housing from 1994 to 1995, when public housing was allowed to be bought and owned by individuals. Brokerages that dealt with rental and home exchanges began to appear. In 2000, public housing was allowed to go on market, giving rise to the first boom of existing home sales, the transaction volume growing from 20 thousand housing units in 2001 to 100 thousand housing units in 2007, just before the financial crisis. The market volume grew by four times (see Fig. 9.1). Brokerages began to sprout and grow during this period, including the later well-known names like 5i5j, Homelink, Zdhouse as well as the Tianjin-based brokerage firm Sunco.

5i5j was the real benchmark during this period. Rental was the then dominant business, but home exchanges and the sales of former public housing accounted for the majority of the transaction volume. Almost all of 5i5j's offices were located in the center of Beijing, within the 3rd Ring Road, where rental and existing home sales were the most active. 5i5j is the pioneer of standardized management. It

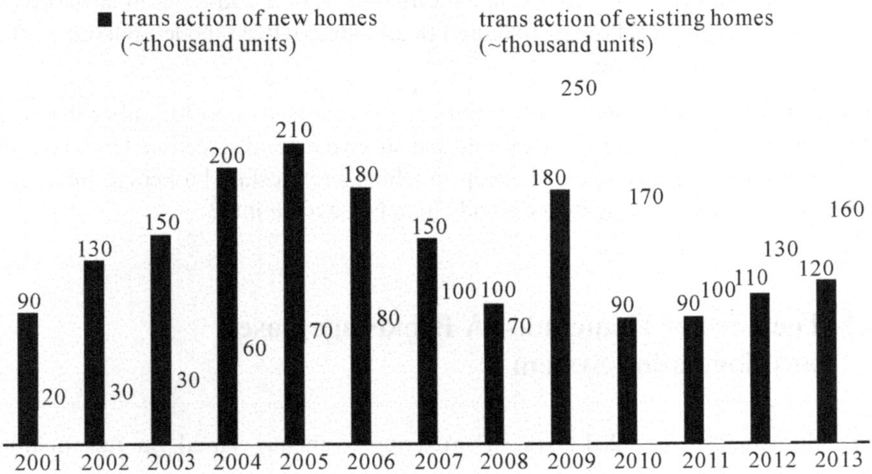

Fig. 9.1 The composition of Beijing's Residential Real Estate Transaction. *Source* Market Research Center, Homelink

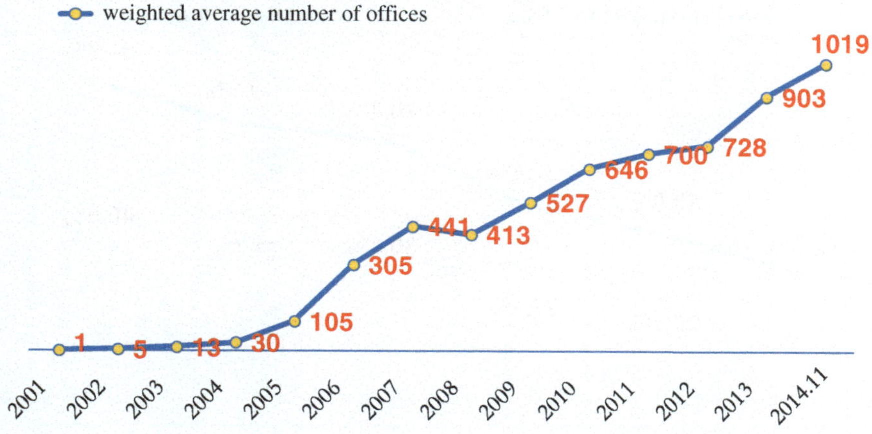

Fig. 9.2 The growth of Home Link's number of offices. *Source* Market Research Center, Homelink

developed its ERP (Enterprise Resource Planning) system and call center, enabling its four networks to work simultaneously, namely the intranet, the Internet, the telephone network and the offline franchising network. This was the typical model of the brokerage industry during that period.

Homelink was relatively weaker and had fewer offices. Homelink started in 2001 with one office only, and grew to 30 offices in 2005, but then Homelink expanded rapidly in the next two years, owning over 300 offices in 2007 (see Fig. 9.2). Zdhouse, however, already had 1000 offices in 2007. It had been growing with dazzling speed until it later perished in its own madness. To conclude, 5i5j was the most well established, Zdhouse the biggest, while Homelink was still in its infancy, carefully building its brand profile and word-of-mouth.

2007 was a watershed year in the real estate market. First, private-ownership housing was beginning to take the place of former public housing and dominate the market. Former public housing still accounted for 60–70 % of the total transactions. The figure fell moderately from 2008 to 2009, until private-ownership housing's market share exceeded 50 % in 2010 and then 80 % in 2014. Second, the industry went through a shakeup during the 2007 financial crisis. Zdhouse fell from its height; 5i5j expanded slowly and cautiously, Centaline remained tepid, Homelink developed rapidly in spite of the global recession, the number of offices growing from 300 offices in 2007 to 500 in 2010. It is interesting to note that Homelink's offices were located outside Beijing's 3rd Ring Road, where private-owned housing was rising rapidly. Homelink was working in a "brokerage vacuum", with almost no competition to speak of. With market share as its top concern, Homelink occupied 32.9 % of its target market in 2010 (see Fig. 9.3).

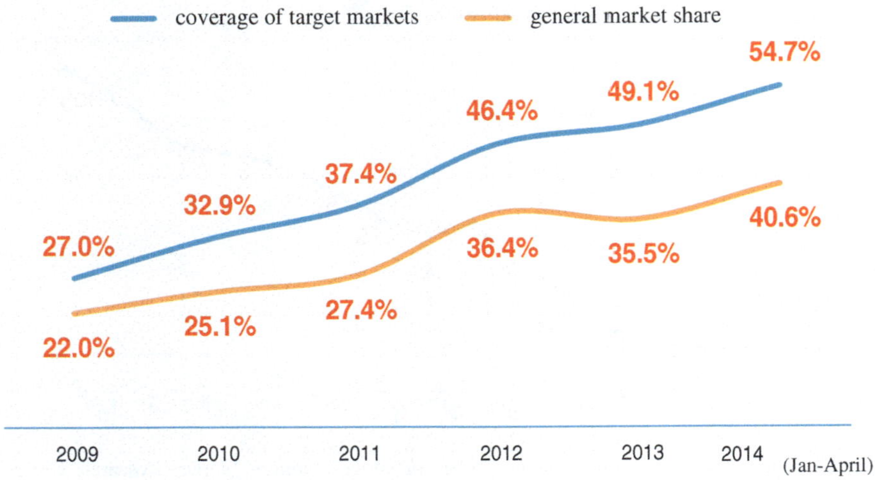

Fig. 9.3 Homelink's share in Beijing's Market. *Source* Market Research Center, Homelink

9.1.1.2 Doing the Right Thing in "No Man's Land"

Doing the right thing while no one else was doing it was the key to Homelink's success.

There were two things that Homelink did right during the first boom of the real estate brokerage industry, especially from 2000 to 2005. First, Homelink did not expand aggressively like Zdhouse. Instead, it chose to improve its service and built brand profile. It practiced buyer-seller-broker tripartite contracts in as early as 2003, refraining from ripping consumers off by getting buyers to pay a higher amount than sellers actually agree on. This is a regular practice today, but quite an innovation back then, when profiting from the discrepancy of prices was the common practice in the real estate brokerage industry. This innovation cost Homelink more than 100 real estate agents, who later left the company. Second, during Homelink's beginning years, it insisted in hiring real estate agents with no experience in the brokerage industry, so that they could train agents in their own ways. It was a slow process, but now the earliest batches of agents have grown into Homelink's office chiefs and regional managers. Training their own agents has given a bonus to the development of the company.

Homelink's refrainment from ripping off consumers has given a brand building bonus as well. In 2003, Homelink was designated by the government as one of the three brokerages that were allowed to deal with sales of homes that were formerly owned by the central government.

In the second real estate boom after 2008, Homelink began to build service standards. The first is risk disclosure in contracts. The second is public notice of consumer complaints. The general public can view all consumer complaints as well as Homelink's responses. Homelink's complaint rate in 2014 was less than

3 ‰ and it was still falling. The third is public notice of selling prices. The fourth is public notice of unwelcome facilities around a property, for example, cemeteries, high-voltage cables, factories and gas stations. In order to avoid possible disputes with its clients, Homelink has also set up a database of "unlucky abodes" where suicides, murders or other irregular deaths have occurred.

The establishment and practice of these standards have enabled Homelink to charge commission at a premium, at 2.7, 0.5 % higher than the average commission rate in China.

9.1.2 Homelink as an IT Company

Homelink transformed from a brokerage firm to an IT company during 2009–2011. In 2009, Homelink worked with a Dalian-based brokerage firm, Goodhope, adopted ERP (Enterprise Resource Planning) system and cooperated with IBM Global Business Service, hiring IBM's top executives to facilitate the transformation of Homelink's service system. Then in 2011, Homelink started "accurate listing campaign" and launched its new online platform. Effective information system and online platform have transformed Homelink from a labor-driven brokerage into an IT company driven by technology.

Homelink expanded as a mature brokerage as well as an IT company during 2012–2014. The company's work flow is managed with SE (Sale Enablement) system and the conversion rate is soaring.

Homelink is 6 times as efficient as its peers. Its success can be attributed to two factors. The first is information system. This is the solution to a labor-intensive industry. Replacement of human labor with powerful information system is consistent with the efficiency-based logic of the industrial revolution. The second is powerful management that is in line with the industrial management. Therefore, Homelink before 2014 can be deemed as the industrialized Homelink, which was not much different from a traditional industrialized enterprise, with workflow restructured in an industrialized model, pursuing efficiency and market share.

The purpose of Sales Enablement is to align the organization's people, processes and systems within an organization to produce deliverables in a managed and repeatable process, to increase conversion and velocity in the sales funnel (see Fig. 9.4).

SE system enables sales in real estate brokerage industry in three aspects.

The first is listing management. Since a listing is the departing point of a sale, maximizing control over listings is naturally the priority. The traditional practice is to increase offices and real estate agents to acquire and manage more listings. SE system will follow each listing, and, according to certain rules, allocate each listing to a "responsibility area", the contact information of which is only accessible to a designated team of real estate agents.

Homelink owns more than 80 % of the listings in its target markets in Beijing. This means that consumers can find most of the listings for sale in Homelink.

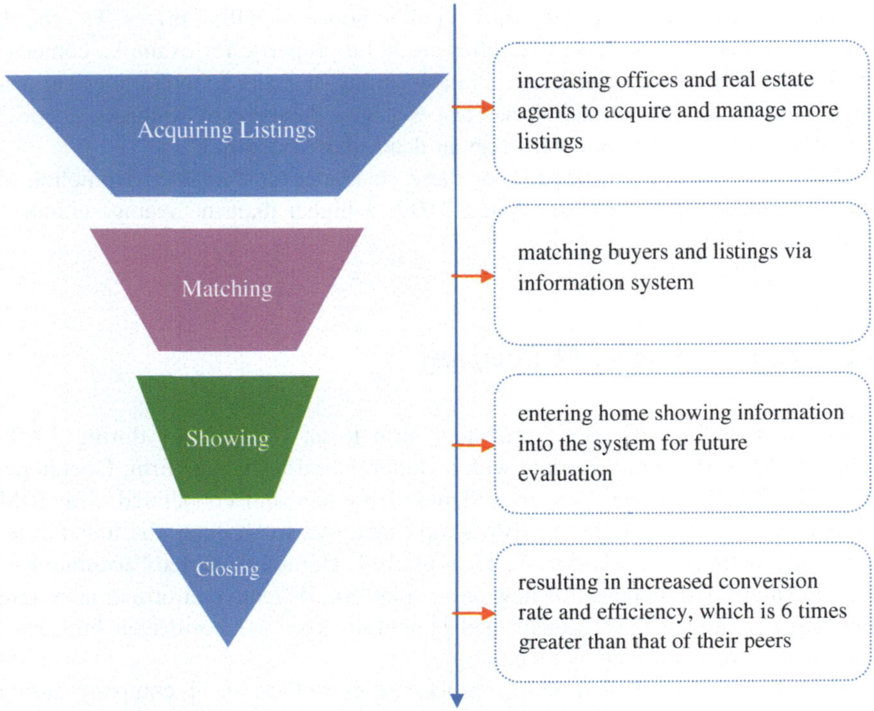

Fig. 9.4 Home Link's SE system. *Source* The Authors

The reason why maximizing listings shall be the first step is that it is the basis of sales. In order to maintain 50 % of the sales in its target market, Homelink shall have control of at least 80 % of the listings. If Homelink aims at a 60 % rate, it has to have almost 100 % of the listings.

The second step is information matching and home showing. The SE system is able to match buyers and listings effectively and efficiently as long as there are enough listings to match buyers' requirements. This will free real estate agents from futile home showings and enable them to show their clients more than one home on a single trip. According to the statistics of 2014, every successful buyer took 4.2 trips and viewed 12.6 housing units in average. Half of the home viewing trips covered at least 5 housing units (see Fig. 9.5).

The last is sales efficiency. A large enough database of listings, efficient information matching and home showing normally guarantee considerable sales efficiency and market share. Homelink's velocity of sales is 2.5 times that of their peers, and comprehensive efficiency 6 times.

Why does Homelink manages to secure only 55 % of the total transactions with its over 80 % share of all listings? This discrepancy is mostly attributed to the inadequacy of real estate agents' negotiating ability. A real estate agent's essential expertise includes the abilities of pricing a property and negotiating with clients, which is similar to the expertise of a securities analyst.

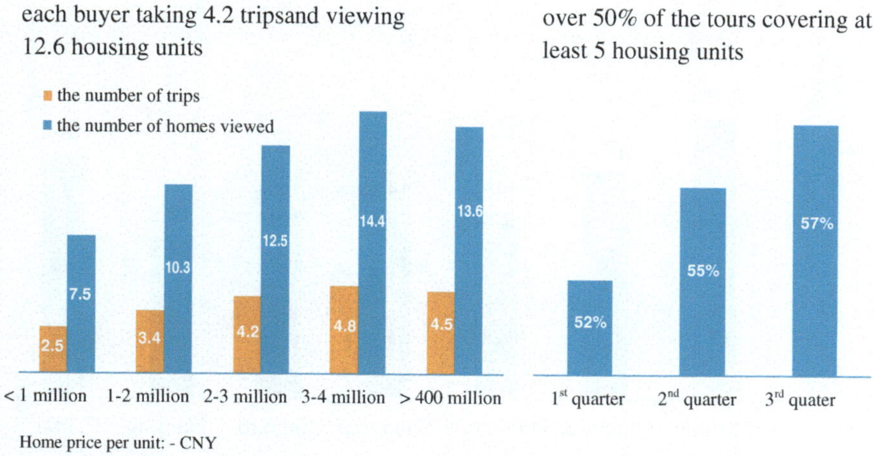

Fig. 9.5 Homelink's showings in Beijing. *Source* Market Research Center, Homelink

Why is Homelink the most efficient real estate company, when all the other companies also have ERP systems? There are largely two reasons. First, most of Homelink's top executives had occupational background in other fields than the real estate brokerage industry. This enables them to take a detached view of Homelink and the real estate industry at large. The second reason lies in Homelink's strong management and control. Information systems are not the essential part as they are not exclusive to a company. Without effective enforcement, information systems are of little value. Most large-scale real estate brokerages adopt information systems, but only those that can rigidly enforce the systems become efficient. The rigid enforcement refers to the enforcement of rules. Competition exists in any industry where resource is limited, but the competition has to be controlled. The efficiency of a company will drop if it has no rules to restrict employee conducts. This is also the reason behind the stark contrast between Centaline HK and Centaline branches in mainland cities of China.

9.1.2.1 Today's Homelink: The Lone Winner on the Pinnacle

Today's Homelink is expanding across China. In 2014, Homelink already had presence in over 10 cities, with over 1500 offices and over 22 thousand real estate agents. Homelink's market share in each city keeps growing. Its market share in Tianjin has reached 27 % (see Fig. 9.6).

Homelink's turnover in 2013 was nine times that of 2008. Commission from existing home sales accounted for 88 % of the total and commission from rentals accounted for the rest (see Fig. 9.7). In 2014, Homelink's financial penetration was 21 %. 47 % of home mortgage in Beijing's market was done through Homelink. Homelink's human efficiency reached the historical high of 27,000 RMB per year in October, 2014.

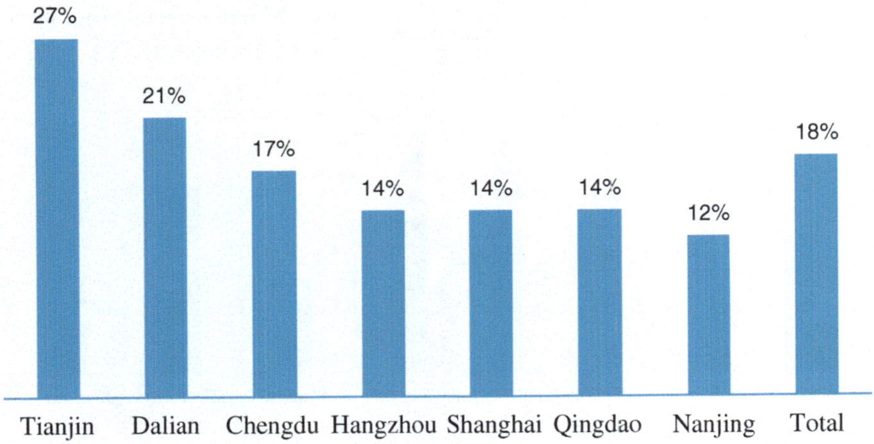

Fig. 9.6 Homelink's market share in different cities. *Source* Market Research Center, Homelink

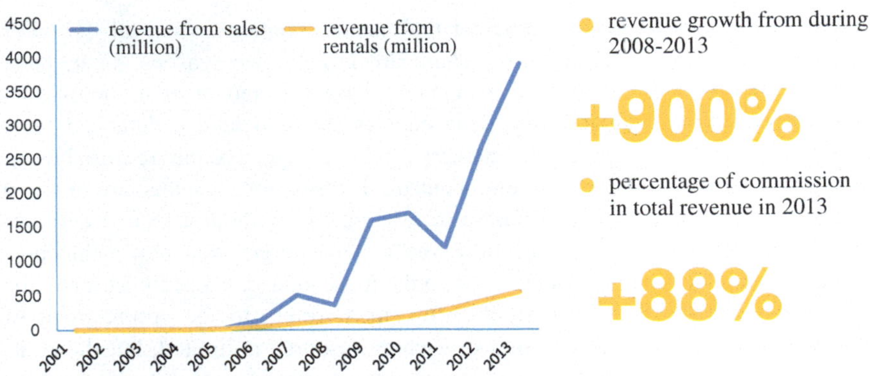

Fig. 9.7 Homelink's revenue growth. *Source* Market Research Center, Home Link

Statistics show that Homelink has become the benchmark of the industry. However, judging from the rise and fall of many big companies, a company's assets often equals the amount of its debt. The past success often becomes the hindrance to reform and progress. Which way is Homelink heading in this time of transformation?

9.2 The Future Homelink—An Internet-Based, Data-Driven Broker's Platform

Homelink identifies itself as a platform company. This is a rather blurry self-identification.

There are only two types of existence in the real estate brokerage industry if one looks at it from an economist's perspective: the market and the brokerages. The existence of brokerages is dependent on the commissions in the real estate market. The border between a brokerage and the market is determined by the discrepancy between the management cost of the brokerage and the commissions in the market. Multiple listing systems in the US are the market makers, who establish easy-to-follow rules and extremely low commission rates. The sellers, buyers and brokers all have their proper places in the market. It is contracted independent brokers that are the dominant players in the market, rather than brokerages. However, multiple listing systems are not able to evaluate real estate agents and determine their credibility. The frontier of a brokerage firm is where multiple listing systems have failed. That explains why franchising companies that help real estate agents build professional profiles are thriving in the US. However, given the high commission rates and lack of market rules in China, brokerage companies become dominant players. The competition between individual brokers has to give way to the competition between brokerage firms. That is why America's franchising brand names are losing their ground to local brokerage companies with strong managing and controlling capacity.

The advent of the Internet age is eliminating information asymmetry and reducing commissions. The performance of real estate agents can be easily followed, evaluated and rated, thus reducing the cost of management. These changes have made it possible for a third type of existence that transcends enterprises and markets—Internet platforms. Internet platforms break the traditional borders between brokerage companies and the market and integrate them into one being. Platforms will be the ultimate structure in the Internet Age. They will defeat brokerage companies and redistribute the resources, breaking the cost-benefit structure of traditional enterprises.

Therefore, Homelink's self-identification as a platform enterprise is self-contradictory. Platforms and enterprises are not mutually inclusive. Homelink will develop into an Internet-based and data-driven platform for real estate agents if it transforms itself successfully.

9.2.1 *What Is an Internet Platform?*

The best analogy of a platform is a city. Normally, as the number of employees in a company increases, the cost of management will rise and the human efficiency will decrease. A company's efficiency decreases as it expands. In contrast, a city becomes more efficient and innovative as its population grows. Research shows that if the working population of a city doubles, the productivity of the city will increase by 20 % (see Fig. 9.8).

What is a platform like and what is it able to provide?

First, a platform provides a support system, in the same way a city provides public facilities like roads, water supply and electricity supply, but does not tell

Fig. 9.8 The city analogy of Internet platforms. *Source* The Authors

each city dweller what to do. It is impossible to maintain a top-down management over the relationship and interaction between individuals on a platform, just as it is impossible to do so in a city.

Second, a platform is a self-adaptive ecosystem. It is more a living thing than a machine. Its "brain", "eyes" and "ears" enable it to adapt to the changing environment and learn and grow in the process.

Third, a platform provides a standardized "language" system, through which transaction and payment can take place, with good value for money.

Fourth, a platform provides only basic public services. There are all sorts of services in a city, but the municipal government is only responsible for infrastructures and basic facilities, with city dwellers taking care of the rest. Facebook and Amazon are platforms like global and borderless cities, which provide basic services, maintain orders and record client reviews.

Fifth, just as in a city, individual freedom must be restricted to safeguad public interests. For example, certain products, like guns, are not allowed on Amazon. Third-party sellers must observe such rules, which will help build a trustworthy system for consumers. The rules of platforms tell one what not to do instead of what to do, unlike the commands given in an industrial management model.

9.2.2 What Is an Internet-Based and Data-Driven Real Estate Platform?

What is an Internet real estate platform supposed to be in the future brokerage industry? Is Homelink marching on the right course? How can Homelink transform itself from an enterprise into a platform? Can Homelink transform into a "city" in the Internet age?

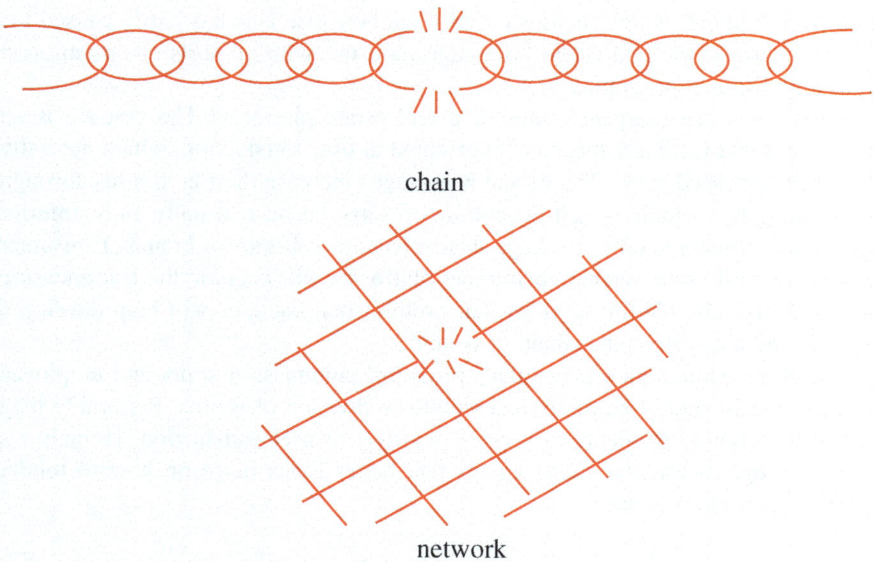

Fig. 9.9 The Chain Model and the Network Model of Management. *Source* The Authors

9.2.2.1 From Enterprise-Based Management Model to a Platform-Based Management Model

Homelink's present management model is an enterprise-based model that manages workflow by breaking it up into various steps, with transaction efficiency as its target. This highly controlling management model belongs to the industrial age, and may not be viable and efficient in the long run for a service industry that features flexibility and interaction. This workflow management model is like a chain (see Fig. 9.9). One mistake in one of the links will impact the rest of the chain. The management model of a platform, however, is like a network, which will remain functioning even when one of the nodes goes wrong.

Homelink needs to provide basic public services to make real estate agents' job easier, which ultimately results in good consumer experience. These public facilities include tools that facilitate real estate agents' work, for example, listing management system, leads management system and transaction management system. They enable real estate agents to respond to consumer needs quickly, rather than following a set procedure mechanically.

9.2.2.2 From Sales-Targeted Rules to Service-Targeted Rules

Most of the innovations in traditional brokerages are targeted at new ways to increase listings and sales, and the rest at commission split models and payment policies. These so called innovations are all sales oriented. It is the typical industrial thinking, which focuses on cost and benefits. This has partly caused the present chaos of the real estate brokerage industry, with all sorts of commission splits and discount programs.

What are service-targeted rules of a real estate platform? The essence is an assessment and feedback mechanism oriented at user satisfaction, which naturally results in increased sales. Traditional brokerages increase their credibility through brand building, which is self-deception of sorts because usually only inferior agents and brokers need to package themselves in well-known brands. Consumer reviews on real estate agents on Internet platforms will become the true measure of credibility. The platforms' rules that prohibit malpractices will help develop a realistic and user-oriented evaluation system.

Therefore, Homelink's new salary program, commission splits and employee ranking system should be more than simplistic division of profits. Preferably they should incorporate elements of service quality and user satisfaction. Homelink's training program for real estate agents had better focus more on how to render good services to consumers.

9.2.2.3 From Revenue-Orientation to Performance-Orientation

Commission is the price of real estate agents' service. It is the most effective means of restricting real estate agents' behavior. A commission split policy is supposed to guide real estate agents toward better service. Presently quite a few real estate brokerages, including Cetaline, Qfang, Homelink and Fang, have declared their new bonus policies, all of which use real estate agents' sales volume as the most important criterion. Is the real estate agent that generates the most revenue the best agent? Does the agent that has closed the most deals gives the greatest consumer satisfaction? The answer may not be positive from a consumer's perspective.

9.2.2.4 A Data-Driven Platform

A data-driven platform is supposed to be Homelink's ultimate form. As intermediaries or match makers between buyers and sellers, Chinese real estate agents' job is negotiating prices. Since there is no "reasonable" price for any transactions and neither buyers nor sellers have any clues concerning prices, the negotiation is often a protracted psychological game. The only solution lies in accurate valuation based on a large collection of transaction data. This will reduce the cost of negotiation and increase consumer satisfaction.

Reviews and ratings of real estate agents are as valuable as transaction data, because they help consumers choose their agents. Data help reduce information asymmetry and it probably is the solution to the trilemmas of the real estate brokerage industry.

Chapter 10
Are the Sharing Economy and the Maker Economy Here to Stay?

Readers Guide

- The average room price on Airbnb is $140/day at present in the US. Airbnb profits are from the 3 % booking fee charged on landlords and 6–12 % service fee charged on tenants. Other income includes cancellation fee and service fee for providing bedding.
- Concern over WeWork is two-fold: one on the rationality of the business model of WeWork and the other from investors' expectations and positioning. Its sustainability depends on whether the concept of co-working can provide stable dividends for members of business starters circle.

Airbnb is a typical representative of the new home sharing economy. Three things account for its popularity. The first is the rapid development of the internet and mobile internet. The second goes to the prosperity of the hotel market in the US. There are undoubtedly websites providing hotel searching, but hotels are usually located in larger cities and fail to provide differentiated service. Family hotels can better meet the demands of leisure tourists such as backpackers. The third reason is the economic crisis in 2008 that made people eager to make money from their homes. The value of Airbnb soared with the application of shared economy and the social element of Facebook to achieve mutual trust among landlords and tenants who can interact and evaluate one another. So far acceptance of the new business is positive with nearly or even more than 50 % of the population in developed countries involved in shared economy, 39 % in the US, 41 % in the UK, and 52 % in Canada,

WeWork is a typical youth service office provider. As a real estate company in the co-working renting market, its annual sales income in 2014 is $0.15 billion with profits close to 30 %. As an estimated $6 billion company, WeWork takes the lead in rapidly adding new members and accumulating resources from online social products and offline hard power.

S. Ba and X. Yang, *"Internet Plus" Pathways to the Transformation of China's Property Sector*, DOI 10.1007/978-981-10-1699-8_10

10.1 Airbnb: A Benchmark for Home Sharing Economy

- Airbnb inspiration came from Joe Gebbia and Brian Chesky, two graduates from Rhode Island School of Design. In 2007, during a conference among the design community in San Francisco, they decided to rent airbeds to participants who failed to book a hotel room so they can use airbeds and share hotel costs with others. Soon they realized the great market potential and promptly put Airbnb into operation online in 2008. Like other C2C searching, home owners uploaded photos of their homes which were fairly confusing. The company virtually stopped growing after the first round of seed money was gone. A decision was made in 2009. The company rented a professional camera in New York and began to take photos house by house to replace all the old pictures. Immediately the weekly sales doubled and the practice became standard when a project team was set up in 2010 to provide photography service to home owners. Traffic soared following that. Now professional photographers are employed in every Airbnb operating city whose photos can bring 2–3 times more orders compared with photos taken by home owners.
- Currently, Airbnb covers more than 34,000 cities in over 190 countries, serving over 25 million customers. The number of rooms available in 2013 was only 300,000, but in 2014, it reached 1 million. In comparison, the number of rooms available by the world's largest hotel group InterContinental Hotel was 687,000 in 2014. Airbnb achieved 37 million room nights in 2014 while the number for InterContinental Hotel in 2014 was 180 million. Airbnb room night number is expected to be 129 million in 2016, surpassing InterContinental Hotel for certain based on its growth rate.

1. C2C Operation Model
   Once home owners post room information on the website, Airbnb photographers will go and take pictures. The rooms will be available once new beddings are supplied by the landlords. Landlords' obligations also include: providing telephone number of the nearest local hospital in the room; providing emergency telephone number; providing smoke alarms and carbon monoxide detectors and other security equipment in the room. Tenants can fill in information about required housing conditions on the company's website. Booking, making payment or cancellation and evaluation can all be done on the main page. Cancellation should be made 24 h prior to the check-in date. Refund refers to the room fee not the service fee.
   Currently, the average room price in the US Airbnb is $140/day, Airbnb profits are from the 3 % booking fee charged on landlords and 6–12 % service fee charged on tenants. Other income includes cancellation fee and service fee for providing bedding.
2. House Recourse Structure and Booking Structure
   There are two types of owners in New York Airbnb: commercial owners and common owners. Those who have three or more than three rental units are

called commercial owners. There are about 1406 commercial owners, accounting for 6 % and about 24,057 common owners, accounting for 94 %. Among the revenue structure generated by owners, commercial owners generated $164 million, accounting for 37 %, while common owners generated $283 million, accounting for 63 %. That is to say, 6 % commercial owners has brought 37 % of the income, while 94 % of the common owners has only brought 63 % of the income. With 3 or more than three rental units, commercial owners can be regarded as small real estate managers who are much more capable than common owners in generating income. The same is true in Los Angeles: companies have the strongest ability to generate income, while individual owners' ability to generate income is the poorest.

Room reservation structures on Airbnb include long-term renting and short-term renting. In New York long-term renting is increasing, while short-term renting is decreasing. In 2013 the proportion of long-term renting exceeded that of the short-term renting. The room types by 2012 are the following, 57 % whole set apartments or houses, 41 % single rooms and 2 % shared rooms.

3. How to Evaluate the Future of Home Sharing?

First, analysis of pure C2C model: From the above data of several relatively mature cities in Airbnb, those who have better ability to generate revenue are landlords and brokerage firms with several houses. Single house owners are less able to generate revenue. If the house is found through an agency, C2C becomes a small B2C, a brokerage service platform. Rivals the Internet real estate companies in China face are not comparable with the US market. When Airizu began to operate B2C in China, it paid around RMB150 Yuan for each room while making only RMB 50–60 Yuan. No effective measures were taken to stop the continuous losses which inevitably led to its failure.

Second, the proportion of long-term renting in New York in Airbnb continues to grow. Nearly 70 % reservations are for renting for more than 90 days. Any Internet rental company can do this which means that the opportunity for a company in China to transform into a lease platform is small.

Third, Tujia was one of the first companies in China to copy Homeaway and Airbnb model. But Tujia owns self-operated houses, with a special off-line management team, and has advantages in getting C-end private houses. In 2013 it started cooperation with Ctrip, offering both online and offline renting. Xiaozhu.com cooperates with 58.com. Short-term renting in China is likely to be dependent on large OTA (online travel agent) or other Internet giants.

Fourth, other opportunities. In China, the effective supply and demand chain of short-term renting+sharing isn't available. Its credit system also lacks market education. The huge success of Airbnb partly comes from the use of Facebook to accumulate popularity. In China, two effective models may be "WeChat+Airbnb" and "Microblog+Airbnb" as WeChat can be used to increase flow and social recognition. The huge success of Didi came after its move to give away Red Packet on WeChat. Family Hotel may very well learn from Didi's marketing strategy.

10.2 WeWork: A Benchmark for Co-working

In the past five years the number of co-working service providers worldwide increased from 300 to nearly 6000, and the number of employees increased from 10,000 to 300,000 due to the birth of more and more venture and small-scale companies. The number of domestic entrepreneurs in China is also growing rapidly, represented by Internet ventures. China's venture capital industry has reached a record high in the amount of investment, the number of agencies, and the level of activity, and can supply funds for the early start-up companies.

The two Chinese companies P2 (joint venture office agency) and YOU+apartment are similar to WeWork, They aim to attract start-up companies in creative industry, S&T and services sectors by building a self-sufficient ecosystem, integrating resources and providing all-round services, thus turning a simple office renting into a venture incubator. So in the eyes of investors, WeWork is not only a real estate company, but also an agent for office leasing and business incubator.

10.2.1 WeWork Operating Model

WeWork primarily collaborates with commercial real estate funds and developers. After taking 1–2 floors of a newly constructed urban renewal landmark with price lower than market about 10 % or more, WeWork will turn the floor into a modern and customized work space with complete social functions and rent out the space to start-up firms at a much higher price than that offered by their competitors.

WeWork profits mainly come from three areas:

First, membership fee and catering service fee. Money is made through lower whole renting fee paid and higher leasing fee charged, together with income from additional service.

Second, the invisible returns, which includes appreciation of the surrounding land price and profit from investment on other seed companies. On site selection, WeWork chooses offices in newly developed zones or renovated buildings in the depressed neighborhoods which means about 10 % discount for rents. WeWork members have reached 14,000. 28 % of the company's revenue comes from small-scale members. When large-scale members move into larger and newer offices of WeWork, smaller members will be upgraded accordingly.

Third, the rents. Although most of WeWork members are starters, and most of them are short term tenants, the company charges high rent per square foot. The rent for a desk is as high as $350 per month. Renting an office of 64 square feet costs $650 per month per person.

10.2.2 How Did WeWork Obtain High Price Difference

The first reason is its perfect supporting services which include security, reception, broadband, printing and other services (such as social welfares).

The second reason is the social activities organized by WeWork. There are bagel and mimosa gatherings every week. Members can also promote their ideas on presentation day, hopefully getting advice from the advertising companies and other voluntary partners free of charge. If lucky, participants may reach verbal agreements and recommend jobs.

The third reason comes from large enterprises who move in and even directly invest in incubation. In 2011, Pepsi sent several staff to WeWork office. On the one hand, these large companies become "mentors" of starters, on the other hand, they take the opportunity to search for potential projects for further incubation investment. They settle in at a very low cost to seek potential customers and purchase needed services as well as acquiring business opportunities and ideas which are hard to quantify.

The fourth reason is the provision of high standard legal and human resources services and resource docking. Its internal social network (WeWork Common, set up in 2014) offers a low cost user qualification. Users only pay about $60 a month for benefits such as booking offices when needed and enjoying favorable support in legal, human resources and other aspects. Users can also exchange and cooperate with other WeWork users through this platform beyond geographical limitation. It is also possible that WeWork will actively serve as a bridge for users in different areas and get paid for the service.

The fourth support comes from government. Government has been attracted by WeWork's potential in promoting local economy and has been eager to provide support to WeWork.

WeWork is more than an online business platform. When more and more resources begin to circulate on this platform, it will be much more than a real estate company.

10.2.3 Risk and Valuation of WeWork

Risks are mainly reflected in three aspects:

The first and the biggest risk is its excessive expansion. The company should stay within a controllable scale to maintain its brand image and a high customer service standard.

Secondly, there is potential strategic confusion in WeWork. Even the founders of WeWork haven't decided whether WeWork should enter smaller cities after settling in 25 large cities in the US and 12 large cities in Europe.

The third risk lies in the heavy asset model of subletting. Long-term lease between WeWork and property owners means that they have fixed expenditures. Cash flow crisis may occur once market demand weakens.

However, WeWork has accumulated millions of dollars of net assets and operating cash flow. Start-up companies the US enjoy favorable financing environment. The majority of WeWork clients are able to complete financing and afford high-end office cost.

Concerns over its valuation focus mainly on the following issues:

Firstly, from the traditional commercial real estate valuation perspective, WeWork's market value is significantly overvalued. According to Wall Street Journal, its market value/revenue ratio in 2014 is close to 100. Being a starter, WeWork's revenue is expected to grow significantly before the market full matures, and the 100 ratio will be reduced. But compared with the traditional high-end rental companies like Regus whose ratio is 18:20, WeWork has a long way to go to reduce the ratio. Venture capital may have been attracted by the infinite value space created by WeWork. The key lies in connecting people and service with strong operating capacity, which is not to be copied easily.

Secondly, disputes on WeWork model are two-fold: one on the rationality of the business model of WeWork and the other from investors' expectations and positioning. Its sustainability depends on whether the concept of co-working can provide stable dividends for members of business starters circle.

Thirdly, users of services similar to WeWork show a very strong demand, but no one can yet tell where the market saturation point is.

Chapter 11
How to Build a Data Ecosystem for Real Estates?

Readers Guide

Since the strong influx of the mobile internet, internet thinking began to infiltrate into real estate valuation services where new demands, new products, and new ideas are bred and a revolutionary restructuring of the industry has started. When traditional valuation services fail to meet the demand of the time, the market is looking for a new one that is comprehensive and multi-faceted.

In China, the outbreak of the existing home market is bound to happen when new home transactions gradually give way to existing home transactions. The existing housing stock has exceeded 100 million units. A conservative estimate of the existing homes in 2020 will be 160 million units when we take into consideration of the present house construction scale. There will be a huge financial services market and after sales market following the large scale existing home transaction.

The traditional valuation service refers to the real estate valuation service provided when people take mortgage to buy or sell a second-hand house. In traditional valuation services, customers and agencies usually contact by way of telephone or Email. 3–4 days are needed for the entire process of valuation service, which includes commission, field survey by appraisers, market research, report drafting, and delivery of the final report to customers. More time and costs are required as the process is not standardized. The traditional valuation service is simple in service manner and content and is used for one time only. It cannot meet the demands for upgraded services at present time as it fails to provide further needed derivative services.

How can the traditional valuation service industry take advantage of the favorable wind generated by the internet? Which is the way to go and which is the way out? It is no longer possible to survive if it stays the old way. Instead it should reassess customer needs, understand the market, master new skills and upgrade its service by imitating international practices, exploring and guiding the domestic market demand, sticking to "catering, upgrading and innovation" in the service content and service pattern, and seeking core competitiveness.

With a strong influx of the mobile Internet, the Internet thought began to penetrate into real estate valuation services; new demands, new products, and new

S. Ba and X. Yang, *"Internet Plus" Pathways to the Transformation of China's Property Sector*, DOI 10.1007/978-981-10-1699-8_11

ideas are constantly derived: a revolutionary restructuring of the industry is quietly initiating. Under this background, it is only too obvious that the traditional valuation service cannot meet the needs of the time; a new valuation service chosen by the market will be more comprehensive and multi-faceted.

11.1 Users' Changing Demands for Property Data

Users' changing demands fall on two aspects. The first one is efficiency for inquiring, pricing, and mass appraisal due to the weakening of legal valuation system. The second demand is for accuracy and sufficiency due to users' need for risk control. Existing valuation institutions fail to meet both requirements. Firstly, the efficiency is low as the valuation operation and report is still conducted manually and both project management and internal management level is low. Secondly, valuation lacks accuracy and support as cases are few and data are insufficient in supporting parameter and price analysis.

In order to meet users' changing demand, an industrial chain of "valuation information digitization" has emerged which includes internet companies such as Fang.com, E-House, fangjia.com, dichankuaiji, and intermediaries that provide online appraisal, e-property dictionary, bank's security appraisal model, and mass property appraisal by tax authority. New solutions are proposed by domestic software companies, bank and finance institutions and property valuation agencies to improve pricing accuracy. One way is called "floor investigation" which aims at building a basic housing data bank and developing an automatic pricing (dynamic pricing and mass appraisal included) system based on regression calculation and benchmark price + modification. The system can be applied in price index, market analysis, personal loan report and mortgage reassessment. An appraisal operation system can be developed based on Excel homelink and simple web model that mainly covers personal home loan reports. Onsite inspecting and collecting tool system can be developed for cell phone and tablet users. Limitations of the above measures may lie in cost, maintenance, precision, valuation type, management and application, etc.

Data is both the source and assurance for high quality valuation. Only when the source is accurate can the valuation efficiency be properly handled.

11.2 What Home Valuation Service Is Expected?

1. Service for existing homes

For a long time the real estate market has been in an asymmetric state where information lacks sufficiency, promptness and transparency. The existing market information may be outdated or unreal. There is strong desire from buyers, sellers, developers and agents for more open, transparent and precise house information. Traditional off-line operation will give way to the new on-line automatic valuation and price indication to make price information more transparent, timely, accurate so as to meet customers' needs and contribute to the success of existing home transactions.

Move, Zillow and CoStar are some of the typical institutions in this area. They all provide service based on real estate information and data. Move owns the permanent franchise of NAR's (National Economic Association) official website, Realtor.com, whose information directly comes from more than 800 MLS in the country, to ensure the completeness, timeliness and accuracy of its data. Zillow's core strength lies in its house valuation to clients, real estate brokers, mortgage companies, and expert home buyers. CoStar provides commercial real estate data related services.

In China, new home transaction will give way to existing home transaction due to the increase of homes. The outbreak of the existing home market is bound to take place. The existing housing stock has exceeded 100 million units. A conservative estimate of the existing homes in 2020 will be 160 million units with the present house construction scale taken into consideration. Market space for the financial services and post-transaction services derived from existing home transaction is enormous.

2. Service for government taxation

The new valuation services can provide more comprehensive basic information and accurate price information on real estate for the tax authorities, thereby avoiding the taxpayers from cheating on real estate information and price. In addition, the bulk of the tax base assessment provides a reference for the government to develop appropriate and reasonable assessment program to guarantee the interest of taxpayers.

Institutions such as Hong Kong Rating and Valuation Department and QV in New Zealand and Australia all provide tax base valuation and other services to government and other decision-making departments based on market valuation. In 2013, 855 staff members of Hong Kong Rating and Valuation Department achieved total income rates of 14.911 billion Yuan.

China is about to levy house tax. It is expected that in the future, the threshold of house taxes in China will be more than 500 billion Yuan. Counting with 1–2.5 % of the tax base valuation fee, the future valuation cost in valuation industry is quite considerable.

3. Service for banks

Traditional bank collateral valuation service is limited to value assessment prior to loan. According to statistics, there are about 40 % of the loan collateralized by real estate in China, and about 80 % in the United States. From the difference we can see the prospects of China's real estate mortgage and valuations for prior loan are promising. With the introduction of the New Basel Capital Accord, banks are required to supervise the risk of post-loan collateral.

The new valuation service will provide banks with timely information to help them make timely and accurate operation with full control of the risk. Traditional valuation service cannot assess massive collateral in a short time. Online valuation service that can provide model calculation in its valuation system is the only way to meet the demand for efficiency and economy.

The US company CoreLogic has a mature business in serving the banking sector, providing lending risk management, collateral management and consulting services for the bank. Listed since 2010, CoreLogic's market has reached $2.831 billion, and its annual revenue in 2013 reached $1.331 billion.

4. Service for real estate investment

In addition to providing real estate information and convenient online valuation services, new valuation services can also provide real estate price potential, and predicted future price based on large data, as well as return on investment, etc., which makes the investor's investment decisions to be more indicative. From making investment decisions to the occurrence and accomplishment of investment behavior, the new real estate valuation services runs throughout the whole process of investment behavior.

In addition to providing services for the banking sector, American CoreLogic, with a strong accumulation of data, also provides services on additional risk analysis in capital market, and real estate dynamic valuation reports etc.

According to statistics, the asset value of the housing stock in China has been more than 200 trillion Yuan. With such a huge gross amount of the stock housing, whether it is used for investment, insurance, and trust funds, or asset management, it needs vast valuation and additional services, of which the new valuation services will be a huge market.

11.3 Upgrading Home Valuation Tools and Operating Systems

In order to cater to the requirements of valuation services in the Internet era, home valuation industry should keep up with the development in information and digitalization to use information technology and big data analysis to create more convenient tools and operating systems. On the one hand, home valuation software should provide tools for valuation companies and appraisers to improve efficiency and management level. On the other hand, related APPs should be developed to serve clients' need in taxation and banking business and to upgrade the efficiency and big data analysis accordingly.

Firstly, potential clients can get real-time valuation through online evaluation system, and place order directly through the system. Fieldworkers can then conduct field survey and transmit real-time data which is one-time and standardized also through the system. By this time, appraisers can issue a standardized and unified appraisal report through the report generating system, which greatly improves the efficiency of the work. All data related will be data stored in foundation database in accordance with real estate appraisal standards, which unifies data storage and application.

Throughout the valuation processes, a modern management platform is established to replace old fashioned small workshops. Information technology operations, and standardized enterprise management shall be realized to improve internal management level.

In addition to online real-time valuations, the valuation system mostly, using tax collection, bank collateral value monitoring and stress testing, oral enquiry and other time-sensitive, big volume, low cost valuation services, by model calculations, efficiently, conveniently, and accurately measure and analyze the value of real estate under different purposes and provide relevant market research, investment reference and other real estate related services.

In short, home valuation tools and operating systems are in urgent need for upgrading to meet the requirements of the time and to enhance the overall service level of home valuation industry.

11.4 The Trends in Home Valuation Service

O2O is a new home valuation service model developed for the full use of the tools and operating systems. It depends on an open application platform for valuation system, combines the "off-line" valuation operations with the "online" valuation. It aims at achieving a closed loop from offline to online operations and a successful transformation to O2O model. It provides diversified online services and perfect online and offline linking. It meets the diversified demands of the time through the integration of big data, big economy, and big market and providing efficient and standardized offline service and other value added services.

1. Diversified online valuation services

Through online evaluation system, it establishes a high-speed and smooth network service channel to provide real-time online valuation, online commission of business, business inquiry, case inquiry, reference value, collateral value monitoring, market research and analysis and other services to achieve efficient and convenient services.

At the same time, it tries to use the most refined zoning for different property types to establish valuation model respectively. And in accordance with billions real transaction data accumulated from multi-channels, it keeps updating and adjusting the reference price in order to ensure the accuracy of the valuation.

2. Perfect online and offline linking

Through online platforms, the task needs to be valuated manually will be transferred to off-line directly. Valuation agency gets orders from online, and provides a variety of credible and legally binding real estate valuation reports.

3. Efficient and standard offline service

Valuation services such as business assignment, site investigation, and report writing will be operated by business process system, site collecting system, and report generation system to provide the standardization and quality of off-line valuation services, to improve appraisers' work efficiency and valuation company's' management.

4. Diversified data value-added services

Faced with massive valuation data, through the development of a variety of data mining algorithms and predictive models, it analyzes the relevance of the data, visually demonstrates the results of analysis and forecasting, and designs new products and services according to these results. The value-added services may include real estate ROI survey analysis, business index analysis of urban residential investment, house (collateral) price, rental index and market analysis research.

11.5 Building a Multi-source and Multi-dimensional Data Ecosystem

Complete, standard and systematic basic data are essential for both the traditional valuation model and the modern O2O model. A powerful data bank represents the core competitiveness and is key to market success.

Therefore, the future lies in establishing a data ecology, collecting diversified data through multiple channels with real-time updates. Data, after being sort under the principle of completeness and accuracy, should be stored in a three-dimensional private database. Relations among data of different levels should be established to integrate data from different areas completely. Standardized data should be applied to all areas and rectified and examined through dynamic application. In this way, through collection, application and examination of data, multi-dimensional data ecology with multiple sources could be formed.

Data ecology should be established based on the following aspects.

1. Multiple data sources

To form a data source system from multiple channels, it is necessary to take advantage of hundreds of millions of trading and lease data accumulated in real-estate industry and integrate data including data from on-site collection, online listing, valuation accumulation, banks, intermediary agents or other agencies, especially those related with real-estate administration, tax administration and planning of government.

2. Comprehensive data

Data of different levels should be stored and related with each other to form an interwoven relational data warehouse. It is useful for valuation agencies, governmental departments (local tax bureau) and financial agencies of banks to construct a three-dimensional private database with multiple levels and realize uniform storage and application of data.

3. Standardized data management

First, data should be inputted into database after the whole procedure of standardizing, examination on completeness and accuracy and valuation on feasibility. Second, all the inputted data should undergo strict data cleaning process according to real-estate data standards to standardize basic attributes and formats of cases. Last, a specialized software system should be set up to record various types, fields and affiliation of real-estate data so that storage and application of data could be unified.

4. Real-time data updates

The time allowed for analyzing the transaction data of second-hand housing market, tax collecting data and market rents, to supplement data of house numbers and addresses for new buildings and to modify and upgrade the database of the system is set at once every 24 h. In this way, matching degree of data could be improved and results of the valuation model could manifest current market situation timely.

5. A three-dimensional data display

Coordinate system based on points or surfaces should be established on data management systematic platform to match data with GIS, to display data of various types and their inner relations more clearly and to display clear GIS positions and dynamic visualized data. With the coordinate system, the problem of unmatched valuation data for the same house could be avoided.

11.6 The Internet + Valuation = ?

Change in the valuation industry is inevitable due to the change of external environment and increasing demands of clients. To keep pace with the time, the industry should focus on client demands and enrich the content of real-estate valuation.

But how to change? The way is to make full use of the Internet and establish the O2O valuation model. It includes two parts. First, clients require online valuation services with functions of online enquiry, ordering and e-reports as well as having an always online expert consultant. To meet clients' real-time requirements, the valuation industry should utilize enormous data information to establish auto-valuation model of different types, and establish an online valuation system with traditional valuation methods or mass valuation techniques.

Second, valuation agencies should realize auto-management of business process to simplify valuation process and realize process-oriented organization. Auto-management of business process includes functions like business handling, task scheduling and arrangement, on-site inspection, report-writing, report auditing, sealing, report-filing, financial charging management, customer feedback and data uploading. It is operated in the form of valuation business process system and it is a combination of online and offline operations. On-site inspection could utilize existing mobile 3G/4G techniques to communicate information, improve database, auto-categorize on-site photos and describe valuation objects through business collecting (inspection) system. Report-writing could be operated on computers through report generation system (valuation auxiliary system) to improve working efficiency while minimizing mistakes made by appraisers.

The nature of valuation automation is an upgrade and transformation of the client service model to be O2O model in valuation service.

Living in the Internet era, clients are embracing brand new valuation services completely different from traditional valuation services. First, they are making enquiries and orders online through WeChat, an online social APP in China.

Second, users enjoy better convenience in operation. When dealing with bank issues, clients needn't input information manually, thus effectively avoiding unnecessary operating mistakes as the E-reports can conduct real-time communication as well as auto-aggregation of data.

Moreover, valuation agencies will match with financial agencies including banks so that valuation services are unified and shared by all three parties, thus completing the whole process of pre-loan consultation of real estate mortgage, mid-loan assessment and post-loan value reassessment. E-reports can effectively collect and keep data to build a real estate mortgage databank and share standardized information of basic data and assessment parameters. It's convenient for financial agencies like banks to manage collaterals.

O2O model in valuation industry has turned "Internet plus" into a reality. It has enabled clients to embrace brand new services, an answer to the call of our time and of the industry.

Chapter 12
Long-Term Apartment Rentals for Youth—A New Frontier

Readers Guide

- Current apartment renting market is dominated by professional "head-tenants" and individual home owners. Brand apartment market is small and dispersed, leaving a huge space for future market integration. Home owners possess limited amount of homes from a few to less than 100 sets. They are often confronted with management problems caused by rents, tenancy terms and apartment types. As for professional head-tenants, they may turn a three-bedroom apartment into a dozen small rooms for the co-called group-renting. However, as serious security risks lurk in group-renting, it is banned in many cities.
- Current apartment renting industry operates on a pattern of "housing trust, standardized decoration and after-renting services", which is costly in terms of economy, time and operation. Fund return may also take a long time. The advantages are favorable cash flow, derivative revenues and market space. It can be predicted that some long-term rental company tycoons will emerge in China in the near future.

As an emerging force in the leasing market, long-term rental apartment market is a frontier. According to some rough estimation, the market size of leasing in China is over trillions of RMB Yuan, which provides an enormous space for market development. This also explains why long-term rental apartment market has attracted extensive attention. We can inspect the market from the following aspects.

First, heavy flow of migrants causes great demands of rental apartments. The floating population in China is over 0.2 billion, and young people, most of whom requiring rental apartments, take a large proportion. Statistics suggest that more than 0.13 billion young people are renting houses for living creating a rental market size of over 0.4 trillion RMB. As large cities with the heaviest flow of migrants, Beijing, Shanghai and Shenzhen have larger market space for rental apartment industry. Take Shanghai as an example, according to statistics of the Ministry of Public Security, the population of Shanghai has reached 40 million,

S. Ba and X. Yang, *"Internet Plus" Pathways to the Transformation of China's Property Sector*, DOI 10.1007/978-981-10-1699-8_12

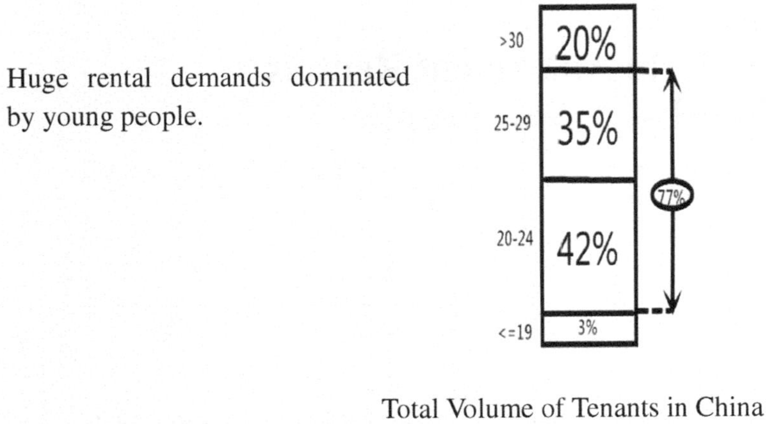

Fig. 12.1 Young tenants taking the lead

including 25 million permanent residents and 15 million floating population and the annual net inflow on average is about 0.7–0.9 million. This explains why Shanghai has become a target area of apartment-rental industry.

Second, the youth's demand for renting is not met by traditional leasing market. Statistics show that 77 % of tenants are under 30 (see Fig. 12.1), and the majority are those born after 1985. Once they start their career these post-85s usually demand long-term rental apartments. Brought up with favorable living standards, most post-85s cannot accept poor living conditions provided by traditional "head-tenants". They attach importance to living quality, individuality, social networks, and an atmosphere with thoughts and culture. This demand is not understood by the traditional rental market, nor met by it, thus creating space for long-term rental apartment market for young people. The emerging brand apartment rental companies begin to take the demand into consideration and cater to the new requirements of young people.

Third, Current apartment renting market is predominated by professional head-tenants and individual home owners. Apartment with a brand market is extremely dispersed and small. The apartment with a brand industry has great opportunities of integrating in the future. The numbers of apartments owned by individuals are limited, no more than 100. On the other hand, individual home owners are often confronted with management problems by differences of rents, tenancy terms and apartment types. As for professional head-tenants, they divide apartments with three bedrooms and a sitting room or three bedrooms and two sitting rooms into a dozen small rooms, and then they rent these small rooms separately to different tenants. This is the so-called group-renting. However, as group-renting apartments usually have serious security risks, they are banned in many cities. At this time, a brand apartment market is just starting in China, but in the US, its largest apartment management company owns over 0.2 million apartments and 60 % are brand apartments. The Chinese market is more localized and scattered because tenants have specific requirements on location and landlords have limited managing scope. The cost is relatively high and requirement on investment is also high. In Beijing, there are around 500 apartment brands and more than 8 million tenants. Beijing Ziroom Company is the largest apartment rental company in China which only owns 30,000 apartments.

Fourth, changes in customers behavior has brought potential opportunities for application of Internet in rental apartment market. The result of Online House Renting Investigation on March of 2015 shows that 54.2 % of people who search for rental apartments online are from second or third-tier cities, while those from Beijing, Shanghai, Guangzhou and Shenzhen only account for 47.4 %. The proportion of people who once utilized mobile phones to search for rental apartments and people who are willing to publish information of rental apartment online account for 76.9 and 60.1 % respectively. It is obvious that the development trend of the internet is irresistible. Internet companies should attach importance to the fact that mobile phone apps have been accepted by most users for rental apartment information and online transaction. From the perspective of landlords, increasing number of them started to take advantage of Internet to publish rental apartment information. Therefore, what apartment renting sites should do is to select and optimize online information to offer the most authentic information to potential customers with the most user-friendly methods.

With such enormous potentials, how will the rental apartment market evolve? How should we analyze and predict the future of the industry? In the following parts, we will analyze and discuss these from multiple perspectives.

12.1 The History of Long-Term Apartment Rental

The serviced apartment is originated from Timeshare hotels in France in 1976. Timeshare hotels, namely, are properties which customers purchased rights to use within a period of time every year. In 1980, the serviced apartment emerged in New York and became a major development direction of New York property developers. Since the middle and late period of 1990s, high-end serviced apartments emerged in Shanghai. The target customers of these serviced apartments are senior managers of foreign enterprises who demand long-term rental apartments.

In 1998, the welfare-oriented distribution policy of public housing was abolished. The real estate market maintained a rapid growth for over a decade after 2002. During this period, head-tenant came into existence. They rented out apartments of which they hold the right to use. The market became larger and brands emerged. After standardization of managing systems and operation methods, so-called apartment rental companies were established.

Large-scale serviced apartments came into being in 2002. Since national income was not high enough at that time, Yopark Corporation set its target group as senior managers of foreign enterprises. In 2003, China's entry into WTO attracted a large number of global Top 500 enterprises. Senior managers from

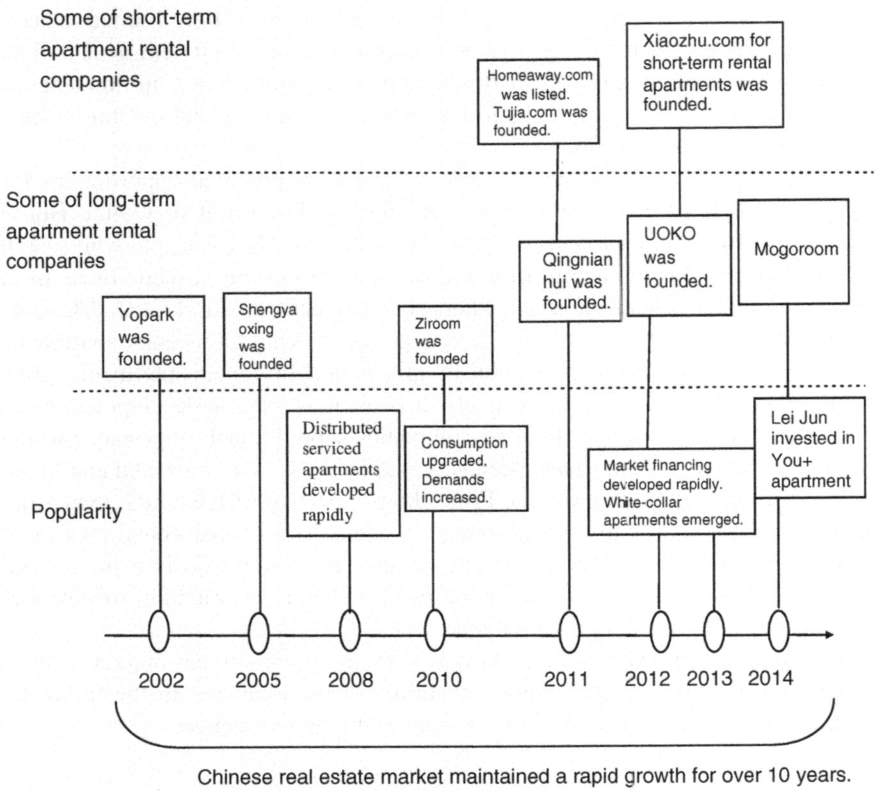

Fig. 12.2 The brief history of serviced apartment industry

these enterprises increased the demands for high-end apartments. At that time, Yopark's rivals are overseas high-end apartment rental companies, like Ascott of Singapore. Domestic employees of foreign enterprises disliked the idea of living in hotels. Therefore, Yopark quickly exploited domestic high-end apartment market with facilities of five-star standard, unified shuttle bus system, staff with uniforms, price 20–30 % lower than rivals from overseas. On the other hand, the capability of forming a community also contributed to its success. In 2005, the Legend Capital planned to invest in Yopark, but the investment was then cancelled for the failure in negotiation on some specific conditions. Yopark had been a leading enterprise in the high-end rental apartment market before that event. In recent year, Yopark's growth rate has decreased. In 2011, it only had 1000 apartments.

The 2008 Beijing Olympic Games contributed to the rapid growth of individual serviced apartments. However, the following global financial crisis hindered the development of these individual serviced apartments. Later, most of them were resold to apartment rental companies (see Fig. 12.2).

2010 witnessed the upgrade of consumption and the transformation of demands as the rise of post 1985s. Long-term serviced apartments of chain brands replaced traditional rental apartments to some extent with its better living experience and cost performance. Shengyaoxing Corporation took the advantage of Shanghai World Expo to expand its market with 45 community service centers. It has become the top brand of middle and high-end market in Shanghai. Shengyaoxing blended characters of centralized and individual rental apartments, initiating a new managing method in China. From 2010 to 2012, apartment rental companies owned 100–300 rooms on average.

The word "apartment" became most popular in 2011. In March 2011, HomeAway, a website for reserving rental apartments, went public. Its assessed value was once up to $2 billion. Later, many domestic companies like Tujia and Airizu began to imitate its operation pattern. Tujia operates and manages its own rental apartments in name of Sweethome, which is an integration of online and offline services of short-term rental apartment market. With Tujia's quick marketing methods, the mass came to know what rental apartment market is.

From 2012 to 2013, the real-estate market maintained a stable supply-demand relationship, which led to the demands for individual group-renting apartments. As the comprehensive development of white-collar apartments, many apartment rental companies with great development potential came into the market. These companies included UOKO, Qing Ke and Mofang, but they were not well-known then. During this period, rooms operated by the leading apartment rental companies reached 1000 sets.

Lei Jun invested in You+ Apartment in Guangzhou in November, 2014. Apartment was then a hotspot internet issue. Although active capital market and the internet promoted the development of apartment rental market, the number of current domestic apartment rental companies of large scale (turnover is over 0.1 billion RMB) is less than 5, and few of these companies are make profits yet. The apartment industry in China is still in the period of low profits and high costs.

12.2 The Industrial Chain of Long-Term Apartment Rental

Long-term rental apartment industry (B2C) is distinctly different from traditional head-tenant pattern (C2C) (Fig. 12.3).

First, with better brand recognition and premium control, apartment rental companies have a better chance to decrease contract violation of tenants and home owners.

Second, compared with traditional head-tenants, apartment rental companies have better performance in talent-cultivating, reprocessing, house-maintaining, supply chain management and systematic management.

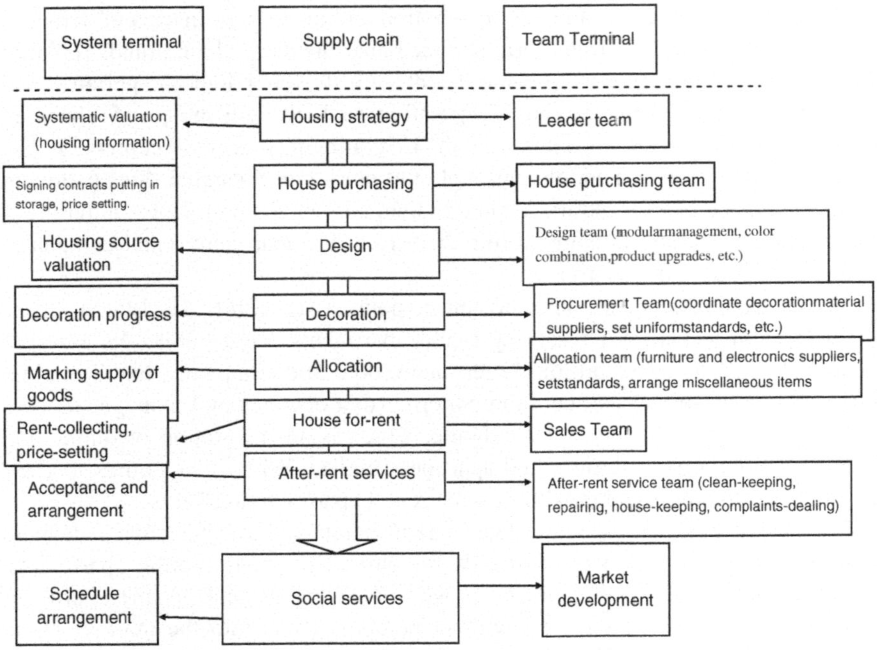

Fig. 12.3 Supply chain system of qualified long-term apartment rental companies (individual)

Third, apartment rental companies can manage cash flow better. They are more willing to take more houses while it is difficult for head-tenants to break the regional boundary who tend to seek for price spread when taking homes.

Fourth, apartment rental companies have greater potential in developing tenants socializing, financial cooperation, and cooperation with local businessmen, as well as deepening supply chain and product chain systems.

Fierce competition is inevitable between the companies and head-tenants for home taking. It is predicted that apartment rental companies will take the lead in the future, prompted by capitals, improvement of industry environment, and maturity of supply chain system.

12.3 The Target Markets of Long-Term Apartment Rental

Current apartment renting industry operates on a pattern of "housing trust, standardized decoration and after-renting services", which is costly in terms of economy, time and operation. Fund return may also take a long time. The advantages are favorable cash flow, derivative revenues and market space. It can be predicted that some long-term rental company tycoon will emerge in China in the near future.

Both rental apartment industry and real estate business work on fixed assets and are regionalized. Because long term rental apartment service is localized, the industry

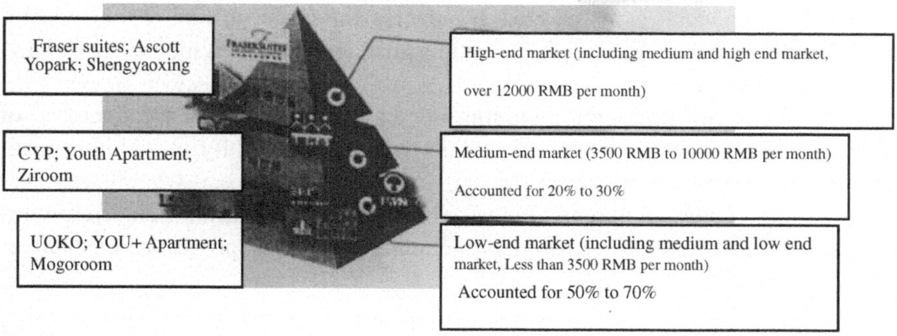

Fig. 12.4 Different apartment rental enterprises with different target customers

has limited managing scope and a scattered market. Currently, white-collar apartments are in first-tier cities like Beijing, Shanghai, Guangzhou and Shenzhen and developed second-tier cities like Chengdu, Wuhan and Hangzhou. With a large mobile population, high demand for rental apartments, abundant room resources, these cities provide favorable development conditions for youth apartment rental companies.

With the rise of quality apartment rental companies, the industry will undergo integration and transformation. Head-tenants in certain areas may still focus on being "small and beautiful", but will expand through acquisition and cooperation once the supply chain and capital chain are more mature. A big market test will occur in 2015 and 2016, when Ziroom entered into the market in Shanghai, Qingke started to exploit market in Hangzhou and UOKO began its business in Beijing, all for cross-regional market development.

Similar with the development of express hotels, long-term apartment rental industry could at least provide market space for its top 10 enterprises with regional characters. Some quality enterprises may develop cross-regional markets.

Different apartment rental enterprises have different target customers, which can be divided into the following three types (see Fig. 12.4): gold collar (senior managers, foreigners), white collar and blue collar.

12.3.1 High-End Market (Including Medium and High End Market)

The target customers of this market are senior managers of enterprises and foreigners. They are reluctant to live in hotels while demanding high living standard. They prefer serviced apartments or long-term rental apartments with services. Singaporean enterprises like Ascott and Frasers Suites are leading the market with little competitive pressure. As for Chinese enterprises, Yopark and Shengyaoxing with community property asset management orientation have a good prospect. However, current high-end apartment rental industry involving foreign affairs is faced with the following problems:

The 2008 financial crisis exerted an adverse influence on real estate industry and financial industry. The number of senior managers of foreign enterprises leaving China is increasing.

Confronted with problems including decrease of single expense, increase of labor cost, market involving foreign affairs will have difficulty in making breakthrough in development in the future.

In the future, apartment rental industry involving foreign affairs can offer multi-business chain services for customers including study tour programs, exchanges, mandarin-teaching, etc.

12.3.2 Medium-End Market

From 2011 to 2013, many youth apartment rental companies entered the market. The most obvious difference between medium-end market and low-end market is that medium-end market can offer better services. For example, a centralized medium-end apartment may have a large public area like stores, reading rooms, fitting rooms, bars, and it may organize regular offline activities. However, the reception desk of a low-end apartment may only serve as a financial department.

12.3.3 Low-End Market

The market mainly involves apartments for people who are applying for jobs or preparing for postgraduate entrance exams and staff dormitories. This kind of apartment is of low cost, usually renting bed space with necessities of life. There are large demands for this market currently, and I will analyze it later in detail.

Comparing the three types of markets, the white-collar market is of huge market space but fierce competition. Although there are still not many enterprises in medium and high end market for gold collar and blue collar workers, medium to high end market has advantage of high renewal rate. Medium and low end apartments for white collar only have rental period of 8–9 months. Before a company builds up its scale and brand name, it is important for the company to ensure stable renewal rate to decrease cost as the cost of attracting new customers is rather high.

12.4 Apartment Blocks

The stable supply-demand relationship of real estate market provides great opportunities for apartment rental companies. There are two types of apartment rental companies, blocks and individual ones. Vacancy rate, renewal rate and profit rate are important factors affecting the operation of apartment rental companies.

Companies have to take these factors as well as their own situations into consideration for further development. However, leading enterprises like Ziroom are developing well with both two types.

I. Apartment blocks

Apartment blocks operate on traditional business pattern. They usually rent whole commercial buildings first and then upgrade these buildings. Since business transformation is a one-off investment, centralized apartment rental companies will start business later than individual ones. On the other hand, due to the high rents of CBD and limited house sources, most apartment blocks are set in suburbs. The key is to realize refined development with low-cost property management.

The long-term rental apartment block is very different from short-term serviced apartments and economical express hotels on serve density, application of channels and labor cost, in spite of their similarities on property management and decoration. (see Table 12.1).

Table 12.1 Comparison between apartments blocks and short-term serviced apartments

	Long-term apartments blocks	Short-term serviced apartments
Rental period	Three months to several years	Several days to one or two months
Property management	Long-term rental apartments did better at property management. It needs more space for property management than express hotels	
Cash flow	Favorable cash flow and financial leverage. Long-term rental apartments have revenues received in advance, which includes deposit and rents	Cash revenues
Service density	Limited services with low frequency	High density services required daily
Cost of channels	Low cost of channels caused by industry characters. No need of OTA distribution (it may be needed in the future)	Hotels and short-term serviced apartments need distribution channels to solve selling problems, thus distribution cost is high. Distribution costs take up about 15 %
Labor cost	It only needs three to six people to provide daily services for the whole building	It needs 6–8 times that of a long-term rental apartment needs
Efficiency (revenue earned per square meter)	Low efficiency. However, deducting distribution cost and operation cost, excellent long-term rental apartments can achieve the same net interest rate as short-term apartments	Short-term rental apartments and serviced apartments can produce higher efficiency (revenue earned per square meter)

Current apartment rental companies like You+, Cypalife, Youth Apartment, Ziroom and Mofang offer apartment blocks. Among others, You+ invested by Lei Jun targets at entrepreneurs. With a defined position, You+ takes the perspective of entrepreneurs when designing the whole building and separate rooms. For example, its location is near Science & technology Park with hammocks in the bedrooms and no kitchen. One of the founders of You+ is also the founder of ChekuCafé, who is familiar with demands of entrepreneurs. He hopes that the entrepreneur apartment can be upgraded to entrepreneur community in the future to satisfy clients' sense of belonging and sense of identity.

Future development opportunities for apartment rental industry may come from its market segments. For example, New Starting Point targets at meeting requirements of the blue collar workers while Miyouroom targets at female clients.

Blue collar workers are less particular about housing, New Starting Point provides them with inexpensive rooms like staff dormitories. They can accommodate 6, 8 or 10 people in one room. They can realize return on investment in 2 years on average and have higher efficiency. On the other hand, the central government is working on ensuring security of group renting. Government set favorable policies for the development of this market and cooperate with enterprises to finance New Starting Point. In this way, enterprises can have quality staff dormitories.

12.5 Individual Apartments

Individual long-term rental apartments are still in the primary period of development. Its pattern is relatively simple. Companies got houses from individual home owners and rent rooms out. With standardized services and transformation, individual apartment rental companies can have complete capital management solution, provide customers with brand-new renting experiences and meet requirements of the blue-collar and the white-collar.

In three years, Ziroom of Lianjia has developed its own mature product system. The company has several product lines and various decoration styles. Users can reserve rooms and pay rents online. It also has a point system, with which customers can get rewards. The company is experienced at organizing offline activities. Each activity it organized can attract hundreds of people.

As for Mogoroom and YOKO, although they are temporarily smaller than Ziroom, they develop rather rapidly due to rich experience of two founders accumulated while working in tourism and real estate industry. YOKO sets second-tier cities as its target market and has relatively few rivals. Recently, it has claimed to enter Beijing, a market of high transaction per customer. Mogoroom has expanded its house sources from 0 to 5000 rooms in a year since 2014. Since its rooms are located near subway stations, it has been popular among the white collar workers. Moreover, it provides tenants with fiber-optic network of 100 M to meet their business and recreational requirements.

Table 12.2 Large-scale expansion of individual rental apartments

Characters	Summary
Expansion	Compared with centralized apartments, individual apartments include various departments and a huge operating system. Reasonable expansion rate can help individual apartments produce scale effect
Multiple house source selections	Individual apartments aim to provide convenient transportation and timely repair for customers. Customers can select rooms of high cost performance online. It requires that apartment rental companies should have abundant houses to form a brand and provide selections for customers
Competition for capitals and talents	Current apartment rental companies, especially individual ones, require large amount of capitals for purchasing houses and operation and management. Companies with strong team capacity, early market development experience and good services can dominate the market, but they should take consideration of their own development characters

Individual apartment rental companies will form ladder-shaped scale by 2016. Big apartment rental companies will expand their market to more cities and acquire medium or small-sized companies. But big companies should control the pace of expansion. Some of medium or small-sized companies can focus on their markets and improve their services. With good management of product, control and costs, they can also realize development. (See Table 12.2).

1. Home owner end: providing capital management cooperation solutions

Under traditional pattern, apartment rental companies will offer landlords rents regularly. Individual apartment rental companies provide comprehensive rental solution for individual landlords. Landlords are suppliers as well as the demand side. To provide more capital management cooperation solutions is an improvement welcomed by risk-takers.

In this regard, Ziroom and Qingke had made a stride by the marketization of operation. From contracting the housing to leasing out, the operation can be completed in 8 days for decorated houses and about 22 days for undecorated houses.

2. Client end: realizing the integration of rent, service fee, and value added service and social traffic

After signing three-to-five years hosting contract with home owners, apartment operators will decorate the entrusted housing with standardized design, such as IKEA furniture, home electrical appliance of famous brands, unified color painting and then rent house to customers according to various time and space arrangement. In this way, apartment business can profit from the price margin and the rent increase with the former caused by the transferring from wholesale to retail

Table 12.3 Profitable ways from clients' end

Cash flow	Contents	Related Cost
The price margin between leasing the whole apartment and leasing segmented compartment	Lease the bedrooms and the compartments segmented from living room (N + 1). The price margin is the gap between the total rent and the total cost	Decoration, electrical household appliance, house rent, channel cost
Service fee	Every room receives cleaning service twice a month, repairing service at any time and high broadband speed, with 10–15 % service fee	WiFi fee, cleaning and repairing cost and so on
Value-added service	Value added service or financial consumption provided to customers with special need, such as oven, takeout laundry, mahjong and so on	Depending on specific cases
Cash flow from social traffic	Given that apartments are well operated with stable customer flow, apartment business can implant advertising cooperate with convenience store and group purchasing financial products and so on	Depending on specific cases

and the latter resulted from housing redecoration. At present time, the investment pay-off period is about 3 years, maybe 2 years given that it is well operated (Table 12.3).

Apart from traditional profitable ways such as rent margin and service fee, apartment business keeps trying employing financial products. For instance, the cooperation in consumption loan between apartment rental business and banks, such as Nanjing Bank and Beijing Bank, has become popular. Banks pay apartment rental companies 2 year's rent while tenants pay the monthly rent with credit card. In this way, apartment rental companies can invest with future cash flow while tenants needn't pay the first three months' rent at one time along with a certain amount of deposit.

At the moment, individual apartment business is still at the exploration stage in terms of the decoration, furnishing, and the integration of online and offline service as well as whether the service is satisfactory or not. More new services will be launched with the growing number of regular tenants and increasingly abundant capital so as to make service fee worthy. In addition, cooperation with other enterprises will be highlighted in the future for large-scale distribute apartment companies. For example, cooperating with cinemas, group purchasing, laundry, fresh home delivery, various banking and financing service, intelligent electrical household appliance, all these are good ways of transferring population flow to cash flow.

3. Housing problems for individual apartments

Firstly, apartment standard setting. Property source is a key problem apartment rental companies face. Now it seems that enterprises always take their own advantages into consideration when choosing apartments to rent. An example is the dependence of Ziroom on Lianjia. When opening a new market, it is important to set up standard for home selection such as the age of the buildings because a building over 20 years may require certain repair fee. Other factors include passenger flow and population flow in the area, value-added space of the property rent (for instance, comparing Zhabei, Yangpu and Xuhui in Shanghai), whether rough-cast houses are acceptable or not. All of these should be taken into consideration.

Individual apartment renting adopts dynamic leasing strategy, varying between investment strategy or conservative strategy. Low efficiency may occur during the time of rapid growth, which is necessary at a specific time and for some specific purpose. Strategically, vacant period, renewal rate, subletting rate should be taken into consideration. High renewal rate and subletting rate show that products are market-acceptable and that the market share is expanding when the reputation remains good.

Secondly, getting homes. Meticulous division of labor can improve efficiency. If stuff can rent and lease houses, housing performance evaluation can be demonstrated directly. However, with the expanding business, the efficiency improvement must rely on meticulous division of labor. At the moment, to some extent, apartment rental companies still rely on intermediary in terms of acquiring housing resource information. In the future, with the market becoming more and more mature, the portion of voluntary house-owners will go up.

Thirdly, home cost. Take Shanghai as an example. It is difficult to rent homes in downtown area as self-occupation rate and leasing rate is 8 to 2 with various apartment companies and relatively large head-tenants. Of course, if apartment rental companies will rent then at any cost, the housing resource will not be a problem anymore. If so, the problem is that when and at what price the companies should acquire the homes, which should take their own strategic planning into consideration. The breakthrough in house renting, information concerning leasing rate, self-occupation rate, circulation rate and unit price of different rooms are all closely related to companies' three-to-five-year operation strategy.

Apartment block rental companies should refer to hotel business when acquiring homes. Hotel managers aim to maximize RevPar (actual annual revenue per rentable room) by increasing leasing rate and unit price because room income for three-star hotel or below counts for a large portion in their total turnover, which is especially true for express hotels due to low service income.

Fourthly, renting strategy. The home-renting strategy goes through the following phases: random home-renting (easily affected by capital), regional quotation (fixed price can be realized when the quotation in a residential quarter is more than 25 %), trusteeship (leading apartment rental companies are light asset provider, only selling their brands and serving developers and various types of home-owners).

4. System problems

System controls the whole process of finding homes—taking homes—commercialization—inventory—leasing—after leasing. A powerful system collects various operating data such as how much it costs to get tenants from different channels, customer's inquiry, customers' site-visiting, dealing as well as conversion rate of all the above procedures.

Besides, a system consists of different sub-systems, including official website, enterprise interior management system, and house-owner management system, which is the most distinct difference between apartment rental companies and traditional middleman landlord. Couples who own rental apartments and middle landlord can well manage the housing rental information by deploying Excel. However, when the number of apartments is more than several hundred or reaching ten thousand or more, traditional head-tenants can't manage their business without a reliable system.

Long term renting apartment ERP system emphasizes the accurate description of the demand. Otherwise, it will redo the task. A properly running system can clearly demonstrate the ratio between house for rent and house rented out, resulting in a good cash flow. In order to well manage the business and evaluate the profitability of an apartment, many factors should be taken into consideration, such as estimated rent fee, cost caused by taking over the apartments, space available and decoration cost.

12.6 Apartment Blocks Versus Individual Apartments

A simple comparison between apartment blocks vs individual apartments is made in Table 12.4. These two types of businesses adopt completely different operating modes.

The centralized-style enterprises tend to be more diversified in the channels of acquiring housing resources. At the moment, they are exploring ways to cooperate with developers.

With the end of property-value-added era and the coming of property-management era, it may be not promising in the sales of newly constructed buildings. Therefore, it is estimated that developers are willing to construct property for rent and strengthen the cooperation with brand apartment rental enterprises.

There are three modes for future cooperation: (1) the real estate developers sell the apartments with leasing contract, i.e., the apartments are owned by individuals but operated by apartment rental companies with brand output. (2) Developers directly authorize operating companies to operate the apartment rental business. (3) The third mode is similar to REITs mode in which funds provide capital, companies operate and the profits are shared.

From the perspective of profit index, due to its natural attributes, apartment block rental business has a shorter payback period. Compared with individual

Table 12.4 Comparisons between apartment block and individual apartment

Business	Apartment block	Individual apartment
Form	Companies always rent the whole building, redecorating them with same style, equipping them with same services. The rent is related to property cost, location and decoration class	Companies take over the apartment from individual house-owners in different residence quarter. The abetments are rent out with the famous brands with unified decoration and furniture
Requirements on product development	In form, the companies similar to small developers, requiring a thorough understanding of the building, facing various difficulties in development of products	In spite of lower requirement on development, companies have extremely high requirement on products, such as decoration cost control, color matching, and repetitive testing of the product market
Rental mode	According to the development requirements, the building is always leased as a whole	The apartment is ways shared by many tenants. A three-bedroom flat may be leased to 3 or 4 different tenants (the living room is usually be separated to 2 compartments). The rent of each room varies based on their class. The apartment may be leased out as a whole
Housing resource	The companies have difficulties in taking over suitable housing resource and are facing fierce competition from economy hotel. Their properties are always failure properties from real estate developers. Therefore, price-favored property is the key to the success of the centralized apartment	Generally, companies take over the flats from individual house-owners by signing 3-to-5-year trusteeship contract with them. However, it takes a long time to reach a large scale. The strategy of taking over houses from the owner is always a challenge for individual apartment rental enterprises
Cash flow	Large-scale of investment in the primary stage	Monthly payment ensures good cash flow, thus individual apartment rental enterprises have enough flow cash to take over another apartment
Standardization	Centralized apartments are easier to be standardized to establish a brand. Centralized management leads to a strong sense of social community	It has a high management requirement. Due to diversified housing resources and large cost absorption, it is not easy to be standardized and to establish a brand

(continued)

Table 12.4 (continued)

Business	Apartment block	Individual apartment
Management system	It has a relatively lower management system duo to its high management efficiency. In the later stage, the management cost is lower, manifesting in lower human resources compared with individual apartment	As the individual apartment management is related to intermediary companies, decoration companies, property management companies and IT companies, it needs powerful ERP system to integrate the management effectively. Especially when there are a large number of apartments, high-efficient system is the key
Status quo	The rent in first-tier cities such as Beijing and Shanghai can support the development of apartment block rental business	Due to high property cost and low rent in the second-tier cities, apartment blocks may lead to low gross profit. Therefore, individual apartment is more suitable in second-tier cities
Capital intervention	Mainly rely on capital fund	One is long-term fund featuring in dollar-pool with high risk. The other is strategic investment intervention with prearranged strategic layout
A comparison between domestic and foreign companies	Ascott and Fraser Suites are two apartment block rental companies. The parent company of Ascott is CapitaLand, a property developer. Ascott can take over the whole building easily. With the good location of the housing resources, Ascott take high-end apartments with average rent more than $20,000 as its target market. However, most of the domestic apartment rental companies are adopting individual style	
Typical enterprises	Youth Street, Ziroom, Cubic City Apartment	Mogoroom, Qingke

Data resource the Internet, the author

apartment renting, it is more likely to launch high-end products. Analyzed from the current contract violation rate and management difficulties, apartment block rental business with its high product positing accuracy is doing much better. In the future, it is more likely to launch competitive social products. As we can see, You+ apartment is gradually growing from an individual entrepreneurship to be an entrepreneurial community.

From the perspective of long-term scale, more attention should be paid to individual apartment renting. As small owners possess individual housing resource, the rental companies should pay attention to issues as house-take-over speed, house-take-over strategy, vacancy rate, and operating cost. As it usually take 3–5 years for rental business to take over an apartment, the increasing burden on rent, talent reserve, and after-leasing management should be taken into consideration.

12.7 Potential Problems and Their Solutions in Long-Term Apartment Rentals

The long-term apartment rental business has developed well for more than a decade since 2002. But it didn't become a hotspot until 2014 when the internet and capital helped to boom the industry. But we still it at the primary development stage. The increasing investment won't lead to fundamental changes in the industry. The core of the apartment still lies in the inventory turnover and management capacity. The main challenges the apartment rental industry is facing can be summarized as follows.

1. Common problems in long-term apartment rental business

The first one is location selection. Current location selection is not conducted scientifically. Companies usually rent a low-price property according to a rough judgment, leasing the apartment when the rent price is increased. KFC offers a site selection model that has enabled its great business success. KFC has very professional outlet-launching model and research report to guide their site selection. Factors in the model include human flow, traffic, and price level in the neighborhood and so on. However, rental companies' site selection often depends on personal judgment.

The second problem lies in property-take-over cost. For instance, the rent of a two-bedroom and one-living-room apartment in Xujiahui, Shanghai is 10,000 RMB. In order to take over the house, a company paid the full commission of 10,000 RMB instead of the usual ratio which is 35 %.

The third problem deals with the prediction of the increase in the property price and the forward rent. The price margin is usually determined by the gap between property costs spent by apartment rental enterprises and the forward price. It can be affected by other factors as well. One factor is the amount of available homes. For instance, in the old center of Shanghai, there are only a small number of neighborhoods with more than 1000 apartments with 80 % self-occupation rate, which means only about 200 units available for renting. Usually there are more than 3 head-tenants and many private landlords. Therefore, the shortage of housing resource determines the cost, period and the difficulties of renting the property. The other factor is that it is more difficult to estimate the rent which is constricted by the traffic conditions and business facilities.

The next problem concerns vacancy rate and turnaround time. Inventory checking comes after taking over properties. Inventory includes actual inventory after rent-free period. If the apartment isn't leased out after the free-rent period, there comes vacancy period. Turnover period starts from taking over the property, from decorating to leasing which needs efficient operating ability.

Distribution channel and marketing expense exert more problems. Current distribution channels are not adequate. Low-end apartments are mainly advertised in www.58.com while high-end apartments are promoted through intermediary outlet at a high expense. In addition, companies may purchase many key words on mobile end or PC for quicker customers search.

The sixth problem is the IT system. Professional head-tenants have poor business performance due to the absence of IT system. At the moment, many companies are at a primary stage, dealing with statistics by using Excel.

The seventh problem deals with interval energy consumption calculation which remains unsolved today.

The last problem is profit. This is the biggest question at the moment. A newly set-up company should realize that it will take a long time before making profit, usually 3 or 4 years. It will take a well-managed company 3 years to make profits and longer for poorly-managed companies.

2. Possible way-out: smart apartment management

One development trend might be smart apartments which combine long-term rental apartment, intelligent household appliances, IT system and the Internet of things. In this regard, possible solutions in need are as follows:

Firstly, timely monitoring of the renting status of apartments. In the future, a terminus or a mobile phone can be deployed to know the renting status of apartments in real time. It is ridiculous to think that many businessmen today have no idea about the renting status of the apartments they are about to rent.

Secondly, security surveillance. When it comes to group renting or shared renting, security is of great importance.

Thirdly, intelligent access control and lock. In many cases, intelligent access control is operated when Wi-Fi is available. However, Wi-Fi will be out of date many years later. In addition, Wi-Fi availability is restricted by distance.

Fourthly, customized housing service and stay-in experience.

Next, self-help house visiting service.

Finally, accurate interval energy consumption calculation.

12.8 Secular Trends in Long-Term Apartment Rental

The widely discussed important points at the moment are still at a shallow level including apartment leasing platform, after-leasing platform, community asset management platform, middleman landlord platform and apartment socialization platform. As for the possible trends in the future, they can be thoroughly discussed from the following aspects:

Firstly, simple housing leasing is gradually becoming house-owner property asset management which is the target all the apartment rental companies will be working for. In the future, a large number of developer and brokers might be involved in the property asset management.

Secondly, centralized whole renting will be replaced by housing trusteeship. As a heavy asset model, whole renting is not promising in the future. The whole renting necessary at the beginning because companies can then set the price. However, the model is not sustainable once the company brand begins to gain popularity. The solution is trusteeship.

Thirdly, mono-regional business will gradually give way to multi-regional business. Nowadays, many companies choose to expand their business to other cities before the business in their base is adequately developed and can be copied. The normal practice should be establishing a solid base to be number one in the local market instead of expanding business into more cities because renting has a much localized market.

Fourthly, the income source is changing from traditional leasing to upgraded leasing consumption combined with financial products.

Fifthly, the individual management will integrate with centralized management so as to form a community-based management pattern.

Sixthly, real estate developers will collaborate with apartment operators to co-establish apartment business. In the future, be it subletting or whole leasing, the differences lie in products nor the business mode. And the two key index which can evaluate the strength of an apartment rental business are firstly, the size of the asset, the number of rooms for rent and the tenants, secondly, whether it makes profits or not.

12.9 The Future of China's Long-Term Apartment Rental—A Prediction Based on EQR's Development

EQR (Equity Residential Properties) the largest American apartment rental company was established in 1969. With the development of REITs (real estate trust investment fund),American apartment REITs kept an annual revenue growth rate of 8 %. Later EQR became the first listed REITs in the US. Now, as a member of the SandP 500 Indices, with 27.5 billion dollars market value, it targets at purchasing, developing and managing high-end apartments. It possesses more than 300 hundred properties and 110,000 apartments nationwide. The development of EQR can provide reference for China's apartment rental companies.

1. A steady rental market is essential to the development of EQR, which has been fully manifested in three aspects:

Firstly, steady rate of return. Over the last 15 years REITs in the US has maintained approximately an annual increase of 3 % on rent (see Fig. 12.5) with 5 % vacancy rate. High vacancy and decreased rent only occurred during the 2008–2010 financial crises (see Fig. 12.6).

Secondly, a steadily growing demand for renting. The gradually increasing age of first marriage ensure the high demand for rental market.

Thirdly, strong renting demand from the young people. House price in major American cities is very high compared with people's income. China has a similar situation. In some cities, the ratio between house price and income comes to be 10:1. It will take a college graduate 5–10 years to buy an apartment. When both the rental demand and personnel mobility across regions is high, China sees a favorable environment for the development of apartment rental industry.

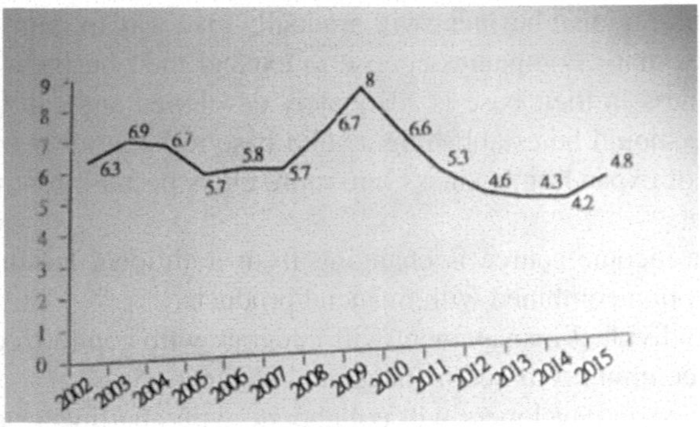

Fig. 12.5 The housing vacancy rate in the US 2002–2015. *Data source* author

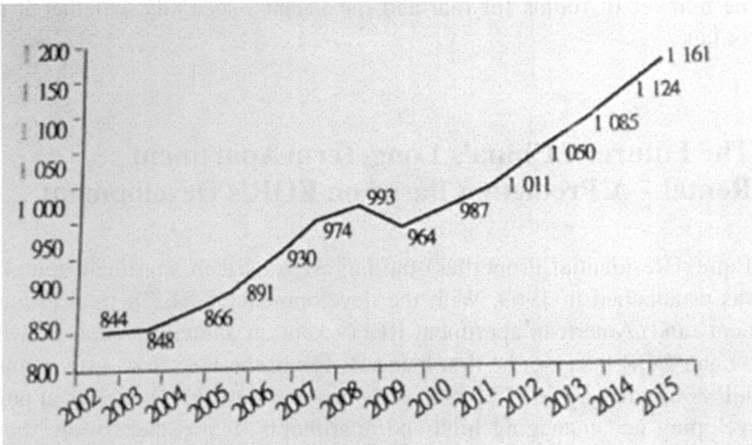

Fig. 12.6 Effective rent in apartment rental business 2002–2015

At their primary capital accumulation period, young people's choice of buying or renting a home is affected by the differences between mortgage payment and rent. When homes are too expensive, the market favors renting. This is the reason why an increasing number of American apartment rental companies develop business in core cities.

2. The history of EQR

First period 1993–2001, characterized by large scale financing and acquisition. Since its listing, EQR has conducted large-scale financing and started seven-year-long apartment acquisition nationwide, reaching a peak of 230,000 sets of apartment in 2002 through the use of capital (see Fig. 12.7).

Its large-scale development contributes to a diverse EQR market (the white-collars, the blue-collars, the seniors and students), improving brand awareness and customer loyalty. As EQR apartments is widely spread across ten states in the US,

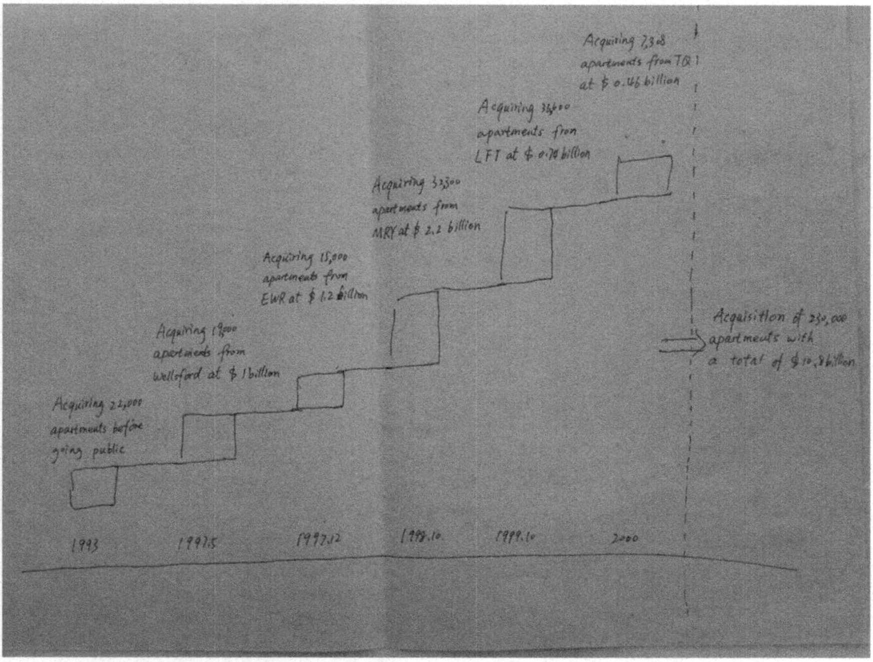

Fig. 12.7 EQR acquisition 1993–2000

tenants can accomplish cross-city sub renting, which increases the rental renewal rate and achieves the largest value of tenants by ensuring same high-quality living standards.

1993, 22,000 sets before listing

In May 1997, 1 billion US dollars for 19,000 sets from Wellsford

In December 1997, 1.2 billion US dollars for 15,000 sets from EWR

In November 1998, 2.2 billion US dollars for 32,300 sets from MRY

In November, 1999, 0.74 billion US dollars for 36,600 sets from FLT

In 2000, 0.46 billion US dollars for 7380 sets from TQ

Total: From 1993 to 2000, EQR spent a total of 10.8 billion US dollars on purchasing 230,000 sets of apartment.

The market scale helped EQR to realize diversified profit-making. By collaborating with insurance companies and advertisers, EQR gained revenue of 1.6 million dollars from the large browsing quantity of its online business.

Second period 2002–2012. EQR began to strip off low-yielding assets and streamline business scope. In 2000, EQR launched furniture business and purchased GLOBE. Later EQR sold the business and rented furniture instead to focus on apartment rental business. In 2003, EQR sold its old property market and marched in the rapid growing housing rental market, concluded a series of property purchase deals, streamlined its management and changed its target market. REITs survived the sub-prime mortgage crisis much better than real estate companies. Its prudent financial strategy also helped EQR through the financial crisis.

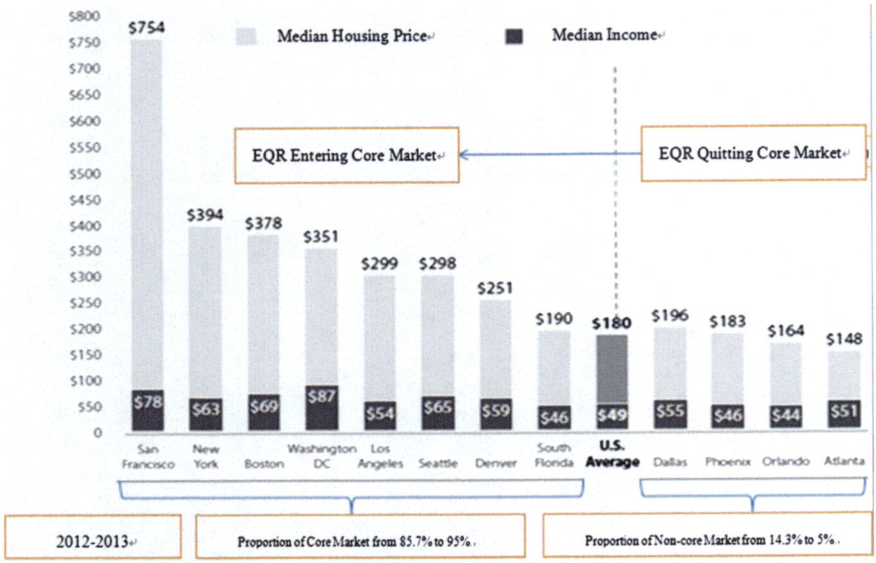

Fig. 12.8 The distribution of EQR core market in 2013. *Data source* Author

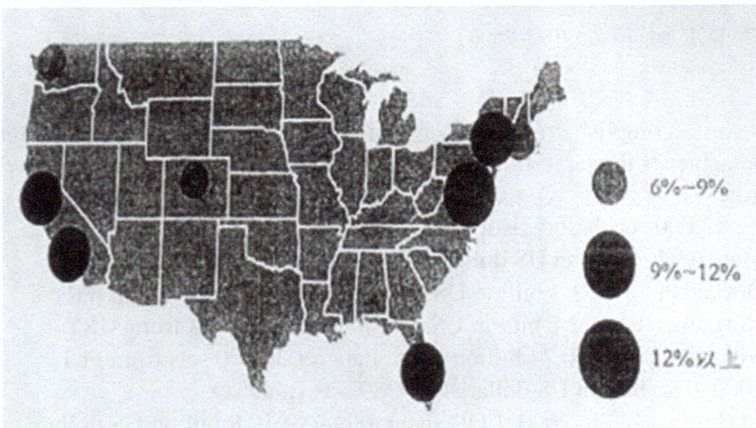

Fig. 12.9 The distribution of EQR core market in 2014. *Data source* Author

Third period, 2012 till now. Starting from 2012, EQR kept giving up its non-core business and concentrating on its core market. Apartment business market share shrank from 14.3 to 5 % and core market share increased from 85.7 to 95 % (see Figs. 12.8 and 12.9).

Thanks to the strategy of focusing on core cities, the current average rent level of EQR is even higher than that of the whole industry compared with several years ago. The favorable rental market and the company's management experience of 20 plus years contributed to the low vacancy rate in EQR. In addition, continuous rental demand is assured by the sound income of urban tenants and economic recovery.

Hence, EQR established the strategy of making cities like San Francisco, New York, Washington D. C., Boston, and Miami as the core market.

1. What China can learn from EQR

The apartment rental industry in China differs greatly from that in the US. In comparison, the development of REITs in China is still at the primary stage with low brand recognition. Apartment rental market is not yet the mainstream housing market. Only a small number of apartment rental companies generate steady revenue from rent. Young people's home consumption upgrading is also at the initial phase.

Same as what we have observed in retail industry, real estate industry and post-automobile industry, China will not duplicate the American way in the apartment rental industry either, even though the basic industrial laws remain unchanged and we do need to study the American market. America's today doesn't mean the future of China. Any industry in China will take a different path as China faces a fragile tradition, rapid development of the internet and a huge consumption demand. Chinese apartment rental industry won't be an exception (see Table 12.5). The reasons are as follows.

Table 12.5 Comparison of apartment rental industry in China and the US

	The US	China
Operation means	American companies adopt financial operation methods, focusing on capital operation, merge and acquisition. With large number of properties, American companies can build apartment and run the rental business by themselves	Chinese companies adopt real estate operation means, indirectly possessing properties by means of whole-renting
Development phase	The development is at advanced stage. By using financial means such as REITs, the number of its brand high-quality apartments has reached hundreds of thousands	The development is at the primary stage with no scale merits. By using cash flow to rent the apartment, the number of apartments for rent of leading companies is just 30,000
Average property quality	Relatively high	Relatively low
Financing cost	It is diversified in financial instruments, smooth in financial channel and low in financing cost	It has limited financial leverage with high financial cost
Rental return rate	8–12 %	2–4 %
Internet application	In the largest American apartment renting company REITs, 65 % of the rental contracts are done online, which greatly reducing field-visiting frequency	Companies still mainly rely on intermediary agencies for customer resource. However, the number of online transaction of brand apartment rental companies is increasing

Data resource the Internet, the author

Firstly, the apartment rental industry in China will not wait for REITs' maturity for its own development. Venture capital, the New Tertiary Board, and listed companies in secondary market will play a more significant role in the large-scale development and cross-regional integration of apartment rental companies. The development pattern of EQR has made it clear that due to the localization of the industry, the rise of national apartment rental companies should depend on capital, merge and acquisition. We should not count on government's efforts to promote REITs. We'd rather believe that the mainstream will be the spontaneous and interest-driven primary and secondary markets based on a capital market. The two predictable paths are: one, VC-dominated inter-city merge and acquisition. In other words, one or more than one large-sized VC institutions will invest in different brand companies located in different cities and then integrate them. Secondly, it is inter-city merge and acquisition dominated by listed companies. Currently, domestic listed real estate enterprises are exploring transformation paths. It is estimated that some listed enterprises will continue to integrate with localized apartment rental industry and then March into the property management market.

Secondly, the Youth Apartment business in China will skyrocket as a result of poor traditional apartment renting experience, low brand profile, increasing youth renting demand, and the powerful intervention of the internet. China's apartment companies, compared with those in the US, have two distinct features. First, brand companies will rise more rapidly. The weaker the tradition is, the more rapidly the new industry develops and the more profound effects the internet will exert, as proven in other industries. Secondly, the apartment operation in China will become more heavily set. Apartment rental industry requires strong operation capability and lean management. Although internet technology can improve the efficiency of renting and leasing process, it is more important to have efficient operation to reduce the rotation time. Therefore, Chinese rental apartment companies will be more heavily engaged in the whole business process. However, the heavier the rental business, the deeper its guarding moats.

Thirdly, same as the market in the US, Chinese rental companies concentrate on core cities. Urban demographic structure and its rental demand structure makes the first-tier cities the ideal destination. There are three reasons. Firstly, highly concentrated demand for renting business in first-tier cities. Secondly, a large number of population and existing homes serves as a solid foundation for large-scale business development. Thirdly, unit room prices are higher in core cities. Take Chengdu as an example. Although the renting demand is high, the unit renting price is low. As Beijing is so much larger than Chengdu, it takes a cyclist to circle Chengdu three times to match the same distance in Beijing. Therefore the turnover and scale of the business is not significant unless the unit price is taken into consideration.

The manufacturer's authorised representative in the EU is Springer Nature Customer Service Centre GmbH, Europaplatz 3, 69115 Heidelberg, Germany. If you have any concerns regarding our products, please contact ProductSafety@springernature.com

Printed and bound by CPI Group (UK) Ltd, Croydon, CR0 4YY
25/09/2026
02222900-0019